UTOPIAN GENDERSCAPES

UTOPIAN GENDERSCAPES

Rhetorics of Women's Work in the Early Industrial Age

MICHELLE C. SMITH

Southern Illinois University Press
Carbondale

Southern Illinois University Press
www.siupress.com

Printed in the United States of America

24 23 22 21 4 3 2 1

Cover illustration: Haymaking. Photo 790 (cropped), manuscript group 354: Old Economy Village Collection. Old Economy Village Archives, Pennsylvania Historical and Museum Commission, Ambridge, PA.

Library of Congress Cataloging-in-Publication Data
Names: Smith, Michelle (Michelle Christine), author.
Title: Utopian genderscapes : rhetorics of women's work in the early industrial age / Michelle C. Smith.
Identifiers: LCCN 2020049754 (print) | LCCN 2020049755 (ebook) |ISBN 9780809338351 (paperback) | ISBN 9780809338368 (ebook)
Subjects: LCSH: Women—Employment—United States—History—19th century. | Sex role—United States—History—19th century. | Utopias—United States—History—19th century. | Rhetoric—Social aspects—United States. | Feminist theory.
Classification: LCC HD6095 .S569 2021(print) | LCC HD6095(ebook) | DDC 331.40973/09034—dcundefined
LC record available at https://lccn.loc.gov/2020049754
LC ebook record available at https://lccn.loc.gov/2020049755

Printed on recycled paper ♻

For my sister

CONTENTS

FIGURES AND TABLE

ACKNOWLEDGMENTS

This project began with a hunch that there was a story to be told about women in intentional—or utopian—communities. This hunch sprouted from two seeds planted in my college years: a women's studies field trip to Twin Oaks, Virginia (a thriving community founded in 1967), as part of my education in the incomparable WILL* program at the University of Richmond, and a six-week stay at Blueberry Hill, a cohousing community outside Washington D.C. (I thank Tom, Mary Helen, and the Erickson family for this life-changing experience). Given the long germination of this project, I owe gratitude to more people than I can name here.

This research took root in the fertile soil of the rhetoric and composition program at Penn State, under the guidance of my mentors and committee members Cheryl Glenn, Jack Selzer, and Hester Blum. Cheryl, you have been a model of generosity and listening as I found my way through this quirky project: thank you for your day-or-night mentoring and for always giving me the "full-on Cheryl Glenn." Jack, thank you for believing in me, always, and for your faith that road bumps along the way are just the colorful stories I'll get to tell once I get where I'm going. Hester, you helped me see the potential of this project to comment on a specific moment and phenomenon in American history. While at Penn State, this project also benefited from the insights and intellectual camaraderie of Rebecca Wilson Lundin, Una Kimokeo-Goes, Brandy Scalise, Michael Faris, Jenell Johnson, Stacy Sheriff, and Heather Adams. Heather, your feedback and companionship has been irreplaceable throughout this journey.

Over the years, numerous colleagues have nurtured this project through its intermediate stages. During my brief time at Whitworth University, Doug Downs, Fred Johnson, and Megan Hershey helped me adjust to life as a professor and encouraged me to continue prioritizing my research. Over several years at Marist College, I enjoyed the friendship, wisdom, and mentorship of Angela Laflen, Eileen Curley, and Danielle Langfield. The entire School of Liberal Arts at Marist (particularly the indomitable History Department) taught me the meaning of collegiality and the ways that, at our best, academics can and should support one another. I continue to seek opportunities to pay this forward. At Clemson University, I am humbled and bolstered by amazing colleagues in rhetoric and composition, particularly Megan Eatman, Cynthia Haynes, and Jordan Frith, and in my department, especially Erin, Walt, Mike, Brian, Elizabeth, Angela, Andy, Lee, Maya, Cameron, David, and Clare.

This book has been enriched by my participation in thriving interdisciplinary networks in the study of intentional communities and feminist rhetorics. I received early support and encouragement from the Communal Studies Association and the Center for Communal Studies at the University of Southern Indiana. In addition, the community of feminist rhetoricians has been invaluable to my growth as a scholar, critic, and teacher during the writing of this book. I am especially grateful for the extrainstitutional mentorship of Jess Enoch and David Gold and the discerning commentary and exuberant friendship of Risa Applegarth, Sarah Hallenbeck, and Lindsay Rose Russell. I am indebted to Sarah and to Megan Eatman for generously reading (and rereading) chapter drafts and to Lindsay for my title.

This project has received crucial support from several institutions, not least of which are the archives at the heart of this study. Sarah Buffington, curator of the Old Economy Village Archives, has worked alongside me to unearth traces of women's work in the Harmony Society. I am also grateful to Abigail Lawton at the Oneida Community Mansion House, the librarians and staff at the Special Collections Research Center at Syracuse Libraries and the Massachusetts Historical Society, and the artists and institutions that granted the use of their images and materials. Various academic librarians—especially Sandy Stelts at Penn State and Camille Cooper at Clemson University—have provided vital assistance and access to critical (re)sources. This research was supported by a National Endowment for the Humanities Summer Stipend and internal funding from the English Department at Penn State, the School of Liberal Arts at Marist College, and, at Clemson University, the Humanities Hub, the College of Architecture, Arts, and Humanities, and the Division of Research. I especially thank the English Department at Clemson University for my pre-tenure research leave. This project found a home at Southern Illinois University Press, where editor Kristine Priddy shepherded it along and two anonymous reviewers offered feedback that made this book a better version of itself. A version of chapter 2 originally appeared as "'Indoor Duties' in Utopia: Archival Recalcitrance and Methodologies of Lived Experience" in *College English* 80, no. 6 (2018): 517–38 (copyright 2018 by the National Council of Teachers of English; used with permission).

Finally, I could not have written this book without the unflagging support of family and friends. This book is a testament to the influence of my mother, a staunch feminist who died during the early stages of this project—from the wall art I grew up with ("A Woman's Place is in the Home—And She Should Go There Directly after Work" and "A Woman's Place Is in the House—And the Senate") to her own monograph, *Gender in the Workplace* (apples and trees, right?). My father gave me my love of theory and analysis, both essential to processing this material and to loving the process. My sister Meghan, to whom I dedicate this book, is my partner in decoding the norms of gendered labor that pervade our lives and my role model in her unfailing dedication to work that is more than work and to all those parts of life we are told are mutually incompatible. Time spent with her, Leo, Jack, and Robert has been a source of joy and laughter, rest and renewal. Many friends have lifted my heart and my spirits along the way, but I retain a special place in my heart for my Richmond "family" (you know who you are). And to the Bonsalls—Jon, Kathy, Mary Kay, Kate, Matt, Dan, Megan, Abby, Emily, and Maggie—thank you for the long dinners and the love.

I have the most incredible luck to be sharing my life with Dan Bonsall—amore, best friend, confidante, cheerleader, and in-house librarian—without whom not. To Dan and Callum: I love you and cherish the adventure of creating our own little intentional community.

UTOPIAN GENDERSCAPES

1. ECOLOGIES OF WOMEN'S WORK

Feminist Historiography and Material Rhetorics

In 1907, a journalist named Alvan F. Sanborn wrote a cautionary article for *Good Housekeeping* called "The Revolt from Family Ties." In the article, Sanborn associates contemporary critiques of the family by feminists such as Charlotte Perkins Gilman and Elsie Clews Parsons with the utopian fervor of the mid-nineteenth century.[1] In Sanborn's telling, the communal experiments of the Shakers, the Mormons, the German Amana Colonies, John Humphrey Noyes's Oneida, and the transcendentalist Brook Farm (as well as its close neighbor, Bronson Alcott's Fruitlands) are a history of assaults on the nuclear family, attempts "to persuade their fellows to break away from the traditional family life" (167). Sanborn seeks to "remind the public, whose memory is proverbially short," of the ostensible failure of these communities, which should "give us pause" when considering present-day reforms (167, 170). Decades prior, contemporary commenters prefigured Sanborn by assessing midcentury utopian communities as having "cast aside the family"—"at war with the whole principle of family responsibilities, support, and ties of relationship" ("Social Communities" 445; "The Last of a 'Community'" 127). This threat was particularly salient in the middle decades of the nineteenth century, when the American family stood as a symbol of continuity and security amid the social and economic turmoil of industrialization. But how, specifically, did utopian communities threaten the family?

One clue comes in an alternative response to midcentury intentional communities.[2] For Mary Roberts Coolidge, a pioneer of women's studies, the significance of these experiments lay in their prospects for women. From the 1820s to 1880s, a striking array of intentional communities offered female members a "larger and more prophetic atmosphere," promoting "the development of exceptional women whose careers were in themselves a contradiction of the accepted views as to feminine capacity" (261). Alongside and in contrast to new opportunities in factory work, wage labor, and urban life, utopian experiments underscored the expanding possibilities for women's lives. Such communities were *lived arguments* for increasing women's access to education, self-culture, and a variety of careers: "Then, as now, whenever a thinking man came to know such a woman, he ever afterwards had an enlarged idea of what women might become under the stimulus of broadened opportunities" (262). For Coolidge, then, the greatest significance of utopian communities was their embodied testimony to the possibility of revising conventional gender relations.

Despite their differing conclusions, Sanborn and Coolidge both highlight intentional communities' reconfiguration of women's roles. In this they were not alone: nineteenth-century commentators also oriented their praise and blame of utopian communities around questions of gender. Critics insisted that changing women's roles would undermine the nuclear family and the American home, a threat only loosely tied to the social structure of the community in question.[3] In such accounts, as in contemporary public discourse, ostensible concern for the family functions as a dog whistle for alarm over changes in women's status: an instance of synecdoche where the whole (the family) serves as a veiled reference to one constituent part (women). For other contemporaries, intentional communities promised to liberate women by revising men's and women's work. An 1856 article in the *United States Magazine*, deploring "the pecuniary dependence of woman," praised intentional communities as a step toward a future society "so organized that both sexes may, by virtuous industry, secure a competence," such that women will no longer be forced "to assume the bond of marriage as an equivalent for bread and raiment" ("Social Communities"). Following Nathan Stormer's approach to public memory as a "conduit of contestation (as opposed to a topic to be debated)," public debate over intentional communities functioned "not as a dispute awaiting resolution but rather as a way of orienting struggle around new ways of living" (4). For midcentury Americans, intentional communities—as a practice or an object of public valuation—were one means of coming to terms with the new social and labor dynamics of the Industrial Revolution.

In this light, *Utopian Genderscapes* reads midcentury intentional communities as a suggestive yet underexplored discursive and material site for American constructions of gender, labor, and industrialism. In the 1840s alone, the United States housed eighty-four active utopian communities (Fogarty, *Dictionary*). As Ralph Waldo Emerson quipped, "We are all a little wild with numberless projects of social reform; not a reading man but has a draft of a new community in his waistcoat pocket" (qtd. in D. Hayden, *Seven* 9). These communal efforts involved significant reconfigurations of labor and gender as midcentury utopian communities attempted to cope with "the crisis of transition from preindustrial to more modern forms of family and social life" (Foster, *Religion* 4). Their coping strategies involved alternative systems of labor that opposed industrial trends toward individualism, hierarchy, and the pursuit of wealth. But trying out new labor models also necessitated a reconsideration of women's roles and work.[4] As they grappled with new patterns of industrial labor, intentional communities redrew divisions between men's and women's work, raising and engaging the broader question: what would industrialism mean for women's work? Throughout this book, I engage the 1840s as a kairotic moment where Americans explored the affordances of industrialism before it calcified into more rigid forms in the second half of the century.

This book has three principal aims: (*1*) to illustrate the material-discursive construction of women's work in nineteenth-century intentional communities; (*2*) to consider these communities as instances of the gender reforms that were thinkable—that fell within the boundaries of the possible—in the mid-nineteenth century; and (*3*) to approach these communities as case studies of how industrialization shaped enduring configurations that differentiated labor across not only gender but also class and race. In the following chapters, I pursue these aims through an analysis of three distinct communities. The transcendentalist Brook Farm community in West Roxbury, Massachusetts (1841–47)—where Unitarian ministers and other Boston intellectual lights tried their hand at self-subsistence—is the focus of chapter 2 as well as the most famous of the three communities, commonly celebrated as an egalitarian space tragically undermined by its leaders' attention to philosophy at the expense of pragmatics. Chapter 3 introduces the long-lived Harmony Society (1804–1905)—a community of religious Separatists fleeing persecution in Germany—whose members relocated several times before settling north of Pittsburgh in 1825, where the immigrant community was renowned for its worldly successes and policy of celibacy (satirized by Lord Byron in *Don Juan*). Finally, chapter 4 takes up the infamous upstate New York Oneida Community (1848–81), which shocked the American public with its practices of "complex marriage" (a highly structured polyamory) and "male continence" (an early form of birth control), among other eccentricities. Each body chapter focuses on women's domestic, professional, or reproductive labor in a particular community, framing that labor in light of the community's history and situating it as a rhetorical negotiation within the larger material-discursive landscape of women's work during U.S. industrialization. Because the boundaries of women's domestic, professional, and reproductive labor are often blurred and relational, there is a fruitful slippage among these categories as negotiated by the midcentury women and communities at the heart of this study.

Utopian Genderscapes is a feminist history of rhetoric mapping constructions of gendered labor in the mid-nineteenth century United States. I pursue this task through a theoretical framework I call *ecologies of gender*, which I develop further in the next section. This approach is premised on the view that careers, workspaces, and work tasks are differently gendered in different times and places and that *what counts as work*—a perennial concern for women's labor—is negotiable rather than given (see also Hallenbeck and Smith). Thus, I foreground the rhetorical-material production of gendered work within each community rather than explicit written or spoken arguments about gender. Though community leaders and members did circulate their visions through speaking or writing—notably through community newspapers—I locate the primary rhetorical force of utopian communities in their embodied and material practices.[5] Similarly, while this project acknowledges women's work as a site of rhetorical invention, my examination of women's rhetorics is primarily deployed as a means to illuminate midcentury ecologies of gendered labor. Finally, by minimizing intention, this book's ecological approach forgoes simple binaries of resistance and compliance. As much as intentional communities were borne of *resistance* to contemporary trends, they were also *of* their age: thus, I analyze their innovations as an indication of what gender reforms were thinkable and achievable in the mid-nineteenth century. Drawing on conversations in feminist historiography and material rhetorics, *Utopian Genderscapes* articulates the networks of bodies, spaces, objects, and discourses that comprised women's work within each community, intervened in larger rhetorics of women's work, and initiated patterns of gendered labor that persist today.

As a study of rhetorics of gendered labor, this project engages concerns that extend beyond utopian spaces and the mid-nineteenth century. This study takes as its object the construction of the persistent, counterfactual-yet-normative understanding of work spaces, practices, and identities as opposed to home. Because this binary particularly disadvantages women—while also unevenly affecting differently situated women—unpacking its production is an important feminist undertaking. Thus, this project answers Jessica Enoch's call "to explore the often-thorny relationship between feminism and work" (*Domestic Occupations* 185). In pursuing this task, I consider the joint articulation of the labor of re/production. That is, I maintain that to fully understand the lives and work of women, we must consider the labor of reproduction and production together.[6] The erasure and invisibility of much of women's work is an enduring problem, and studies of the rhetoric of women's work can help reveal the ideological and rhetorical maneuvers that render some women's work invisible, natural, or inconsequential. Significantly, many of these rhetorical patterns emerged during the Industrial Revolution.

In the following chapters, *Utopian Genderscapes* explores material-rhetorical structures that discount women's work as real work and divide women's labor from men's. As I pursue this task, I illuminate three rhetorical tropes that permeate the ecologies of gendered labor in this study. My investigation of domestic labor at Brook Farm highlights the role of *teleological rhetorics* in explaining (*logos*) women's housework with reference to the presumed end or purpose (*telos*) of woman (as wife, mother, and caretaker). Rather than framing rhetorics of gender as static and essentialist, teleology directs our attention to the *trajectories* of gendered ecologies, as in midcentury discourses of working women "unfitting" themselves for future roles as wives and mothers. In the Harmony Society, the case of the extraordinary woman professional illuminates how rhetorics of *exceptionalism* promote false narratives of "trickle-down feminism," implying that one woman's success automatically increases other women's access to professional status. In this light, success stories about individual women often serve to mystify and reify structural inequities in specific workplaces and broader educational and economic institutions. Finally, I examine rhetorics of *choice* that oppose women's reproductive and productive labor in the Oneida Community, illustrating how such rhetorics bolster zero-sum logics regarding work and family. Even as familial logics pervade women's treatment and opportunities in the workplace, women are simultaneously positioned as needing to choose between irreconcilable career and family roles and identities. By articulating work as a crucial node in the rhetorical construction of gender, I identify rhetorics of teleology, exceptionalism, and choice as central to historical and contemporary ecologies of gender.

A central argument of this book is that constructs of gendered labor are never only about gender. Teleology, exceptionalism, and choice operate in midcentury ecologies of gender so as to divide work by class, race, ethnicity, geography, education, and religion—as well as gender. The domestic ideal of a woman's purpose and eventual aim in life as directed toward a *telos* of home and family is deeply raced and classed. Women of color or working-class women, in particular, whose lives fall outside this imagined white, middle-class trajectory, find their identities, lives, and work unrecognizable within dominant frameworks. In the professions, success stories about individual women as tokens often imply that their achievements are the just reward for exceptional personal qualities rather than the result of cultural and structural privilege. Similarly, the illusion of free and unfettered choice eschews how women's decisions are framed by economic, educational, geographic, and other constraints that operate unevenly across class, race, ethnicity, education, and so on. By directing attention to the personal rather than the social, structural, or institutional, rhetorics of exceptionalism and choice are complicit in maintaining unequal life chances. As I argue throughout this book, such rhetorics of gendered labor function to increase divides among women and preclude alliances on the basis of gender.

As the breadth of utopian experimentation in the period attests, midcentury industrialization disrupted existing norms so as to simultaneously invite resistance and open a space of possibility. In this time of flux, intentional communities modeled alternative configurations of women's work, modifying the value accorded housework, women's access to diverse occupations, and interactions between work and family. Individually, the chapters to follow illustrate the gendering or regendering of particular kinds of labor in a unique space and time. Together, they offer a better understanding of what midcentury norms of gendered labor proved mutable or recalcitrant and what rhetorical-material factors facilitated and impeded change. On the whole, the constructs of gendered work during industrialism speak to gendered work today, especially insofar as attempts to reform or revise women's work continue to falter along lines of race or class. Ultimately, the industrial *telos* toward specialization, hierarchy, and sequestration undermined the utopian projects of the age. Nevertheless, by examining the rhetorical contours of gendered labor in utopian communities, we gain a deeper understanding of both the enduring patterns that emerged in the Industrial Revolution and the communities that embodied a counternarrative to those trends. The remainder of this introduction elaborates the theoretical framework, historical background, and methodological approach of this study.

ECOLOGIES OF GENDER

My turn to ecologies builds on scholarship comprising the so-called "material turn" in rhetorical studies. This body of work emphasizes that, given the interanimation of language and the material world, rhetoricians can no longer think of texts as their sole or primary point of investigation. Nor can they think of texts as operating *on* or responding *to* a context that texts themselves stand above or apart from. Instead, rhetoric "must diffuse outward to include the material environment, things (including the technological), our own embodiment, and a complex understanding of ecological relationality as participating in rhetorical practices and their theorization" (Rickert 3). Besides adding spaces, bodies, things, animals, and tasks to our objects of study, material rhetoricians have reworked central rhetorical concepts such as agency (Cooper), intention (Blair), situation (Edbauer), and context (Rickert), among others. Throughout this book, I consider the implications of these contributions for feminist rhetoricians, scholars whose work has performed its own revisions and reimaginings of rhetorical history and theory. Specifically, what does our increasing awareness of the interconnections among words and things, spaces and discourse, tropes and bodies mean for feminist historiography? How might these concerns animate the selection, analysis, and weighting of our sources? How might we apply our expanded understanding of rhetoric to the historical examination of gender? I theorize ecologies of gender as one way of broaching these questions and articulating the productive convergence and tension between material and feminist rhetorics.[7]

To elaborate further, I describe below three premises that inform my analysis, as a way of defining what I mean by ecologies of gender and how a study of gendered ecologies proceeds. What does it mean to view gender as ecological? How does this stance diverge from other potential ways of understanding gender? I use ecologies of gender as a shorthand for the notion that *gendering is an emergent and ongoing rhetorical process resulting from the intra-actions of human and nonhuman bodies.* My approach builds on a tradition of feminist rhetorical scholarship often traced back to Barbara Biesecker's 1992 article "Coming to Terms," which suggested that dominant approaches were "fenc[ing] out a vast array of collective rhetorical practices to which there belongs no proper name" and "deflect[ing] critical attention away from those structures of oppression larger than individual consciousness and will" (340, 342). In contrast, the hallmark characteristic of an ecological approach to gender is its view of the production of gender as dispersed and contingent. This view insists that constructions of gender are not solely the result of willed, intentional actions by particular human individuals or groups. As a result, an ecological view suggests that disrupting gendered constructions is no simple affair—striving to intervene in gendered ecologies might be compared to "riding a bicycle on a gravel road" (Bennett 38). Conversely, an ecological approach may be seen as weakening our ability to hold individuals to account for their participation in perpetuating misogyny. Yet if this model sacrifices the clarity and simplicity of a more instrumental approach, it does so in favor of a feminist materialist approach that does not minimize the body—and material oppression and violence—in its concentration on discursive constructions of gender.[8]

Constructions of gender are rhetorical and variable. That is, gender is a production and performance, varying across space and time, rather than eternal and given. Gendered ecologies vary just as natural ecologies vary: according to the local networks in and through which they emerge. This perspective builds on the longstanding efforts of feminist rhetoricians to gender our understanding of the practice, theory, and history of rhetoric, including both the recovery of historical women rhetors as well as the theoretical and methodological revisions that writing women into the history of rhetoric requires.[9] Once it was established that women were indeed practicing rhetoric, often in spaces from which they had been historically or culturally excluded, scholars began to ask how those spaces and practices had come to be gendered masculine in the first place. That is, they began explicating the history and rhetoric of gender itself, recognizing gender as rhetorical insofar as human beings require convincing, over and over, consciously or unconsciously, that gender is a meaningful category for understanding ourselves and our world.[10] Roxanne Mountford's *The Gendered Pulpit* is exemplary of this transition, examining the gendering of the space of the pulpit through literary and religious texts before considering how women preachers inhabit, repurpose, resist, and comply with that gendering. Her study situates novels, preaching manuals, sacred architecture, church congregations, and women preachers as part of a gendered ecology. Ecologies of gender are one way that feminist rhetoricians might answer Jessica Enoch's call to consider "the numerous possibilities that emerge when the historiographic concern becomes the history of rhetorical gendering rather than the gendered rereading of the rhetorical tradition" ("Releasing Hold" 72).

Though ecologies of gender as a theoretical approach might be applied to nearly any facet of gendered experience, I identify *work* as a particularly salient node in ecologies of gender, central to the gendering of spaces, bodies, tasks, and objects. Rhetorics of work touch on nearly all aspects of women's lives and intersect private and public domains often depicted as separate. For example, nineteenth-century schools were reframed as domestic spaces in an effort to recruit women as teachers; similarly, World War II childcare centers were assessed in the postwar moment as inadequate substitutes for the nuclear family home (Enoch, *Domestic Occupations*). These competing spatial rhetorics had important consequences for female teachers and working mothers and variously gendered their inhabitants as "natural teachers," "patriotic women workers," and "insufficient mothers and homemakers." Similarly, feminist rhetoricians have traced the rhetorical-material gendering and regendering of work tasks and spaces associated with World War II factories, invention, and U.S. Navy submarines (see Jack, "Acts"; Hallenbeck, "Inventing"; and Buchanan, "A Few Good"). My project joins this recent work in exploring the ways that gender is constructed and reconstructed, the boundaries of "women's work" shifting and drawn anew in often surprising ways. More broadly, I suggest that work and gender co-construct one another insofar as ideas about work fundamentally shape understandings of gender, and vice versa—indeed, it is sometimes difficult to tell where ideas about work end and ideas about gender begin.

Gender emerges from the intra-actions of humans and nonhumans.[11] By stressing that gender is both rhetorical and ecological, I move beyond determinist or instrumentalist models that view gender as the result of intentional rhetorical action by individual or collective human agents. Thus, ecologies of gender decenter humans as the sole locus of agency and dethrone human intention as the point of initiation for rhetoric, suggesting "a wider social field of distribution" for gendered rhetorics (Edbauer 13). Indeed, the rhetorical circulation of gender often happens in everyday, not-explicitly-persuasive encounters that are nonetheless rhetorical. Rhetorics of gender "do not always emerge from the deliberate efforts of individual women or groups of women. Often, they do not emerge from the deliberate efforts of anyone at all but as the unintended by-products of the social institutions that surround us" (Hallenbeck, "Toward" 24). In this light, my project considers not only "the places where rhetorics travel and are deployed but also the external social, economic, and political influences that serve as exigencies for particular . . . arguments about women" (Dingo, *Networking* 17). In this light, pursuing ecologies of gender can help feminist rhetoricians avoid designating historical scapegoats or heroines, instead considering the holistic emergence of gender norms as a product of innumerable interactions beyond the control of individual or collective human activity.

Though a feminist perspective continues to center the experience of women and other marginalized groups, ecologies of gender call us to consider how nonhumans share in, facilitate, or resist that marginalization. An ecological perspective suggests that rhetoric is not the sole province of humans, that "rhetoric emerges not solely from one or between multiple intentional human being(s) but from the entangled associations among various things, human and otherwise, that constitute everyday life" (Walsh et al. 438). For instance, it is important to consider how gendered technologies—ranging from washing machines and dishwashers to the birth control pill—succeed or fail in liberating women from domestic drudgery or reproductive determinism, respectively (see Cowan; Adams). Regardless of our attempts to enlist them in our projects—commercial, industrial, social, and political—nonhumans often do more or other than we expect, exceeding our intentions and displaying their own thing-power (see Bennett). This nonhuman excess participates in ecologies of gender alongside human designs and projects. Thus, an ecological stance attempts to do justice to a view of gender as produced through spaces, bodies, objects, and tasks—as well as texts.

Constructions of gender are not random or arbitrary. In opening gender to an ecological perspective, the attention to nonhuman forces and the contingent nature of gendered constructions can imply that gender just "happens," as if by chance. For instance, Bruno Latour argues that "no explanation is stronger or more powerful than providing connections among unrelated elements or showing how one element holds many others" ("On Actor-Network" 375). But an ecologist of gender is not content to simply map these connections without considering "the nature and quality of those associations" (Walsh et al. 456). For instance, a material-feminist study of World War II factory rhetorics concludes that the "arrangements of space, time, bodies, and dress" in these factories are "not separate or arbitrary," as they produce and reproduce gender difference (Jack, "Acts" 288–89). In the context of this study, the systemic social and economic devaluing of labor associated with femininity or performed by women does not just *happen*. As Jennifer Bay cautions,

> While rhetorical studies is having a field day with nonhuman objects, the nonhumans we encounter every day are still being left out: the housekeeping assistant who cleans your room at a conference hotel while you are at sessions; the migrant worker who picked the strawberries you ate for breakfast; the Chinese woman who assembled your iPhone. (Walsh et al. 448)

Tellingly, Bay's examples center on the intersections of gendered labor with class, race, and ethnicity. As we "flatten" the contributions of humans and nonhumans, we need to be wary of how flattening relationships *among humans* can mask and perpetuate privilege.

Ecologies of gender are never *only* about gender. Latour's maxim—"Nothing can be reduced to anything else, nothing can be deduced from anything else, everything may be allied to everything else"—urges an irreductionist approach that refuses simple or singular explanations (*Pasteurization* 163). But where Latour's irreductionism is aimed at reincorporating nonhumans into our (his)stories, feminist rhetoricians might embrace irreductionism in service of other forms of intersectionality. To paraphrase philosopher Barbara Cassin, we need to bear in mind that some humans have been and still are considered or treated as nonhuman: "The Sophists were a little like plants, *homoioi phutoi*, but so were women, slaves, children, and animals. None were human. . . . these materialities of other sorts are always already nonhuman" (Walsh et al. 448). In this light, feminist rhetoricians' embrace of material rhetorics might focus less on things in themselves and more on "the complex material-discursive process by which bodies become things" (Walsh et al. 446). In sum, when we engage in ecological historical inquiry through the node of gender, we should not rest comfortably with the narratives we produce. As Jenny (Edbauer) Rice cautions, "it is necessary for the ecologist to include 'the presence of many *objectors*' in her objective account" (Walsh et al. 436). For an ecologist of gender, these objectors are often the subjects gendered as women whose classed and raced experiences are muffled in both dominant historical narratives and the archive itself.

The three premises I have outlined as defining ecologies of gender are essential for understanding gender as it was re/produced in the midcentury United States. Gender in this period was indeed highly variable, as illustrated by, among other phenomena, the association of factory work first with women and children, and later with male immigrants. The age of industrialization also incorporated many new nonhumans into gendered assemblages: specific inventions like sewing machines, national infrastructure like railroads, and abstract constructs like "wages" as a newly dominant form of compensation. Finally, midcentury gender ideals were far from arbitrary in their work to define womanhood as essentially white and middle class, positioning black and working-class women as its foil or as victims to be saved.

INDUSTRIAL ASSEMBLAGES

The unprecedented social, economic, and cultural shifts accompanying industrialization are central to both subjects at the heart of this study: midcentury utopianism and women's work. On the whole, *Utopian Genderscapes* asks that we consider intentional communities in light of not only their overt successes or failures but also their larger significance as lived testaments to the possibility of different constructions of gendered space, practices, and labor in the early industrial age. In what follows, I provide an initial exploration of the intersections of these concerns with industrialization in the midcentury United States.

The late eighteenth and early nineteenth centuries witnessed the rapid spread and development of U.S. industrialization. The first cotton and textile mills opened in the 1780s and 1790s (alongside the invention of the cotton gin in 1793)—precursors to the famed Boston Manufacturing Company mills of Waltham and Lowell. Transportation underwent its own "revolution," between the first steamboat in 1807, the opening of the Erie Canal in 1825, and the establishment of the Baltimore and Ohio Railroad in 1830. By 1850, America boasted over thirty-five hundred miles of canals, and railroad mileage tripled in the 1840s (Laurie 22). While the 1807 Embargo Act, which cut off British exports, ensured that these new modes of transportation would be largely dedicated to internal trade, inventions such as the mechanical reaper (1831), the refrigerator (1835), and the steel plow (1837) changed work from the ground up. Amid these developments, the American economy shifted steadily out of agriculture, which dropped from 75 percent of the labor force to just 36 percent over the course of the century (Margo 3). Much of this labor moved into manufacturing, which, while nearly nonexistent before 1820, employed just under a third of all non-farm workers by 1840 and reached a fairly stable level (37 percent of the total labor force) by 1860 (Margo 7–8). The labor force itself surged in the 1840s—accounting for all aggregate change prior to the Civil War—due largely to a sharp increase in Irish-Catholic immigration (Margo 3).

The Industrial Revolution irrevocably changed "work" in nineteenth-century America. With improvements in transportation between 1790 and 1840, the market revolution discouraged "the making of goods for immediate use in favor of producing commodities for exchange in the marketplace" (Laurie 15). Work in the market economy gravitated from agricultural communities and artisanal shops to manufacturing centers. As the factory model emerged, work tasks were specialized and routinized (as well as deskilled), completed at a higher pace and intensity, and subject to increasing discipline and supervision. At the same time, this transition was gradual, uneven, and geographically varied—for much of the nineteenth century the subsistence economy existed in tension with the new market economy.[12] During this transition, the unrest of industrialization fostered new utopian projects as well as enduring changes to women's work.

Midcentury Utopianism

Mid-nineteenth-century America teemed with possibility. The optimistic *ethos* of seemingly daily inventions and innovations spilled over into ideas about reinventing Americans' personal, spiritual, and political lives. As President John Tyler (1841–45) quipped, "There is nothing like the elbow room of a new country." One notable facet of this cultural and imaginative "elbow room" was "a tolerance of communitarian ventures which Americans today would hardly find credible" (Durnbaugh 72). Indeed, Americans not only tolerated but also celebrated the many utopian ventures in their midst. Brook Farm alone welcomed four thousand visitors in a single year, and communities of all stripes featured prominently as tourist destinations and subjects of American and European travel writing.

Unlike the contemporary stereotype of utopian communities withdrawing from the world, based largely on popular views of "hippie communes" of the 1960s and 1970s, nineteenth-century intentional communities were active participants in the political, economic, and social developments and debates of the era. Indeed, noting the common tendency to link these two prominent utopian periods in the nation's past, Anne Rose highlights the risk of overstating the comparison:

> The historical parallel should not obscure the fact that voluntary associations were an even more important agency of social reform in the early nineteenth century. . . . So often were old traditions broken and new conditions met by the concerted action of individuals, in evangelical crusades, workingmen's associations, antislavery conventions, and utopian communities that these associations, rather than the far less flexible mechanism of party politics, must be judged the type of reform organization most appropriate to this society. (ix)

Though utopian activity was a prominent force throughout the nineteenth century, midcentury America—particularly the 1840s—witnessed the high tide of utopian experimentation in response to industrialization. In this context, utopian communities betrayed a "desire to impose order on a society they believed was coming apart at the seams" (Vickers 2). Indeed, contemporary Americans may struggle "to understand, much less appreciate, the depth of faith in individual potential and perfectability" that sparked the sixty utopian communities founded in the 1840s United States "in an effort to meliorate social, educational, economic, and political inequities and injustices" (Delano, *Brook Farm* xv; Eakin).

One strand of this midcentury utopian surge was imported from Europe and had its roots in the Protestant Reformation. As the Reformation stressed personal piety over religious formalism and orthodoxy, many Separatist pietist communities immigrated to the United States with the goal of living their understanding of the good life in a community of shared goods modeled after the apostles. The Labadists, settling in Maryland in 1683, were the first in a chain of pietist groups including the Mennonites, Amish, Hutterites, and Shakers, as well as smaller settlements such as the Zoar Community of Ohio, the Amana Society in Iowa, and the Ephrata Cloister in Pennsylvania. The Harmony Society (1804–1905)—the subject of chapter 3—joined this tradition of pietist communities, emigrating from the Württemberg region of Germany in 1804 after increasing persecution and harassment from religious and government leaders. The community eventually established three settlements: Harmony, in Butler County, Pennsylvania (1804–14); New Harmony, on the Wabash River in Posey County, Indiana (1814–25); and Economy, on the Ohio River eighteen miles northwest of Pittsburgh, Pennsylvania (1825–1905). Like other pietist communities, the Harmonists were millennialists who endorsed celibacy and followed a prophet, theirs being George Rapp. Numbering around eight hundred members at their peak, the Harmonists attempted to live a pure and holy life in preparation for the millennium that they believed would come in their lifetime. Like many other communities founded by charismatic religious or secular leaders, the Harmony Society lost some of its vital force after Rapp's death in 1847: from this date, the community adopted a more pragmatic, entrepreneurial philosophy until its dissolution in 1905.

Another strand of midcentury utopianism was secular and homegrown, inspired by the views of Robert Owen and Charles Fourier. Both philosophers and social critics attributed many of society's problems to industrialization, and Owenite communities in the United States and Europe practiced socialist ideas of cooperative labor. Owen himself founded New Harmony, Indiana, which purchased its ready-made communal dwellings from the Harmonists when they decamped for Pennsylvania in 1825. Similarly, Fourier created a system of "phalanxes," communities meant to gather people with all types of personalities. Fourier promoted communitarianism as a model of reform that could leapfrog incremental political change but also avoid unnecessary violence (such as the French Revolution). Around thirty Fourierist U.S. communities were formed between 1843 and 1845, including the Hopedale Community in Massachusetts and the North American Phalanx in New Jersey. In the Owenite or Fourierist model, intentional communities were seen as a lever of social change. Brook Farm (1841–47)—the focus of chapter 2—combined New England transcendentalism with Fourier's associationism. In 1841, the community established itself in West Roxbury, Massachusetts, about eight miles from Boston. The renowned community functioned on a much smaller scale than the Harmony Society, eventually including around thirty-two associates (who had each purchased a five-hundred-dollar share in the joint stock company), though the community also housed boarders, students, and members who could not afford to buy a share. In 1844, Brook Farm officially adopted Fourier's model. Many members rebelled against the increasing rigidity of Fourier's schema compared with the early "transcendental days," and financial difficulties required unpopular retrenchments in food, drink, and leisure. Eventually, a smallpox outbreak and a fire spelled the end for this small New England community, which had an outsized impact on the American imagination in its time and since.

Though these religious and political—pietist and socialist—underpinnings may seem quite distinct, they fermented in midcentury America into a potent mix of communal impulses that sparked intentional communities with shared practices and goals. This mixture is suggestively illustrated by the Oneida Community (1848–81), the brainchild of John Humphrey Noyes, who held that the millennium had already happened and thus one could live a sinless life (a belief known as perfectionism). As a homegrown American community, Oneida shared many qualities with pietist, Separatist groups: relocation due to public hostility, millennialism, and a charismatic leader—surprisingly, Oneida's notorious practice of complex or polyamorous marriage sprung from similar religious tenets as the equally notorious celibacy of the Shakers and Harmonists. Oneida also shared with both secular and pietist communities a commitment to employing each individual according to their powers of mind and body. Indeed, all these communities advocated, whether in secular or religious terms, a view of labor as sacred, as helping to develop each individual as fully as possible. This commitment to shared, equal labor was based in a desire to overcome sexual as well as class inequality. As a group, intentional communities implemented innovative practices regarding women's roles and work. One aspect of their rejection of convention was that children should be raised communally rather than under the primary care of biological parents. Though Marx and Engels would later dismiss nineteenth-century "utopian socialism" in favor of their own "scientific socialism," many of the principles championed by midcentury intentional communities—collectivism, egalitarianism, the rejection of capitalism and individualism—reflect a softer version of communism, what Benjamin Kunkel terms "Marxish" thought.

Conditions in industrializing America called for new ways of thinking about labor. The new market economy was in direct tension with the subsistence economy. American workers were "acutely aware of their class interests" and "fought the transformation of their labor power into a commodity to be bought and sold like any other merchandise" (Laurie 9). Men and women especially resisted the regimentation of the factory, and employers confronted "the difficulties of molding a factory workforce out of a pre-industrial population" (Margo 28). Workers who transitioned from farm to factory worked more annual hours in indoor labor that varied less by season. An early labor movement in the 1820s, known as "radicalism," fought for bread-and-butter causes such as shorter hours, higher wages, and better working conditions rather than systemic overhaul (Margo 30). But conditions continued to deteriorate. By 1832, five hundred cotton mills in New England competed by cutting costs (Freeman 66). Wage cuts in the 1830s sparked national labor protests "in which the language of republicanism and the spirit of the Revolution were invoked to mobilize workers against what was seen as an emerging tyranny of economic power" (Freeman 66–67). In this context, the views of social reformers and critics such as Orestes Brownson, Alexis de Tocqueville, and Seth Luther spread, suggesting that the antidemocratic ethos of the factory system was essential rather than circumstantial. Increased immigration contributed to a surplus of labor, which disincentivized employers from responding to worker demands.[13] Union organizing diminished with the economic panic of 1837 and the depression of the 1840s, prompting reform-minded individuals to look elsewhere for solutions to the alienation and dehumanization of industrial labor.

One place they looked was to the utopian communities that emerged in areas where industrialism flourished (fig. 1.1). Early U.S. settlements on the coasts or in river valleys were closely tied to European markets, whereas interior settlements lived a primarily subsistence life. Over time, a land shortage in the Northeast caused an agrarian crisis, and men and women worked to supplement income through market activities. "In the struggle to maintain a traditional way of life, the farming families of southeastern New England were pioneering the changeover to capitalist methods of production" (Stokes 7). By the 1840s, when the largest spate of utopian organizing occurred, the market economy was in ascendance throughout the north. Intentional communities emerged around the

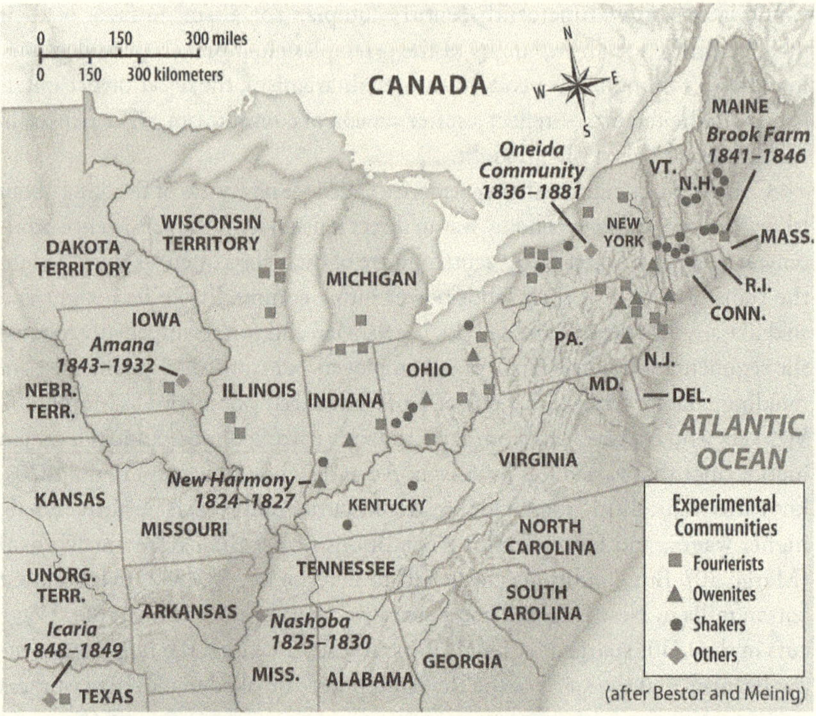

Fig. 1.1. "Major Communal Experiments before 1860." From Rebecca Edwards et al., *America's History*, 9th ed., p. 312; copyright 2018 by Bedford/St. Martin's; all rights reserved; used by permission of the publisher Macmillan Learning.

country, but the vast majority formed in New England and the mid-Atlantic. New York was particularly prolific, spawning the Shakers, Oneida, and the Mormons. In the South, which industrialized later (and debatably only partially) in the nineteenth century, intentional communities were far less common. The national transition out of agriculture was more rapid in New England, where farmers accounted for less than 40 percent of the workforce by the onset of the Civil War (Margo 7). In comparison, the south was the only region with a majority of workers still in farming by 1900 (7). In this light, I extend Lawrence Foster's depiction of Oneida as a strategy for coping with "the crisis of transition from pre-industrial to more modern forms of family and social life" to midcentury intentional communities writ large (*Religion* 4).

In contrast to utopian scholarship that focuses on one community in great depth, *Utopian Genderscapes* breaks new ground as a monograph considering gendered labor across three distinct communities: Brook Farm, the Harmony Society, and the Oneida Community. In so doing, I offer a new take on the rhetorical significance of intentional communities. Perhaps due to the cultural and ideological baggage of the term "utopia," intentional communities are often remembered and considered through an evaluative lens, qualifying entire communities—or particular aspects of those communities—as successes or failures (see Pitzer; Sargent, "Three Faces"). For instance, some scholarship associates a community's success with longevity (Kanter), a questionable marker given that many communities did not intend to be permanent. *Utopian Genderscapes* looks beyond success and failure by considering these communities in terms of their rhetorical significance within midcentury ecologies of gender. While a conventional rhetorical approach to these communities might focus, as many historical accounts do, on the founders' goals, my ecological approach decenters intention to consider the emergent rhetorics of gender in these spaces. The analyses in the chapters to follow excavate the often-ambivalent legacies of these experiments in living. While utopian communities do offer significant lived alternatives to contemporary practices of gendered labor, *Utopian Genderscapes* also illustrates the limits of these reforms, limits that result from the communities' participation in, rather than exemption from, larger nineteenth-century ecologies of gender.

I locate the rhetorical significance of intentional communities in their reconfigurations of women's work in the early industrial age. As an 1856 article in the *United States Magazine* remarked, "It is noticeable that all these communities, numerous as they have been, accord equality of social position and political rights to woman" ("Social Communities" 445). In Shaker communities, women worked collaboratively and rotated among jobs, and Owenites and Fourierists adopted communal housekeeping to free women for industrial work. Even as communities such as the Shakers, Oneida, and the Mormons were largely patriarchal in their philosophy, their practices allowed for an unusual degree of participation by women. In this light, I articulate midcentury utopian experimentation as part of an ecology or assemblage that questioned new industrial forms of labor and gender. This stance is based not in a claim that intentional communities perceived themselves in this way—though the direct passage of ideas, individuals, inventions, and goods between these communities does not foreclose such an interpretation. Rather, I suggest that these communities collectively operated as *arguments on the landscape* with suasive force for midcentury notions of gender and labor. Gesturing toward this collective impact, an 1844 article in the *New York Herald* observed that, "though of little influence individually, yet the impulses which they communicated to the popular mind, and the variety of elements they combine and exercise, make them powerful" ("Wonderful Progress of the New Philosophy").

Women's Work and the Industrial Revolution

When intentional communities formed in response to the Industrial Revolution, they entered the conversation about women's work. At the start of the century, 8 percent of free females age sixteen or older were in the workforce, a number that climbed to 11 percent by midcentury (Margo 4). Many of these women entered new positions in the industrial economy: the 1850 census recorded 225,922 women and 731,137 men in manufacturing (Abbott 81).[14] Women also occupied professions deemed appropriate for their sex: nursing was a popular option, and women comprised between 65 and 80 percent of teachers in every region (Kelley 10). In addition, some privileged women found considerable success in the "female economy," running stores that catered specifically to women, such as millinery shops (Gamber 5). Printing also deserves attention as "a skilled trade in which women have long been employed" but in which they have been consistently outnumbered by men (Abbott 86). Throughout the nineteenth century, women's work varied significantly by marital status, geography, race, and ethnicity: the rate of married women in the workforce hovered around 5 percent, lower than in the late 1700s (Margo 4–5). Women in cities were more likely to work, as were black women, in part because of the lower economic status of black men.

Perhaps the biggest change in women's work with the onset of industrialization was the decline in household production. By 1830, industrial manufacture superseded home spinning and weaving: "When the first boats made their trip westward on the Erie Canal in 1825, New York homesteads turned out a total of 16.5 million yards of textiles or nearly 9 yards per capita. Ten years later those figures were halved . . . by 1855 total production was under one million yards and per capita output was no more than one-third of a yard" (Laurie 24). This transition was duplicated in Pennsylvania in the 1830s and continued westward. Yet the decline of home production did not mean that women's domestic work ceased to be productive:

> The deepening intrusion of market relations into family economies involved all sorts of different women in selling commodities, making commodities, buying commodities, turning parts of their homes into commodities, disposing of their time and skill as commodities. Even for the middle class, the idea is no longer tenable that the world of most women was remote from the market, that their labor had no cash value, that their homes were not also places of work, both paid and unpaid. (Stanley 78)

In midcentury America, wives' roles as "budget managers, boardinghouse keepers, industrial homeworkers, or wage earners . . . were essential, not supplementary"

(Greenwald 9). Moreover, women's unpaid household labor—the primary work of both married and unmarried women throughout the century—made important contributions to familial, local, and national economies.[15] Women's housework encompassed a variety of subsistence-producing activities that allowed employers to pay men less than a subsistence wage: thus, housework "had a value without having a price" (Boydston, "To Earn" 13). Indeed, the home was at the heart of new property and wage relations in both southern and northern households. As historian Amy Dru Stanley explains, "The unity of production and reproduction based on dependent labor within the household ought to be seen as characteristic of *both* free and slave society" (82).

Women also seized new work opportunities outside the home. By 1860, twenty-five thousand women (one-fourth of the entire labor force) worked in manufacturing—two-thirds of whom were in the clothing trades (Stansell 108). Prior to the Civil War, factory work was dominated by children and young single women—whose work was less valuable in agriculture—before midcentury immigrants replaced them as another cheap labor force. Mill owners preferred to hire young women for several reasons: they were a revolving labor force (not a permanent proletariat), they were used to hard work, and their employment avoided the social stigma of child labor. Factory work was deeply segregated by sex: by 1860, just three industries in New York City employed 90 percent of the city's working women (Stansell 105). Predictably, factory work was also subject to a sexual division of labor: women tended the machines while men held positions in construction, maintenance and repair, and supervision or management. The minute, repetitive tasks of factory work were believed to resemble sewing, and this analogy between low status, low pay, low-skill industrial work and women's historical work in the home thus participated in classifying certain factory work as "women's work." On the whole, female wage earning was most common among blacks, immigrants, and the laboring poor, "the renowned case of Yankee farm girls employed at the Lowell mills notwithstanding" (Stanley 79).

Perhaps the least understood form of women's work in the mid-nineteenth century is "putting-out" or "outwork." In the putting-out system, women workers labored at home, producing intermediate goods later crafted into finished products. This model was adopted first in textiles and then by other industries like sewing and shoemaking. As a precursor to the working patterns of sweatshops, "'outworkers' performed ever more finely subdivided tasks for which they were almost always paid by the piece" (Margo 29). By 1850, shoemaking had been broken down into forty distinct steps (Laurie 41). As Alexis de Tocqueville commented on his 1831–32 tour of the country, "What astonishes me is not so much the marvelous grandeur of some undertakings, as the innumerable magnitude of small ones" (qtd. in Laurie 45). Outwork was largely completed in the worker's lodging (often cramped, with poor lighting and ventilation) and was "synonymous with women's work" (Stansell 106). By contracting out as much of the labor as possible, employers passed on the costs of space, light, fuel, and tools to their outworkers. Given the dispersed nature of the work, outworkers had little chance to protest their exploitation in a system that recruited women's patriarchal subordination within the family into industrial work.[16]

By changing the nature, location, pay, and conditions of men's and women's work, the market economy destabilized ideologies of gender. As Stanley argues, "What we know as the market revolution posed a momentous moral problem that contemporaries, in the first instance, understood as a problem of gender" (74). For many men, work for wages was demasculinizing, as Enlightenment thought viewed persons who labored for others as dependents. Indeed, wage labor was legally categorized with marriage and slavery as a domestic relationship. In this context, changing work relations demanded a renegotiation of what men and women owed one another, particularly within marriage:

> In a period when the productive household economy was disappearing and the family wage economy had yet fully to take shape . . . hard times and the irregularity of employment made many husbands poor providers and weakened their control of their families. At the same time, female wage work, however lowly, provided many women some means of support apart from men. (Stanley 81)

Married women also gained the right to own and dispose of property and wages over the course of the 1830s. To counter these challenges to the gender order, Americans adopted a language of separate spheres that aimed to restore masculine privilege to male wage workers.[17] This project joins Stanley in conceiving of separate spheres as a coping rather than descriptive mechanism, as "the first fruits—not the last word—of an effort to rethink the social and cultural problems posed by the spread of free market relations" (77).

The new market economy also had implications for relations among women. In contrast to Gerda Lerner's well-known formulation of the 1830s lady and mill girl, Faye Dudden suggests that, "in fact, the lady's opposite number was more apt to be the domestic" (46). For more affluent, white families, the mid-nineteenth century effected the separation of the idealized wife and mother from devalued subsistence labor. Daughters of middle-class families were "withdrawn from housework in favor of expanded education and training in genteel accomplishments during an extended period of girlhood" (Dudden 47). Middle- and upper-class women were encouraged to embrace a new domestic ideal, a model in which "being a lady . . . meant *not* doing certain kinds of housework" (Stansell

159). In midcentury American cities, 15–30 percent of all households included live-in domestic servants who took on the work of heating and cleaning the house, with laundry distinguished as the most onerous and first-delegated task (Dudden 1). For white housewives, supervising servants was one way of ameliorating the more negative, isolating aspects of the "cult of domesticity." And changes in the nature of domestic service further distanced women who served from women who were served.

While eighteenth-century "help" had worked alongside housewives in producing goods for the market, nineteenth-century "domestics" worked longer hours completing mundane and taxing household labor that housewives declined to perform themselves. Like factory hands, midcentury domestics were subject to increasing work discipline and surveillance. Tellingly, free blacks were denied the title of "help," reinforcing the understanding of domestic service as a degraded form of labor (Dudden 33). Though wages for domestics were as low as any other women's work—at $1.50/week in 1835—the provision of room and board made domestic service an economically sound option. Nevertheless, domestic work remained the least popular option for women workers and thus became closely identified with particular populations who lacked other options. Early nineteenth-century domestic servants were a mix of rural and urban, native and immigrant, black and white, freeborn and slave women. But the midcentury influx of immigrants made race and ethnicity an increasingly important factor in women's work. As this new population flooded the workforce in the 1840s and 1850s, Irish women fleeing the famine replaced Yankee farm women in the textile industry and displaced black women domestics into specialized positions as laundresses, charwomen, and maids—in 1855, only 3 percent of the servants in New York City were black (Stansell 157). By midcentury, domestic work was associated with Irish women in their teens and twenties: available evidence suggests that "almost every young Irish woman who came to America spent some time in domestic service" (Dudden 62). Amid these shifts, class tensions surfaced in the form of the midcentury "servant problem." Midcentury publications and personal accounts are rife with references to the difficulty of finding, training, and keeping good servants.[18] With the influx of Irish immigrants, Irish domestics—"Bridgets" and "Biddys"—were excoriated in a powerful confluence of ethnic and religious prejudice.[19] Even when public discourse framed working-class and immigrant women sympathetically, they were seen as needing an intervention.[20] In this way, domestics were subject not only to their mistresses' standards for cooking and cleaning but also to their desire to "improve" immigrant servants through benevolence and missionary work.[21]

The midcentury period was also a tumultuous time for women's industrial work. Speed-ups and wage cuts in the mid- and late 1840s made New

England textile mills less desirable and respectable employment destinations for women. In the wake of the 1830s strikes and the movement for a ten hour workday, fewer young New Englanders were coming to mill towns. On the whole, increases in women's wages slowed or stalled as new cheap labor arrived via immigrant populations. The situation was similarly grim for outworkers: "Piece rates generally declined and the pace and intensity of outwork increased in the late 1840s and early 1850s, as immigrants glutted labor markets in cities" (Margo 29). New sewing machines drove piece rates so low that fifteen- to eighteen-hour workdays were not uncommon, and seamstresses who couldn't afford to buy one of the new sewing machines (invented in 1846) were forced to work for someone who could. Thus, the outwork system began to evolve into the sweatshop model, as "women and girls began to work in the 1850s for unmarried journeymen in the same capacities as wives and daughters who assisted tailors in their own homes" (Stansell 117). New technologies also participated in the biological experience of class: "A practiced observer like Virginia Penny could recognize a seamstress on the street by her peculiar stooped carriage" (Stansell 113–114).

Despite a wave of strikes and protests in the 1820s and 1830s, women's labor activism had little effect on public opinion about industrial working conditions. In 1825, New York seamstresses led the first all-women's strike in the country, followed by shoe binders in Lynn, Massachusetts; Baltimore seamstresses; and New York bookbinders. The Lowell factory girls went on strike in 1834 and 1836, protesting conditions that were worsening by almost any measure: a study of four New England mills found that, between 1836 and 1850, productivity increased by half, while wages increased by only 4 percent (Freeman 65–66). Still, European visitors to Lowell found it "a commercial Utopia," at least when compared to English factory cities (Freeman 43). Though labor operative Seth Luther reframed the mills as "*Paradise Lost*," the Waltham-Lowell system continued to represent "industrialism in political and cultural discourse, a pole for criticism and, more often, praise of a new type of society" (Freeman 70, 58). Public opinion advised women labor activists to limit their work so men could make more money and protect them. Indeed, workingmen's assistance in these battles "depended on how much, in a given trade, a customary sexual division of labor legitimated the women's presence" (Stansell 142). On the whole, public commentary remained ambivalent at best about women's role in the new industrial economy; responses to women's activism suggested that, if they were unsatisfied, perhaps they didn't belong in such work in the first place.

In recent decades, feminist rhetoricians have begun incorporating women's work into the history of rhetoric. In one sense, feminist rhetoricians have always studied women's work: rhetoric *is* women's work. But we haven't always considered women's rhetoric as a means of self-support, as prey to the same issues of professionalism and work-life "balance" as other occupations.[22] Recently, scholars have turned from addressing rhetoric *as* women's work to considering the workplace as a site for rhetorical production. Notably, much of this scholarship has illuminated rhetorical strategies by which women negotiate their gender in hostile professions. For example, Susan Wells's *Out of the Dead House* identifies women physicians' rhetorical strategies of masquerade and travesty, eschewing or foregrounding their gender (5–6). Similarly, Carolyn Skinner examines how women physicians' ethos combines femininity with medical expertise and authority (*Women Physicians*). Indeed, women breaking new professional ground often face a rhetorical dilemma: either embrace a false gender-blind anonymity to comply with the field's discursive norms (Jack, *Science*) or use more marginal genres (popular texts, personal writing) to regender the profession and "recruit" other women (Applegarth, *Rhetoric*). Through their study of women's entry into male-dominated fields, these projects indicate a new direction for feminist rhetorical scholarship—examining how professions are gendered and regendered, how workers are gendered in and through their labor, and how bodies, spaces, and objects participate in this rhetorical gendering. My project joins this growing body of scholarship examining work as a crucial node in the rhetorical construction of gender. Specifically, in its study of women's work during the Industrial Revolution, *Utopian Genderscapes* explores the inaugural moment of many norms and practices of gendered labor that continue to structure women's lives and opportunities today: the rise of the factory, the shift of labor from home-spaces to workplaces, the invention of housework, the role of birth control and childcare, the question of compensation, and the feminization of particular kinds of labor.

As I have suggested here, the United States in the 1840s inhabited a moment of transition or crisis for industrialization and women's work. In this turbulent moment, with its potent mix of promise for the future and threat of a lost past, Americans turned to utopian communities in an attempt to help steer these rapid social and economic changes. Midcentury utopianism responded to an industrializing moment in which norms of gendered labor were in flux and under construction. As the century progressed, understandings of gender and labor coalesced and calcified, especially in the industrial centers of the Northeast and Midwest where utopianism once thrived:

> Northern workers, to be sure, played a major role in ridding the United States of the scourge of chattel slavery but never did eliminate what they called "wage slavery." Nor did they overcome their own sexism,

> racial intolerance, and cultural chauvinism. If anything, in the 1890s they were more suspicious of women and blacks than they had been in the 1820s. They also gradually embraced a contracting vision of what was possible or desirable. (Laurie 14)

As men's paid labor came to define their masculinity, women's work in or outside the home distinguished among different kinds of womanhood (true, new, Christian, immoral, or deviant), labels tellingly deployed along class, race, and ethnic divisions. Through this analysis of rhetorics of women's work in three utopian communities, I suggest that the contemporary relevance of *work* for our cultural understanding of *gender* was cemented during the Industrial Revolution.

MATERIAL FEMINIST METHODS AND METHODOLOGIES

The ecological approach adopted here involves not only a theoretical view of gender as rhetorical and variable, human and extrahuman, and power laden rather than arbitrary but also a set of methodological practices. The ensuing chapters reconstruct women's work in midcentury utopian communities through an ecological analysis of diverse archival materials. This analysis aims to unpack not only the texts that historical, gendered bodies leave behind but also, to the extent possible, the lived experience of gender in particular historical moments.[23] I trace the circulation and re/production of gender norms in these artifacts, without attributing their rhetorical functions to the intentions of individual speakers, writers, and actors. I echo Jane Bennett by interpreting human responses to situations as more a question of "fermentation" than "deliberation" (103).[24] The archives mined in this study provide a rich sense of the fermenting forces undergirding communal experiments, gender roles, and women's work during the early industrial age.

The following chapters draw on archival evidence gathered and sifted over many years, and my experiences in these sites are crucial to this project's genesis and evolution. I first visited Old Economy Village in Ambridge, Pennsylvania—the historic site of the Harmony Society—as a graduate student. While I was initially focused on Gertrude Rapp's leadership of the community's silk industry, I strove in a second visit to unearth other extant evidence (much of it, challengingly for me, in German) of women's work and experience in the community, including that of the "silk girls" who worked under Rapp as well as German maids and indentured servants. These fragments complicated the alluringly celebratory story of Rapp's entrepreneurship. My second archival site is the Brook Farm materials at the Massachusetts Historical Society in

Boston. Unlike Oneida and Harmony, Brook Farm is not memorialized in a physical site beyond a few small plaques near the original community grounds. As a result, the community's records are more far-flung. Fortunately, intense historical and scholarly interest has helped preserve the accounts and memoirs of former members, many of which are available in print or online. While the historical society is a wonderful place to do research, this archival site inevitably felt quite removed from the community itself. My third and final archival site is the Oneida Community Collection at Syracuse University, thirty or so miles from the historic venue where visitors (and overnight guests!) can see the community's extant buildings, grounds, and materials. The scope of the library's Oneida holdings is truly overwhelming, with box after box of letters, clippings, memoirs, and notebooks—30.5 linear feet of material. Despite its relocation away from the community grounds, the library's sheer volume of materials provides researchers a sense of immersion in Oneida's past.

Building from these archives, the chapters that follow exhibit three key methodological moves. First, I invert or collapse the conventional distinction between figure and ground, or rhetoric and context. In this approach, "the surrounding environment becomes understood as more than a neutral, objective stage on which human drama and activity play out or the objective, at-hand material we source, craft, and use" (Rickert 9). For example, in my analyses, documents such as lists, reports, and rosters receive equal attention and weight to women's accounts of their work. This approach allows me "to get beyond the text-context dilemma by turning texts into actants linked to other actants in complex chains of activity" (Walsh et al. 456). Indeed, for feminist rhetoricians, gender norms are not just the *context* for women's speaking: the constant (re)negotiation and (re)construction of gender is the *subject* of our research. While studies of women's rhetoric explore context, in large part, as a means of illuminating women's rhetorical strategies, studies of rhetorical gendering explore the symbolic actions of gendered individuals as a means of unpacking the material-rhetorical circulation of gender in and beyond those texts.

Second, my analyses trace constellations and connections among stakeholders, places, texts, objects, and practices. In contrast to "mapping" methodologies that parse rhetorical situations into separate elements, this approach enacts a "movement" methodology, following a rhetoric's "circulating ecology of effects, enactments, and events" (Edbauer 9). In other words, I work to "bracket the discrete elements of rhetoric, audience, and exigence" and "attune to the *processes* that both comprise and extend the rhetorics" (Edbauer 19). One benefit of this approach for feminist rhetoricians is its refusal of gendered boundaries and binaries. Indeed, I argue that we cannot understand the rhetorical-material construction of gendered labor without considering production and reproduction together, a stance signified by my use of "re/production" throughout this text. To this end, I adapt Lynn O'Brien Hallstein's conceptualization of "mothering rhetorics" to larger rhetorics of gendered labor. O'Brien Hallstein argues that the rhetoric of motherhood includes both "rhetorics of reproduction (rhetorics about the reproductive function of women/mothers)" and "reproducing rhetorics (the rhetorical reproduction of ideological systems and logics of contemporary culture)" (2). Her configuration is reminiscent of Althusser's insight that, while "the relations of production are first reproduced by the materiality of the processes of production and circulation," ideological relations are also "immediately present in the same processes" (qtd. in Coole and Frost 34–35). Similarly, the following chapters demonstrate how ideas about women's reproductive roles accompany them to work and notions regarding women's paid, professional, or industrial work haunt the home.

Third, I depict ecologies of gender as textured and uneven. Despite the promise of ecological approaches, the "ontological flattening" of material rhetoric can run contrary to feminist aims. Locating constellations and networks does not in itself suggest why some nodes in those configurations exert more power than others.[25] To counter this flattening, material feminists draw our attention to the "translations" and "delegations" of labor not just between humans and nonhumans but between (some) humans and (other) humans.[26] Thus, feminist scholarship aiming to redress the silencing of women's voices must work to avoid resilencing women who fall outside dominant feminist narratives. In particular, feminist rhetoricians should be wary of how Western feminism has elided the experience of women marginalized by class, race, ethnicity, sexuality, religion, education, or nationality. As we craft textured, uneven accounts of gender, we must allow these voices "to *object* to their status as examples merely waiting to be aggregated" (Walsh et al. 436). As the following chapters suggest, when white, middle-class women seek parity with white, middle-class men, their attempts to associate themselves with work and roles construed as masculine relegates traditionally feminine work to less privileged working-class women, immigrant women, and women of color. From the nineteenth century to the present, "right to work" feminist arguments forestall potential alliances along gender lines and mask white women's complicity with unequal rhetorical-material configurations.

Methodologically, *Utopian Genderscapes* explores the promise of ecological approaches to rhetorical historiography. I mobilize archival sources to examine the re/production of gender in utopian communities through the complex interplay of leaders' visions, members' goals, and the affordances of the social and material environment. I restore a radical contingency to these histories, revealing possibilities that, however short-lived, participated in the gendered rhetorics of the time. Utopian communities, even when widely depicted as failures, illuminate what was possible in a specific historical moment. In writing this book, I strove to maintain my sense of surprise at these possibilities, restoring fluidity to historical gender roles often conceived as rigid and inflexible and countering teleological narratives of women progressing gradually but steadily "out of the home" and into positions of cultural, political, and professional power. By approaching historical rhetorics of gender as in flux, I obey the historiographical mandate to restore a sense of possibility to the histories I tell, to combat views of the past as settled and inevitable, and to cultivate an awareness that things might have been and might yet be otherwise.

Chapter 2, "Domestic Rhetorics: The Invention of Housework at Brook Farm," begins with the work most commonly associated with women through an examination of domestic labor in the famous transcendentalist community. Founded outside of Boston by middle- to upper-class academics and clergy, Brook Farm aimed to bridge the increasing gap between classes by providing its members with a variety of work. By examining the letters and memoirs of Brook Farm's women—as well as lesser-known internal records and meeting minutes—I suggest that women were not fully included in the community's promise to value and redistribute mental and physical labor equally. Moreover, the redefinition of women's work in the community did not overturn the teleological view of housework as part of woman's purpose. While women at Brook Farm enjoyed access to conventionally masculine roles and tasks, there was no corresponding shift of men into traditionally feminine domestic roles. As a result, the teleological devaluation of housework—understood as drudgery and associated with women's bodies—remained. In response, Brook Farm's female founders recruited working-class women, sought opportunities to participate in market labor, and positioned themselves as "domestic managers." Visitors to Brook Farm perceived the communal system of housework as an improvement over housewives laboring in isolated homes. Yet as Brook Farm's practices muddied the rhetorical boundaries of men's and women's work, they deepened class divides, cementing the association of housework with working-class women.

Chapter 3, "Professional Rhetorics: Silk Raising in the Harmony Society," explores the most contested arena of women's work through the case of this German pietist community. The Harmonists immigrated to the United States to live according to their religious beliefs, including pacifism and celibacy. In the United States, they were known as successful entrepreneurs and innovators, a reputation owed in large part to the society's silk industry, led by Gertrude Rapp, the granddaughter of the community's founder. Indeed, Rapp became an unlikely minor celebrity—an exemplar of the "professional woman"—and a case study of exceptionalist rhetorics in "success stories" of women's professional work. Rapp's access to this exceptional identity was fostered by a combination of material conditions and rhetorical strategies: seizing the affordances of the new postal service, improved writing technologies, and the nascent state of the silk industry, Rapp conducted her business through correspondence and framed her labor in patriotic and professional terms. At the same time, however, Rapp's acclaim as an exceptional "professional woman" was limited in its effects on other women or larger rhetorics of gendered labor. The effects of her success were circumscribed by the increasing feminization of the silk industry, spatial limitations, and a tokenism that denied the role of privilege in her success. In the end, the case of the Harmonist silk industry underscores that "success stories" of individual women often disguise or reify the gendered dynamics that confront women in the actual spaces of their work.

Chapter 4, "Reproductive Rhetorics: The Work of Motherhood at Oneida," investigates women's least visible work through a study of motherhood in the notorious Oneida Community. Founded in upstate New York by the charismatic John Humphrey Noyes, Oneida drew public hostility for its radical practices, most notably "complex marriage," broadly understood as a form of free love. But the community's most radical tenet was arguably its redefinition of motherhood, including an unusual form of birth control ("male continence") and communal childcare. Liberated from unwanted pregnancy and burdensome childcare, Oneida women were free to participate in the community's masculine industries, such as the trap shop. Yet internal accounts and documents show that, regardless of the rhetoric of women's individual choices, cultural motherhood consistently reasserted itself: in the continued assumption that housework and childcare, while not limited to biological mothers, was labor rightfully belonging to women; in the workplace association of women with "feminine" industries or tasks; and in the expectation that Oneida's women would complete "mothering work" for the community at large. The tension between the community's rhetoric of choice and the restrictions that operated in practice exacerbated divides among women—between members and hired workers or women differentiated by the community's unwritten but consequential religious hierarchy or caste system. In the end, Oneida failed to offer a plausible model of working motherhood and thus inadvertently reinforced the larger cultural opposition—the need to "choose"—between work and motherhood.

In Chapter 5, "Arguments on the Landscape: Rhetorics of Gendered Labor Now and Then," I call for additional attention to rhetorics of gendered labor, articulating the richness of this area of study for feminist rhetoricians. I also explore utopian tropes in contemporary debates surrounding women's work, including continued attempts to redistribute or redefine housework, efforts to increase women's representation in corporate leadership and male-dominated professions, and the barrage of advice aiming to help women manage reproduction so they can "have it all." Finally, I consider the place of utopian tropes in public memory to illuminate how common patterns in depictions of historical and contemporary intentional communities forestall utopian thought and action in the present. This final chapter illustrates that utopia is more than the site for this study: it is an integral part of the rhetorics through which we approach problems and solutions regarding gender in the workplace.

2. DOMESTIC RHETORICS

The Invention of Housework at Brook Farm

Perhaps the least-known innovation of mid-nineteenth-century industrialism is what scholars have dubbed the "invention of housework." As Ruth Schwartz Cowan explains, "Prior to industrialization the word *housework* would probably have been nonsensical since . . . almost all people worked in or on the grounds of a house, their own, or someone else's" (18). As women's productive work (spinning, weaving, shoemaking, and so on) moved into the factory, work in the home came to be understood in opposition to labor for the market, erecting rigid distinctions between categories that had long been blurred in ideology and practice. Respect for housework suffered as wage labor was refigured as independent and masculine rather than subservient. "As a market commodity, male labor was valorized both literally and figuratively by contrast with female housework" (Stanley 85).[1] Indeed, in 1835, Alexis de Tocqueville observed that single American women had more freedom than married women did, largely due to the burdens of housework. To combat these associations, the 1830s cult of the lady depicted housewives as consumers and suggested that "being a lady . . . meant *not* doing certain kinds of housework" (Stansell 159). By 1840, domestic service had become entirely women's work, and yet working women were no more eager to take on this labor than were their bourgeois employers. As Catharine Beecher and Harriet Beecher Stowe lamented in their 1869 domestic tract *The American Woman's Home*, "We are continually harrowed with tales of the sufferings of distressed needle-women, and yet women will encounter all these chances of ruin and starvation rather than make up their minds to permanent domestic service. Now, what is the matter with domestic service?" (313). Beecher and Stowe's perplexity aside, Americans had decided: housework was drudgery.

In this context, utopian communities such as Brook Farm promised alternative ways of managing household labor. The transcendentalist community operated from 1841 to 1847 in West Roxbury, Massachusetts, about eight miles west of Boston (fig. 2.1). Brook Farm aimed to resist the social ills of industrialization by providing a balance of mental and physical labor for its members, a practice intended to bridge the growing gap between the working and professional classes. Of course, this new view of labor also had implications for women. Brook Farm was seen as a generous space for women and was commonly associated with women's rights.[2] The four thousand visitors the community welcomed in just one year marveled at a system in which "each irons as long as she thinks right" (Brownson 493), which seemed to have overcome "the drudgery of housekeeping on the old plan" ("Brook Farm: Seven Golden Years" 186). According to the *Voice of Industry*—the newspaper of the Lowell Female Labor Reform Association (the nation's first women's union),

> The great Social Problem has here been solved. It has been *proved* that men and women of every variety, character, education, habits, and social position, can be brought together, and, even under tremendous disadvantages, be formed into a harmonious and beautiful Society;—that domestic servitude may be abolished, and all the labors of life, even to the washing of pots and kettles, be made attractive and beautiful . . . ("Brook Farm")[3]

Fig. 2.1. Josiah Wolcott, *Brook Farm with Rainbow*, 1845. Collection of the Massachusetts Historical Society.

Reprinted in outlets such as the *Liberator* (William Lloyd Garrison's abolitionist magazine), among others, such articles shaped Brook Farm's legacy as an egalitarian space. And yet, the conflation of drudgery and servitude in these accounts risks obscuring class relations within the community. Did Brook Farm's success lie in improving the status of housework (addressing housework as "drudgery") or in avoiding the employment of domestic servants (addressing the classed nature of midcentury housework)? Was Brook Farm able to redeem housework as "real work," and, if so, what did this mean for the class dimensions so crucial to the construction of midcentury domestic work?

Historians have debated the impact of Brook Farm's egalitarian rhetoric for its female members, particularly as regards women's work. Indeed, one of the community's most promising tenets was that each individual would choose their own work, and yet women still found themselves responsible for the community's domestic work. How should we understand this reversion to a conventional gendered division of labor? Feminist historian Carol Kolmerten attributes the sexual division of labor to "an ideology of gender" that "reared its ugly head almost from the first" (172). Alternatively, Sterling Delano attributes women's focus on domestic labor to their comfort and experience with this work, concluding: "There was no domestic servitude at Brook Farm because women were free to engage in whatever kind of labor appealed to them" ("We Have Abolished" 12). Yet when community leader Charles Dana bragged that Brook Farm had "abolished Domestic Servitude," he likely meant that the housework of the community was completed without hired help, not that the women cheerfully resigned themselves to their domestic roles (qtd. in Delano, "We Have Abolished" 4). In what follows, I examine the rhetorical structures that continued to define housework as women's work and the rhetorical strategies women used to negotiate this construction.

By exploring these rhetorical forces, this chapter complements recent feminist scholarship on rhetorics of women's work. This body of work has focused, in large part, on the rhetorical situations and strategies of women pursuing careers in male-dominated fields and professions (Wells; Skinner, *Women Physicians*; Applegarth, *Rhetoric*; Jack, *Science*; Buchanan, "A Few Good"; Moseley). However, with a few notable exceptions, feminist rhetoricians have devoted less attention to rhetorical struggles over work in the home. This chapter illuminates rhetorical strategies leveraged by women to position their domestic work as meaningful—as work—and thus provides an important counterpart to studies of women in the workplace. Indeed, as Jessica Enoch shows in her study of <home> as an ideograph framing World War II childcare centers, we need to consider the interdependence of constructions of labor inside and outside the home ("There's No Place"). Similarly, Sarah Hallenbeck describes how purportedly masculine work like invention is colored by the association of women inventors with domestic spaces and motives ("Inventing" 261). While scholars have considered how domestic associations haunt women's work *outside* the home, this chapter examines attempts to apply notions of industrialized labor to women's work *in* the home. Like other midcentury women, women at Brook Farm worked to professionalize housework as a way of distancing themselves from associations with unskilled, unproductive, dirty labor. Thus, I join Enoch and other scholars of domestic science in illuminating the material-rhetorical resonances across industrial and domestic (work)spaces (see Enoch, *Domestic Occupations*; Leavitt; and Stage and Vincenti).

This chapter proceeds from the assumption that housework is constructed in relation to other work completed by women and men, inside and outside the home. Thus, I probe the construction of housework during industrialization by inquiring into not only the facts of women's work but also the significance of that work, particularly its recognition (or lack thereof) as a valued contribution, as real work. To this end, I theorize *teleology* as one way of reframing the construction of housework as "natural" work for women. Fusing *telos* and *logos*, teleology describes the act of explaining (logos) something in reference to an ultimate end or purpose (telos). Though we often think of *telos* as directedness toward a goal or aim, the definition of teleology as "final cause" shows the participation of origins in teleo-logics. Thus, a teleological discourse of gender or gendered labor links origins and ends by implying that this is what one was made for—"that for the sake of which" (Aristotle, *Physics* 199a). Teleology is particularly suited to a study of midcentury housework, which was "described in the prescriptive literature less as purposeful activities required and ordered by the welfare of their individual families than as emanations of an abstract but shared Womanhood" (Boydston, *Home and Work* 145). In this teleological framing, housework emanates from women's nature (origin) as a being designed for this purpose (end). Importantly, teleological understandings of gender and housework materialized unevenly across class and race, with varying impacts for the housewife-employer, the solitary housewife, and the domestic servant.

I offer teleology as an alternative to essentialist framings of rhetorics of gender. Indeed, teleology shares essentialism's focus on nature or biology as the purported source of gender difference: Aristotle imagined teleology as a way of understanding the inner directedness of humans, as well as nature and animals. However, teleology incorporates a sense of development absent from essentialism. Teleology directs our attention to the trajectories of mid-nineteenth-century ecologies of gender rather than more static representations of substance or essence. Thus, teleology situates gender norms in macronarratives of women as evolving and developing toward particular roles and ends, as in midcentury discourses of working women "unfitting" themselves for future roles as wives and mothers. A deviation from this expected life course is framed by teleological rhetorics as a deviation from nature. In this sense, teleology is attuned to the temporal dynamics of rhetorics of gender and embraces the rhetorical ecologist's goal of bringing "the dimension of movement back into our discussions of rhetoric" (Edbauer 20). My analysis of housework at Brook Farm interrogates teleological rhetorics espousing that housework was not real work but rather an inherent part of Woman as a purposeful being—and the implicit challenge to one's gendered status should one not feel interested in or fulfilled by this work.

This chapter returns to archival documents such as letters, memoirs, and records to better understand not just what work the women at Brook Farm did but how that work was understood and framed. When it comes to gendered labor, Brook Farm's practices fell short of its ideals. The community's system of communal housework was innovative, yet the rhetorical construction of housework as invisible, natural, "women's work" persisted. The women's accounts of their work suggest that housework was excluded from the transcendental ideal of engaging and uniting mind and body in a fully developed individual. In response, Brook Farm women, like white middle-class women in general, engaged in "energetic ideological maneuvering" to close the perceived gap between their labor and the industrial marketplace (Domosh and Seager 40). Brook Farm demonstrates that changes in the material conditions of housework may not be enough to overcome the teleological construction of that work as natural, unskilled, or uniquely suited to women. In the end, teleological rhetorics continued to dominate understandings of housework at Brook Farm, and privileged women's attempts to overturn or divert these logics succeeded only in recasting housework as natural for *some*, less privileged, women rather than disrupting its gendered status.

In what follows, I trace the construction of women's work at Brook Farm through several stages. First, I introduce the community's goals, particularly the "transcendental ideal" of labor and its implications for class and gender. Next, I enumerate four aspects of the rhetorical-material construction of women's work at Brook Farm: the dependence of male transcendence on female domestic labor, the persistent view of housework as irredeemable drudgery, the reassignment of housework along class lines, and the attempt to ennoble housework through rhetorics of science and management. Finally, I conclude by considering the class dynamics of teleological rhetorics of domesticity. More broadly, I suggest that studies of rhetorics of work must attend to intersections of gender and class in order to avoid repeating the raced and classed assumptions and absences of Western feminist right-to-work rhetorics.

THE TRANSCENDENTAL IDEAL: LABOR, CLASS, AND GENDER

As a philosophy famed for celebrating thought over action, transcendentalism was perhaps an unexpected player in the utopian fervor of the mid-nineteenth century. The best-known transcendentalists, Ralph Waldo Emerson and Henry David Thoreau, were also famously independent. But another strand of transcendentalism, marked by Orestes Brownson's class critique and George and Sophia Ripley's Brook Farm community, held that the smallest unit of social change was the community, not the individual. Like many intentional communities, Brook Farm hoped to revise the prevailing system of labor in mid-nineteenth-century America. The community's ultimate goal was to provide all members with physical and mental labor adapted to their individual tastes and talents. There was an explicit class emphasis to this program, a hope that providing mental and physical stimulation for all would help bridge the gulf between classes. There was also an implicit promise for women, a suggestion that a community dedicated to sharing the burden of labor among classes might also distribute work more equally among men and women. The founding documents, letters, and early accounts of the community illuminate these initial hopes and goals. The transcendental ideal implied that work could and should be an ennobling pursuit, a means of self-culture. Amid the social disruptions of midcentury industrialization, the materialization of this philosophy at Brook Farm was deeply inflected by class and gender.

Brook Farm grew out of New England transcendentalism, which expressed concerns with growing class inequality during industrialization. The market revolution of the 1830s and 1840s initiated a new social order.[4] Increasing strikes demonstrated that relations between workers and employers were vexed in the early days of the market society.[5] The Boston Transcendental Club tackled these concerns head-on, critiquing social, economic, and political arrangements they saw as interfering in individual self-development, including social inequality based on race, class, or gender. Though transcendentalism as an intellectual movement contained diverse elements, one branch was explicitly reform minded and advocated against slavery and for women's rights. George Ripley was particularly concerned with class inequality in the early industrial age, a concern he shared with Orestes Brownson, whose 1840 essay "The Laboring Classes" offered a controversial and influential critique of the capitalist struggle between merchants and laborers.[6] As Ripley wrote, "I could not feel that my duty was accomplished while there was one human being, within the sphere of my influence, held to unrequited labor at the will of another, destitute of the means of education, or doomed to penury, degradation, and vice by the misfortune of birth" (qtd. in Delano, *Brook Farm* 11). With the communitarian proposals of Charles Fourier also increasing in popularity in the 1840s, Ripley came to view communal living as a promising solution to the ills of the time.

The transcendental ideal viewed labor as a means of addressing individual and collective problems. As he imagined the community that would become Brook Farm, George Ripley articulated his belief that the gap between classes was mirrored and perhaps in part caused by the gap between mind and body in elite individuals (Packer 133). Ripley shared with Emerson a sense that a balance of manual and intellectual labor "would build moral strength and at the same time correct the imbalance of labor and leisure in contemporary society" (Rose 115). Brook Farm's labor goals are eloquently explained in perhaps the most-cited document of the West Roxbury community: Ripley's November 9, 1840, letter seeking Emerson's participation. In this passage, Brook Farm's founder expresses labor reform as one of the primary tenets of his vision:

> Our objects, as you know, are to insure a more natural union between intellectual and manual labor than now exists; to combine the thinker and the worker, as far as possible, in the same individual; to guarantee the highest mental freedom, by providing all with labor, adapted to their tastes and talents, and securing to them the fruits of their industry; to do away with the necessity of menial services, by opening the benefits of education and the profits of labor to all; and thus to prepare a society of liberal, intelligent, and cultivated persons, whose relations with each other would permit a more simple and wholesome life, than can be led amidst the pressure of our competitive institutions. (qtd. in Felton 123–24)

The problem was not so much that labor was degrading in and of itself but that the unequal division and conditions of this labor made it degrading. While both the intellectual and laboring classes would be aided by Ripley's scheme, manual laborers were particularly in need of this intervention. Indeed, later in the letter, Ripley explains that his personal inclinations might take him "in another direction," given his "passion for being independent of the world, and of every man in it" (qtd. in Sams 7). Still, as Ripley confided to the famously autonomous Emerson, however pleasant the prospect of "a city of God, on a small scale of my own," he felt "bound to sacrifice this private feeling, in the hope of a great social good" (qtd. in Sams 7).

Brook Farm and transcendentalism more broadly shared the Puritan view of work as a religious activity and of laboring in one's calling as a means of sanctification. Brook Farmer Georgiana Kirby explains the transcendental view of labor as follows:

> It was argued that labor, far from being a curse, was, and had been, the greatest cause of our continuous development, that it conduced to the health of mind and body, when equally divided among all. But that in our present state, the artisan and laborer were degraded to only one step above chattel-slavery, in order to maintain a few in luxurious idleness. Defrauded of these refined conditions, which he himself had created, the workman lost courage, self-respect, elasticity. (92)

Thus, vocation was a cornerstone of transcendental self-culture, and the choice of occupation should be inspired from within, not imposed from without. Ripley's vision of shared intellectual and manual labor is also represented in the community's constitution, which declares as one of its "Guaranties" that "The Association shall provide such employment for all its members as shall be adapted to their capacities, habits, and tastes; and each member shall select and perform such operations of labor, whether corporal or mental, as shall be deemed best suited to his own endowments and the benefit of the Association" (Brook Farm Association, *Constitution* 8). At the heart of the Brook Farm community is a faith that individuals would be better able to divide their time among mental and physical activity in a community of people doing likewise.

Perhaps the most innovative aspect of the transcendental ideal as applied to labor was the declaration that all labor would be equally compensated and chosen according to individual preference.[7] This was, indeed, one of the tensions haunting the community's labor plans. They trusted that individuals would choose a balance between manual and intellectual pursuits but shied away from enforcing this equilibrium. In an optimistic account of the community's plan published in *The Dial*, Elizabeth Peabody, a central transcendentalist but not a Brook Farm member, described a sentiment of class responsibility. The Brook Farmers hoped members would feel a conscientious drive to avoid the idle temptations others of their class succumbed to, believing that "there was no need of any drudge in society, provided there was no drone" ("Plan").[8] Later in the article, Peabody invokes this theme again: "How dare I be a drone when others are drudges? How dare I sacrifice not only my own, but others' health, in sequestrating myself from my share of bodily labour . . . ?" ("Plan"). The community hoped that the shame of being perceived as an idle "drone" would sufficiently motivate members unaccustomed to hard labor to undertake it voluntarily. Similarly, the community trusted that there would be sufficient interest in the necessary forms of labor that they would not need to hire outside laborers, what Ripley refers to as "menial services." Both convictions would prove misguided: compensation alone could not overcome the sense of certain work as "menial," as "drudgery."[9]

Despite the Farmers' concerns about poverty and the degradation of the working classes, their egalitarian aims were structurally limited by the need for capital. Brook Farm was not, in the usual understanding, a commune—it was a joint-stock corporation. As such, "membership in the association depended upon the ownership of property" (Rose 135). Shares cost $500—the equivalent of just over $16,000 in 2020—and shareholders earned 5 percent annual interest on dividends (though the Farm was never profitable, so this promise remained theoretical). Individuals could join the community *as members* by virtue of a majority vote, but "Associates" had to literally "buy in" to the community. This policy effectively created two classes of individuals in the community, a division reinforced by the fact that only shareholders (associates) could vote. Both members and associates paid for room and board through labor—otherwise they owed four dollars per week (Gura 157). Outside the farm, Massachusetts workers' wages in the 1840s averaged between $4.00 and $4.80 per week (*History* 253). Though Brook Farm's labor conditions were enlightened for the time (with shorter workdays and weeks), the idea that all members were equal was false from the outset, economically.

While motivated largely by class concerns, Brook Farm emerged in a moment when gender norms were similarly unsettled. In the early decades of the market society, men's employment was less stable than previously. Indeed, "hard times and the irregularity of employment made many husbands poor providers and weakened their control of their families. At the same time, female wage work, however lowly, provided many women some means of support apart from men" (Stansell 81). New opportunities for women's work violated the pattern where a woman went from being a dependent in her father's household to being a dependent in her husband's (Stansell 84).[10] As the economic basis of the patriarchal family deteriorated, ideologies of gender were likewise disrupted. Because Enlightenment thought held that individuals who labored for others were dependent, working-class men were demasculinized by their new waged positions (Stanley 84–85). As historian Christine Stansell explains, "the old gender system of household dependencies was disintegrating, but the new one—which would eventually bring about an uneasy reconciliation between women's wage-earning abilities and their subordination to men—had yet to emerge fully" (131). Ideologically, unwaged housework provided a rhetorical resource to address this presumed threat to the gender order, a means of overcoming the analogy between wives and hired men as dependents who labored for others.

Though Brook Farm's explicit aims focused on class, the community was imagined as an egalitarian space for women from the start. As a philosophy, transcendentalism held that there was "no sex in souls," and the Brook Farm Constitution stated that "all rights, privileges, guarantees, and obligations of members expressed or implied . . . shall be understood to belong equally to both sexes" (Wayne 2; qtd. in Kolmerten 172). Husbands and wives were autonomous members, and wives had the power to vote and hold office at a time when wives had little legal or political identity separate from husbands in the larger society. And this was not the community's only intervention in the gender order: Brook Farm women and men were paid equally for their work, the community instituted the first nursery school in the country, and four of the original ten subscribing associates were women (Sams 46). Women benefited, in particular, from the unparalleled intellectual opportunities at the farm, as Georgiana Kirby explains: "The very air seemed to hold more exhilarating qualities than any I had breathed before. Democracy and culture made the animus of the association. Had the world denied you opportunity for education? Here your highest needs should be satisfied" (99). Finally, women had a voice in the community's publications, contributing regularly to the *Harbinger*, the community's newspaper ("Girl's Recollections" 233).

In this context, Brook Farm's labor ideals held particular promise for female members, who were, in theory, free to choose their own work. Indeed, one of the most promising aspects of transcendentalism from a feminist perspective is the notion of vocation. As feminist historian Tiffany Wayne explains, "Transcendentalism provided a language for theorizing gender equality in promoting the philosophical ideal that all humans, regardless of sex, race, or social position, had the right to pursue *self-culture* and to engage in a *vocation*, or life's work, suited to one's individual character and talents" (3, emphasis in original). Moreover, Brook Farmers directly engaged the public discourse of housework as drudgery. As John Codman, who joined the community in 1843, wrote,

> It is often stated that the home circle is the sphere of women, but at times it is a very narrow circle—a very narrowing circle to its occupants. There are thousands who enter it as brilliant young ladies, and come from it at the end of a few years morbid, harassed, depressed. . . . The circle in many cases is so narrow that there is no room for growth. (qtd. in Packer 159)

Thus, Brook Farm hoped that its labor system might save women the drudgery of domestic labor. And, in some regards, it seems they were successful. As Marianne Dwight wrote to her brother in September 1844, "I could not feel contented again with the life of isolated houses, and the conventions of civilization . . . life is so full and rich here, that I feel as if my experience were more valuable, and I were *growing* somewhat faster than when I lived in Boston" (41).[11] However, as I will show, Dwight's experience is shaped less by a redefinition of housework than by a structure that allowed her to minimize her housework, a privilege unequally distributed across women of various classes at Brook Farm as in society at large.

Brook Farm's history and guiding philosophy is generally understood in two periods: the transcendentalist period, from April 1841 to December 43, and the Fourierist period, from 1844 to the community's dissolution in 1847. Though the ideas of Charles Fourier were in circulation amid the transcendentalists and Brook Farmers from the beginning, the community officially adopted Fourierism in 1844. The Fourierist period involved active recruitment of working-class members with practical skills, but many of these new members felt patronized by the original, shareholding group (see table). The Fourierist period also involved a more structured religious practice, sparking arguments about required or voluntary attendance at religious services. For the purposes of this study, Fourier's ideas were promising from the perspective of women's work, advocating for shared domestic work and blurring the distinction between public and private (Hardy 64). Indeed, Fourierists saw communal housekeeping as a way of liberating women from domestic drudgery. Yet the increasing class diversity at the farm did not result in the egalitarian division of labor Fourier or other utopian thinkers imagined. In the end, the teleological construction of housework as linked to women's nature, development, and purpose persisted even as it fell out unevenly across the privileged founding members and new working-class recruits.

THE INVENTION OF HOUSEWORK AT BROOK FARM

However promising the community's ideals of vocation and self-culture, women's work at Brook Farm in many ways resembled women's work in society at large. While the constitution explained that members should be provided employment "whether corporal or mental . . . adapted to their capacities, habits,

Brook Farm Recruitment, 1841–44

Year	*New members*	*Men admitted*	*Women admitted*
1841	10	6	4
1842	18	10	8
1843	4	1	3
1844	67	40	27

Source: adapted from Anne C. Rose, *Transcendentalism as a Social Movement, 1830–1850*, Yale UP, 1981, pp. 234–38.

and tastes," women at Brook Farm primarily completed the traditional, mainly corporal labor apportioned to women: cooking, cleaning, sewing, and childcare. Rising before five o'clock in the morning, the women prepared breakfast in "the Hive," while the men cared for the livestock. Women served the meal and then spent the rest of the morning tidying the kitchen, gardening, and straightening the rooms before devoting most of the afternoon to preparing the supper (Delano, *Brook Farm* 47).

Some scholars interpret this almost immediate reversion to "traditional gender roles" as a question of comfort, with women choosing the labor they have been trained for and accustomed to in their lives outside the farm (Delano, *Brook Farm* 46). In Delano's reading, "members performed whatever type of work appealed to their individual natures. Men might, for instance, devote themselves partially or entirely to domestic chores, just as women might similarly busy themselves with agricultural pursuits" (*Brook Farm* 65). The wording here is telling: whatever men and women "might" have done, this is not what happened. Instead, women's work at Brook Farm looked a lot like women's work elsewhere. More important, the argument that women "chose" domestic work out of comfort overlooks the possibility that Brook Farm might have done more to expand women's vocational options. While women were provided ample opportunity to improve their minds by taking courses in Latin or drawing, studying history or reading Dante in the original Italian, there is no record of courses or professional development for women hoping to pursue agriculture or participate in the farm's various industries, which included printing and shoemaking, among others.

In the remainder of this chapter, I consider the rhetorical-material construction of housework at Brook Farm. This involves working to understand not only how the community's housework resembled or differed from that of a typical household but also how housework was rhetorically perceived and constructed. The women's accounts suggest that housework at Brook Farm was constructed in opposition to conventionally masculine labor, such as farming, that participated in the transcendental ideal. Interestingly, the women's letters also compare housework unfavorably to other women's work in the community; specifically, they articulate this subsistence labor as less rewarding than labor intended for the market. As some women devoted more time to nondomestic pursuits and others assumed managerial roles in the domestic economy, the most grueling housework was relegated to working-class recruits whose position in many ways resembled that of working-class, immigrant, or African American domestic servants throughout the nation. In other words, given the failure to redistribute housework across gender lines, the egalitarian promise of Brook Farm could only be achieved at the expense of other women—falling out along the very class lines the community aimed to unsettle. This analysis suggests, then, that changes in the material conditions of women's work may not be enough to overcome the teleological construction of that work as natural and unskilled.

Housework and the Transcendental Ideal

In a community like Brook Farm, devoted to the idea of labor as valuable and ennobling, work that was not seen and recognized as such would necessarily fall short of the transcendental ideal. Yet Brook Farm's efforts to make all work visible and valued occurred at a time when women's domestic labor was becoming less and less visible. The American economy in 1800 was an agricultural economy: "Work for wages as a way of life was uncommon, and families sought economic independence in ownership of land or physical capital" (Margo 26). The percentage of the U.S. labor force employed in agriculture dropped from 75 to 36 percent between 1800 and 1900, and New England transitioned faster than average, with under 40 percent employment in farming by the Civil War (Margo 7). At the founding of Brook Farm, this subsistence economy was in tension with the market economy, which was in ascendance throughout the North by the 1840s. In this context, industriousness was increasingly associated with moneymaking, an attitude that obscured women's household labor as real work.

These shifts had particular implications for women's lives and work. "As half the society became accustomed to wage labor in the developing American industrial economy, the independent home-based work of the other half began to look like something other than work" (Strasser 185). The myth of the family wage obscured the fact that women's unwaged work was a crucial part of how families got by. As Boydston explains, the unrecognized value of women's work benefited "owners of mills and factories and shops, who were able to pay 'subsistence' wages at levels which in fact represented only a fraction of the real price of workers' survival" ("To Earn" 9). The result was that "housework had a value without having a price," and women's participation in and contributions to the economy were rendered invisible ("To Earn" 9, 11). By the end of the first half of the nineteenth century, when Brook Farm was also nearing its close, "antebellum Americans would embrace a growing conviction that housework was not really labor at all" (Boydston, *Home and Work* 141). One of Brook Farm's successes, from a feminist perspective, was to render housework visible by accounting for women's hours and wages alongside all other work at the farm. Indeed, the community's papers belie a commitment to keeping more and more detailed labor records—resolutions to account for past labor and to have members report their hours and tasks appear in December 1842 and at each of the four meetings in January 1843 (Brook Farm Association, *Records*, Meeting Notes).

While the Brook Farm women may have performed the same kinds of tasks that women completed in a traditional home, they were outnumbered in the community and thus faced a daunting workload. As Marianne Dwight wrote, "There are so many, and so few women to do the work, that we have to be nearly all the time about it" (8). Male associates outnumbered females sixty to thirty-nine between 1841 and 1845, and the women were also responsible for caring for the children, the students, and the boarders, thus compounding "the demand for selflessness" (Rose 186). To keep up with this demand, women workers at times mended two hundred pairs of stockings in one sitting or spent ten or more consecutive hours on their feet in the laundry (Garrison and Myerson 6; Russell 11). Moreover, though residents never exceeded one hundred at any one time, the visitors who came "in shoals" from Boston numbered over four thousand in a single year ("Brook Farm Did 'Pay'"; Haraszti 25). In other words, each woman at Brook Farm likely bore the burden of caring for around twice as many individuals as the average housewife: the size of the average U.S. household was 5.55 in 1850 (Pear). As Carol Kolmerten notes, while founding member Nathaniel Hawthorne was excused from farm work to pursue his writing, Brook Farm's female members enjoyed no such privilege (172).[12]

In theory, Brook Farm's reputedly looser gender roles should have given women some respite from domestic chores. Women's studies scholar Lucy Freibert describes the community's playfulness regarding gender roles and its corresponding effect on labor thusly: "Because such menial tasks were community activities completed in a spirit of play, gender stereotyping of work declined" (76). Yet the women's consistent complaints of overwork suggest that these gender-swapping occasions were aberrations from the day-to-day life of the community. Indeed, Georgiana Kirby's recounting of the experience of a male acquaintance in the community supports this view: "Tom told gay stories about helping the girls with their work, and how jolly they were over it. It was particularly pleasant to lend a hand in the evening when there was no need of hurrying" (109). Visitor accounts also celebrated instances of gender role swapping: "I observed that when the young men went to walk in the woods, . . . they would let two or three children go too, and keep their eye upon them, and so relieve the mothers and make the children happy, and this without troubling themselves either" (Brownson 490). As welcome as such assistance may have been, occasional help with the dishes or childcare likely did little to alter the fact that the women were overwhelmed by the community's physical needs. Moreover, while accounts celebrated the munificence of men who helped with women's work, scenes depicting the inverse are lacking. At its core, domestic labor in Brook Farm was "women's work," regardless of the generosity of men who "lent a hand" from time to time.

At Brook Farm, while the constitution and labor records grant domestic work the same status as farming and other purportedly masculine work, other internal documents reveal the same invisibility of housework that prevailed outside the community. For instance, an 1841 roster listing members and occupations classifies women by the profession of their closest male relative (Rose 132). Sophia Ripley, cofounder and renowned teacher, is listed as "Sophia Ripley—wife (minister)," not according to her own profession (Rose 234). Of the thirty-five women with a recorded occupation, twenty-five are listed by their familial roles—as the wives, sisters, daughters, or mothers of ministers, carpenters, shoemakers, and so on.[13] The assumptions here are powerful: family and domestic obligations are women's primary work, and that work has no title—everyone knows the work of a wife, sister, mother, or daughter. Aside from one teacher and two seamstresses, the profession column for women without male relatives in the community is left blank. Presumably the other five unattached women also brought their domestic capabilities to the farm, but without a familial role to classify them, there is no vocabulary for their contributions (Rose 234–38). Intriguingly, in some cases, class trumps gender. The one married woman listed by her own profession is Caroline Clapp, whose identity as seamstress overrules her identity as wife (Rose 237).

In addition to the invisibility of women workers, the women's accounts of their work suggest that housework was excluded from the transcendental ideal of engaging and uniting mind and body in a fully developed individual. Indeed, a passage from Georgiana Kirby's memoir recounts a debate over this very question:

> Some argued that it must be intrinsically beautiful, or its effects would not be so strengthening and purifying. . . . When the garment is finished on which we have expended our time and skill, what a gratified sense of power ensues; when an apartment is put in thorough order, what compensation one glance around it affords; when a dinner which requires much thought and care is at last on the table, a proper pride on the part of the chef is quite permissible; a completed house gives a similar satisfaction to its builder; and what man's head does not feel lighter at the sight of growing grain which his own hand scattered. (137)

This passage equates men and women's work as both capable of achieving the transcendental ideal. Yet Kirby gives cofounder Sophia Ripley the last word: "I must differ from those of you who find any thing aesthetic in scrubbing, washing, preparing vegetables, etc. . . . I shall never admit that there is any thing ideal in scraping saucepans" (138). Sophia's conclusion is echoed by others like Amelia Russell, who relates that the "poetic phase" of her time at the community "was drowned in the water in which I washed the teacups" (3). Russell goes on, "I cannot invest with poetry our domestic life, which was, of course, monotonous, for we could not carve out any very original way of making beds, cooking, and washing dishes" (58). Such accounts suggest that women's work at Brook Farm failed to reach the standard of labor as a balance and complement to mental and intellectual growth.

Indeed, gendered responsibilities seemed to detract from the other opportunities the community was meant to provide, including leisure. As Marianne Dwight explained, "It seems wrong to lose a moment of so much beauty and prophecy;—I would be abroad in the midst of it all the time. But alas! Indoor duties present their claims" (98). This passage indicates that Dwight felt an obligation to complete unpleasant domestic work despite the community's structural openness about the kind of work men and women might pursue. Similarly, a former female member recalled, "I was at various times during the three years of my stay at the school in the dormitory group, the mending group, the typesetting group and in the dining room group. I liked the latter group the least, especially on pleasant summer evenings when I wished to go out for a walk in the groves or by the brook" ("Girl's Recollections" 233). Given the transcendental focus on a balance of manual and intellectual pursuits—as well as work and leisure—such accounts suggest that women's domestic responsibilities upset this balance.

Finally, there was a recurring suspicion that, in order for men to achieve the transcendental ideal, women must play a supporting role. As a former Brook Farm student noted, "Though all worked, it was the *workers* who did the work, there as elsewhere; while the theorizers theorized beautifully and gave a charm to the common life" (Salisbury). While this passage doesn't identify the "workers" and "theorizers," the women's accounts suggest that the latter were largely the more privileged men, while the former included the women and working-class men. As cofounder Sophia Ripley wrote in her 1841 essay "Woman," "It seems an unknown, or at least an unacknowledged fact, that in the spot where man throws aside his heavy responsibilities, his couch of rest is often prepared by his faithful wife, at the sacrifice of all her quiet contemplation and leisure."

Ripley's wording echoes the logic of artist Lisa Lyons's depiction of women's work in the *other* transcendentalist utopian community, Bronson Alcott's Fruitlands (fig. 2.2). Lyons's cartoon joins Louisa May Alcott's short story "Transcendental Wild Oats" in suggesting that the gendered roles plaguing Brook Farm were representative of the movement as a whole. The overburdened

Abigail Alcott of this cartoon had her counterparts at Brook Farm, women working to compensate for men too preoccupied with their own self-culture to attend to the community's physical needs. As Tiffany Wayne has written of women in transcendentalism more broadly, "By neglecting domestic life, and therefore demanding material or 'worldly' support for their otherworldly intellectual life, male thinkers depended on female domestic support and thus negated the possibility of women pursuing intellectual work" (99). In fact, Margaret Fuller, one of few notable female transcendentalists, declined to join Brook Farm in part due to concerns about her own "repose" if she was to join the community as a writer and philosopher, fearing that other members would always be "judging whether I was worth it or not" (qtd. in Sams 217).[14] It doesn't take much imagination to identify a feminist undertone here, suggesting that the transcendental life of the mind may not have been equally available to men and women. Equally important, not all women's work was equal. As I explore below, the case of women's work at Brook Farm suggests that the rhetorical construction of housework as distinct from real work relied on its (perceived) distance from the market and its increasing association with working-class women and women of color.

Fig. 2.2. Lisa Lyons, "Fruitlands." From *Bohemians: A Graphic History*, edited by Paul Buhle and David Berger, expanded e-book ed., Verso, p. 13.

Domestic Drudgery versus Productive Labor

As a social experiment, Brook Farm was innovative in that it compensated workers equally for all labor, including housework. Yet the sense that housework was not "real work" persisted, even among the women themselves. As historian Laura Shapiro explains, when the Industrial Revolution shifted women's household production to the factory, the work left behind had a different tenor: "With the exception of child-rearing, most of the work a woman did consisted of day-to-day maintenance: feeding and cleaning and mending and feeding and cleaning. Her tasks were fewer but they were distinctly monotonous and in a tangible sense unproductive" (13). Indeed, though many Brook Farm women complained of their domestic chores, they found other labor more rewarding, fulfilling, and enjoyable. The women's accounts suggest that the central factor in classifying women's work as drudgery or productive labor was not wages but rather proximity to the market.

Understandings of the devaluation of housework in the nineteenth century often center on the role of industrialization—especially the increasing understanding of work as tied to wages. As men began working outside home farms and industries, new labor patterns closely associated work with wages for the first time. Thus, one reason housework started to look less like work is that it was outside the wage standard (Boydston, *Home and Work* x). Contemporary scholarship echoes this logic. Indeed, in their discussion of the ways that men's and women's work is differentiated in the public mind, Mona Domosh and Joni Seager include third on their list the idea that "only work for wages is work" (37).

However compelling the account that housework is devalued because it is unwaged, this interpretation cannot explain the case of Brook Farm, where housework was compensated equally with all other work. Individuals earned their room, board, fuel, lighting, and washing through their hourly labor (Brook Farm Association, *Records*, Meeting Notes, Wednesday, September 29, 1841).[15] Popular accounts ascribed such equal compensation the power of overcoming stigma associated with particular work: "The meanest toil was shorn of its disagreeable features as all work was honorable and all workers were on the same level and received the same pay" ("Girl's Recollections"). Evidently, paying women members for their housework made a bold statement. So what accounts for the continuing devaluation of housework? One possible answer surfaces in the women's comparisons of their domestic labor to their other work at the farm. For example, one enterprising group of women started what became known as the "fancy group."[16] These women manufactured small items like caps, collars, capes, undersleeves, and painted knickknacks to sell in Boston.

Members drummed up business in their letters home, and the goods were also marketed locally through Houghton's Shop and in Boston through Holmes and Hutchinson's (Garrison and Myerson 9; Delano, *Brook Farm* 173).

In contrast to their housework, and even their teaching, the fancy group's labor provided women an unparalleled sense of accomplishment and productivity. Though sewing is a conventionally feminine task, selling these items in Boston seemed to elevate this work. Marianne Dwight, one of the leaders of the enterprise, explains her new role as follows:

> I belong to a group for making fancy articles for sale in Boston. . . . We have been very busy at it of late, and Amelia Russell and I are often much amused at the idea of our having turned milliners and makers of cap-tabs. Our manufacture is quite workmanlike. I assure you, we realize considerable money (!!) from this, and hope, women tho' we be, to have by and by the credit of doing some productive labor. (24–25)

Dwight's evident pride in this work stems from the "credit" due their "productive labor," despite their identity as women—here voiced as a self-evident obstacle to receiving credit for one's work. While her domestic labor is, on paper, as valued as men's work, this new venture, with its promise of "considerable money (!!)" is clearly perceived as a more real, more valued contribution.[17] Such letters show that, more than the compensation or wages for their work, it is the price of their goods on the market that designates this work as productive. Dwight stresses that their "manufacture" is "workmanlike" and elsewhere delights in the demand for her items: "I seem to have got myself into business" (qtd. in Delano, *Brook Farm* 173). Amelia Russell also confirms the importance of the link to the market. Her memoir explains: "Besides the necessary domestic labor[,] almost every one was connected with some group whose work would prove more immediately remunerative, or was at least intended to do so; and these occupations were generally more interesting on that account" (111). By these accounts, the market value of the articles elevated this labor above the subsistence work of cooking, cleaning, and housekeeping. Despite receiving compensation for their housework, Brook Farm women continued to see housework as a necessary evil, in contrast to their "real work" in the fancy group.

Tellingly, the long-term goal of the Brook Farm fancy group was to lessen the drudgery of housework. The other women are eager to help with this industry, and Elizabeth Curson regularly loses her "chief helper" whenever Dwight needs assistance completing an order (qtd. in Garrison and Myerson 9, 14). Besides temporarily borrowing workers from the domestic department, Dwight hopes the fancy group will lessen the burden of housework on Brook Farm women over time. "If we have success . . . , it will be very desirable for other ladies to come here on purpose to take a part in our fancy work; then our domestic work which now presses too heavily, will get more divided, and we shall each have less house-work and more fancy work" (33). Without questioning that domestic work will continue to be women's lot, Dwight imagines a better balance between the domestic and entrepreneurial work that she finds so disparate in their personal rewards.

The response of the community to these efforts is difficult to determine, but one clue lies in the labor records. Initially, women doing "fancy work" logged their hours in the "Miscellaneous Series" (Delano, *Brook Farm* 164). But later these hours were logged, instead, in a "Second Mechanical Series" organized, presumably, specifically to house this labor. Delano interprets the new addition as a compliment to the women, "an acknowledgement of the important contribution that women were making to the Association," and remarks that it "should have been called the 'Women's Series,' because the top fifteen Brook Farmers who contributed the most labor to it . . . were all women" (*Brook Farm* 164). Another reading, however, might ask why the women's work couldn't be classified in the existing Mechanical Series. Why invent a new series that was essentially, as Delano admits, a "Women's Series" rather than classify this labor alongside men's mechanical work? In any case, it is significant that the community recognized sewing goods for market as essentially different from sewing for the community, which continued to be logged in the domestic series.

Moreover, the "fancy group" at Brook Farm indicates a broader trend in women's work. Dwight, Russell, and the others were not alone in understanding production for the market as more consequential than production for subsistence. On the whole, the market revolution "discouraged the making of goods for immediate use in favor of producing commodities for exchange in the marketplace" (Laurie 15). As the market began to dominate understandings of labor, housework suffered from its association with subsistence labor. Even though women working from home often sold their labor—or its products—for cash, women's "formal relationship to the market remained ambiguous at best—as men's was not" (Boydston, "To Earn" 11). In actuality, it was not uncommon for housewives to take in sewing, laundry, or craftwork to supplement the family income, though outside of Brook Farm that labor remained primarily invisible and unaccounted for aside from women's personal writings and records.[18] The teleological understanding of housework as woman's purpose meant that women's other work was framed as "extra," as work undertaken according to situation and need, family emergency or financial distress. This teleological rendering prevented women's contributions from substantially challenging broader views of women's work. Moreover, as I will discuss in the next section, as privileged women sought alternatives to housework, they distanced themselves from working-class women who lacked those options.

Domestics, Dirt, and Class

While it is important to understand the construction of housework in opposition to both men's work and other work the women did, there is another important touchstone for housework at Brook Farm. Indeed, while the community is rightly praised for compensating domestic labor, the idea of paying people to do housework was hardly novel. In midcentury America, many women pursued housework as wage work—a fact that further troubles the notion that housework is undervalued because it is unwaged. While white, middle-class housewives may have been expected to do housework for free, the rhetorical construction of housework cannot be understood in isolation from the women who did the same work for pay. Indeed, views of domestic labor at Brook Farm were not immune from the broader association of housework with domestic service. As we will see, the class tensions that haunted Brook Farm from the beginning informed the division of domestic labor among the community's women.

So what was the situation of paid housework at the time of Brook Farm? Any understanding of paid housework before 1870 is hampered by the disinterest of previous decades' censuses in women's work generally and domestic service in particular.[19] Yet scholars have concluded that, in midcentury American cities, 15–30 percent of all households included live-in domestic servants (Dudden 1). The fragmented evidence shows domestic service "as by far the largest single occupation for women, dwarfing alternatives like factory or needle work," at least in cities (Dudden 77). Moreover, there are some clear indications about the composition of the domestic workforce. By 1840, domestic service was entirely women's work (Stansell 155). And what began as a racially and ethnically heterogeneous group of workers in the early nineteenth century became increasingly homogenous by midcentury, as young Irish immigrants displaced black women, who were relegated to specialized situations as laundresses, charwomen, and maids. By 1855, Irish women comprised 74 percent of domestic workers, whereas black women comprised only 3 percent (Stansell 157).[20] The predominance of Irish women in domestic service was truly remarkable: the available cross-sectional data suggests that "almost every young Irish woman who came to America spent some time in domestic service" (Dudden 62).

The status of paid housework was, as today, among the lowest of occupations available to women, even as wages for housework were comparable to outwork or other "women's work." Domestic servants' wages in New York City declined midcentury, falling from two dollars a week in 1800 to one dollar a week between 1845 and 1860 (Stansell 262). Nevertheless, domestic service provided a more reliable income than outwork and, in this way, more closely resembled factory work. Because domestic servants were provided room and board, they were able to save some portion of their wages: from 1819 to 1847, domestic servants accounted for one-half to two-thirds of savings accounts opened annually by unskilled workers at the New York Bank for Savings (Stansell 157). Yet despite the comparatively favorable economic positioning of domestic work, working-class and poor women turned to servant positions only as a last resort. Virginia Penny, a contemporary researcher, found that women preferred mechanical labor over any kind of domestic service because women enjoyed more autonomy off the job and felt they were "more their own mistresses" (qtd. in Stansell 167). While public concern fixated on factory work as leading women to prostitution, domestic service did so far more regularly—indeed, brothel proprietors recruited girls at intelligence or employment offices for domestic servants. Given its low status, domestic service drew upon the most vulnerable populations of women, including widows and women with mental and physical disabilities. Conversely, service eroded women's physical, emotional, and mental well-being: women admitted to New York state asylums at Utica and Willard between 1843 and 1900 included "disproportionately large numbers of foreign-born young women who had worked in domestic service" (Stansell 205).

While Brook Farm spoke of class diversity, the female members whose letters and memoirs persist belonged mainly to the middle class. Local data suggests that these women were likely used to being served. The rate of families with full-time live-in service was 17 percent in Boston in 1845 and 19 percent in Providence in 1855 (Dudden 78). Brook Farm's women, coming from patrician households, no doubt helped with housework back home but also delegated less desirable tasks to others. Increasingly, daughters of middle-class families were "withdrawn from housework in favor of expanded education and training in genteel accomplishments during an extended period of girlhood" (Dudden 47). As Faye Dudden notes, though historian Gerda Lerner famously described the 1830s cult of the lady in opposition to the mill girl, in practice "the lady's opposite number was more apt to be the domestic" (46). Unlike the eighteenth-century practice of hiring help, domestic service created greater class divisions among women: "Some women—ethnic and working-class daughters—were quite likely to work as domestics, while other women—middle-class native-born wives—were quite likely to hire domestics. Women experienced one side or the other of the service relationship, but not both" (Dudden 79).[21] No wonder, then, if privileged women at Brook Farm experienced a conflict between their search for self-culture and the community's eschewal of hired labor.[22]

Media accounts took the community's aims at face value, noting that Brook Farm had "no servants . . . , or rather no hired servants—all the male members being their own valets, and every feminine female member having to act as *femme de chambre* to herself" ("George Ripley" 572). Yet despite their lofty goals, the original members of Brook Farm, united by class privilege as well as ideals, soon felt that they would benefit from recruiting members with more practical work experience. Amelia Russell recalls discussing the community's financial troubles and deciding "to increase the association by admitting members who should bring an industry with them" (25). Thus, in 1844, community leaders circulated a call for new capital and new members, seeking "men and women accustomed to labor, skillful, careful, in good health, and more than all imbued with the idea of Association" to supply the "constant and unwearied labor" necessary for the community's success ("Signs of the Times" 350).

While seeking working-class recruits is not in itself problematic, many remaining documents implicitly or explicitly suggest that Brook Farm was a place where individuals from the "vulgar" classes might be "refined." Here, Brook Farm adopted the rhetoric of moral benevolence, which leveraged the ideology of domesticity to enact a class intervention intended to purge midcentury cities "of the supposed perfidies of working-class life" (Stansell xii). As one female visitor to Brook Farm memorably phrased it, "the true democratic equality may be obtained by *levelling up*, instead of *levelling down*" (Brownson 490, emphasis in original). While positive accounts championed stories of working-class members who had sacrificed "some of the income they were getting by outside work in order to secure the advantages of the Farm to themselves and to their children," those close to the association articulated goals for "improving" the individuals who brought a trade to the community ("Brook Farm: A Social Enterprise" 102). For one, Elizabeth Palmer Peabody saw Brook Farm as tackling one of the "most important problems of human life . . . viz. the reconciliation of labour with cultivation and elegance of mind and manners" ("Community"). Others betrayed the same prejudice when they noted approvingly that the members changed clothes for meals and that the "coarser" inhabitants "were ever ready to copy the good example of their superiors" ("Brook Farm: A Social Enterprise" 102). Such comments gain additional salience in the context of domestic advice literature noting the increased separation between employers and employees, especially at mealtime: Beecher and Stowe remark that employers' increase in "refinement and education . . . make these conditions of close intimacy with more uncultured neighbors disagreeable" (*American Woman's Home* 319). Yet as the change to Fourierism brought more working-class individuals into their midst, there are indications that Brook Farm's founding members were alienated by these new recruits. As one observer noted, after this shift, Brook Farm "soon ceased to attract the interest and favor of Emerson and his coterie; some of the associates, pupils of the school, and boarders, fearing they would lose caste if they remained at Brook Farm, left" (Hinds, *American Communities* 261–62).

While scholars have documented the community's desire to recruit tradesmen, Brook Farm also enlisted working-class women specifically to do housework. Indeed, in the postscript to his letter imploring Emerson to join the community, Ripley explains, "I should like to have a good washerwoman in my parish admitted into the plot. She is certainly not a Minerva or a Venus; but we might educate her two children . . . who otherwise will be doomed to drudge through life" (qtd. in Sams 8). The community's women also recruited a housekeeper. At first, they avoided assigning any individual this role, but they eventually hired a seamstress who "showed so much delicacy and tact," who was "so *fit* that they created for her the office," and the woman joined the community as a member (Brownson 494). Now certainly these recruitment efforts are different from hiring domestic servants. Still, the desire to enroll members specifically from the working classes replicates such attitudes. Sophia Ripley talks about several "girls" who have come to help her with the housework; likely these "girls" are managed in much the same way as domestics in a typical home (Harazsti 18).

Though most of the surviving accounts are from the more privileged women, we do have some record of at least one of these more transient women: Sophia Eastman. Charles Lane, a friend of the community, notes that its members comprised three classes: the "leading portion . . . believe that an improved state of existence would be developed in association"; the second group includes "those who join with the view of bettering their condition, by being exempted from some portion of worldly strife"; and the third consists of "those who have their own development or education, for their principal object" (351). Eastman belonged to this third class, planning to work in exchange for her education. The only remaining trace of her voice is a letter home in July 1843, brimming with her sense of submerged class tensions:

> There is an aristocracy prevailing here, although many complain of being neglected. I think there should be a distinction made, but you know it is against their principle, but they all treat me with as much kindness and respect as though I paid five dollars a week for board. . . . There are three horns blown in the morning, the first is sounded a little before five, the second half past five and the third at six, to call them to breakfast. Immediately after breakfast I proceed to the ironing room, which is to the Pilgrim house (or to the washing room just as they wish me to) and there remain until the horn sounds for dinner, which is half past twelve. The work is very hard and wearing to the constitution. . . . The advantages here are not as good as I imagined neither do I think there can be so much improvement made here as at some other institutions

> but I like [it] very well and I shall probably stay here six months, or a year and perhaps I may finish my education. (qtd. in Sams 80–81)

Eastman senses an aristocratic class in the community, despite the leaders' refusal to draw distinctions and insistence on treating her, as a worker, the same as a paying boarder. Moreover, it is quite clear that Eastman is there to work, in whatever capacity "they wish me to." Indeed, Eastman's feeling of being on call echoed midcentury rhetorics of domestic management that recommended that employers hire domestics by their time rather than by task. As an 1857 *Godey's Lady's Book* article addressed to "Maids of All Work" intoned, "I cannot tell you exactly what I require. I wish you to do whatever work I arrange for you as best suits my convenience and not your own; and you must trust my judgment" (286). For Eastman, access to education seems a primary incentive, though the Brook Farmers saw themselves more as a prep school for universities like Harvard than as public educators.

As interesting as Eastman's account is, the conclusion to her time at the farm is just as telling. Four months after Eastman's letter, George Ripley implores her father to take her back:

> We have thought for a long time that she was not adequate to the work of the place, which for the present is quite severe, and should have proposed her return, if we had not understood that she was making arrangements to that effect, and were unwilling to seem to hurry her departure. . . .
>
> In truth, although a very deserving girl, she is not the kind of person contemplated in our plan of admitting a few pupils to defray their expenses by their services. We are obliged to restrict this arrangement to a very few: to those who are capable of going forward in all sorts of labor. . . .
>
> When Mr. Wellington requested admission for your daughter, we had several applications on hand of the same kind; we told him what we wanted; that the duties were very laborious, the work of the heaviest kind; and that none but a very efficient and experienced person could answer the purpose; but from his description, we decided upon her in preference to four others. We supposed her to be a strong, hearty, Granite-State girl, skilled in all sorts of domestic labor, and capable of taking the lead in the most fatiguing duties. We soon found that this was not the case; and that her labors were more burdensome to her than advantageous to us. She has not performed any labors, however, which are not shared by the most delicate ladies of the Association with cheerfulness and alacrity. (qtd. in Sams 85)

Ripley's letter pairs neatly with Eastman's. He shows the very discomfort at the class implications of the situation that Eastman describes. Sophia's application to join the farm is here judged to have been false advertising. Instead of a "hearty, Granite-State girl," Ripley finds Eastman unwilling or unable to "take the lead in the most fatiguing duties." His closing comment about the zest for labor among the more delicate ladies of the association juxtaposes ironically with the women's general complaints. In any case, while Brook Farm may not have been willing to hire domestic servants, they certainly fired them.

Unfortunately, other than Eastman, the voices of the working-class women who joined or worked at Brook Farm are largely absent from the archives. This absence is structural and temporal. The middle-class women among the community's founders were more likely to have time for writing letters and journals while at Brook Farm and more likely—due to class and educational privilege—to publish memoirs of life in the community afterward. In this way, the archive duplicates the structural inequities of the community. At Brook Farm, freeing some women from housework required associating other kinds of women even more insistently with menial labor. The teleological narrative of housework thus bifurcates along class lines. Domestic service gave working-class women like Eastman an opportunity to learn the domestic arts under the supervision of a housewife, supposedly preparing her for a role that her class standing would likely prevent her from achieving. As in midcentury cities, domestic workers at Brook Farm provided the means for "reform-minded men and women to undertake their energetic forays out into the city to investigate and admonish" (Stansell xii–xiii). Just as the women's perspective is silenced in the community's founding documents, the archive silences the voices of the *other* women who made Brook Farm possible. Nonetheless, once we reconsider the absent presence of these women, even imaginatively, their presence haunts our reading of enduring archival accounts, as the following section shows.[23]

Domestic Management

While working-class recruits such as Sophia Eastman did not have much choice in their role and tenure at Brook Farm, other women forged rhetorical strategies for coping with their imagined or real association with housework. The most common approach, for those who found themselves logging the bulk of their hours in the domestic department, was to position their work as managerial. This technique in fact mirrors societal transitions in domesticity, as wives with means began to define their work in terms of supervision and management, distancing themselves from dirt and grime. Since successful housekeeping relied on the image of "pure women residing in pristine homes," white, middle-class wives needed other women to do the hardest, dirtiest labor—women whose "work and identity confirmed the housewife's daintiness and perfection" (Palmer 138). Just as the fancy group's proximity to the market validated their sewing and painting, these domestic managers bridged the gap between domestic and market-based labor through a rhetoric of management.

The communal nature of housework at Brook Farm facilitated comparisons between domestic and industrial labor. Media accounts praised the productivity of the communal model: "In cooking, washing, ironing, and other pursuits in domestic economy, there is a vast saving of labor. A barrel of coffee may be made in a little more time than is required for making a gallon, and the same remark applies to most dishes" ("Brook Farm Association" 226).[24] At Brook Farm, housework was treated as part of the farm's business from the beginning, with the establishment of a department and director of Domestic Economy in February 1842 (Brook Farm Association, *Records*, Meeting Notes, Monday, February 17, 1842). Women workers were organized into different departments or groups, as Elizabeth Curson describes: she helped the "dish-washers," "clean-uppers," and "menders" with their work before becoming the chief of the dormitory group, in charge of sleeping arrangements and accommodations for the community's many overnight guests and visitors (qtd. in Garrison and Myerson 3–5). Indeed, in comparison to isolated housework off the farm, Brook Farm women raved about such pleasures as the "first rate society in the wash room" (qtd. in Garrison and Myerson 20). And Amelia Russell recalled that while "[a] casual observer would think us occupied solely with the dull routine of our domestic avocations . . . you might have heard a great problem discussed even over the wash-tub by one whose brightness shed light on all around" (12). The structure and organization of housework seems to have helped make domestic labor more tolerable.

Another industrial trope applied to housework at Brook Farm was specialization. Women developed work schedules, moving between particular tasks in a rhythm over the course of the day. For instance, Marianne Dwight describes her daily responsibilities to her brother. After taking "a joyful leave of the nursery and the babies," who "with one exception . . . were not to my taste, and not *such* angels as I love to minister to," she proceeds as follows:

> I wait on the breakfast table (½ hour), help M. A. Ripley clear away breakfast things, etc. (1½ hours), go into the dormitory group till eleven o'clock,—dress for dinner—then over to the Eyrie and sew till dinner time,—half past twelve. Then from half past one or two o'clock until ½ past five, I teach drawing in Pilgrim Hall and sew in the Eyrie. At ½ past five go down to the Hive, to help set the tea table, and afterwards I wash tea cups, etc., till about ½ past seven. (7–8)

Dwight's letters attest to the fact that the women worked long days, but they also show that she particularly enjoyed incorporating drawing lessons into her schedule. In a single nuclear household, there is no such "specialization"; a woman must master all the trades her family requires. Few housewives could exempt themselves from laundry duty, which Amelia Russell declined at Brook Farm, recounting, "I was sent for in great need, but I wisely held to my determination, being myself fully convinced of my total incapacity for usefulness in that line" (36). For the community's founding women, opportunities to specialize and supervise lessened the divisions between housework and men's productive labor.

Moreover, Brook Farm's organization of labor into discreet departments meant that a number of women held managerial responsibilities and titles. In March 1843, the board of directors asked that "the Director of Domestic Economy . . . ascertain the feasibility of making new arrangements for ironing at the Pilgrim House," and on April 2nd, Eleanor Hill and Marianne Ripley were "appointed a committee to consider the subject of alterations in the cooking, sewing, and ironing fixtures" (Brook Farm Association, *Records*, Meeting Notes, April 2, 1843). As the director of the dormitory, Elizabeth Curson displays a supervisor's concerns about losing her workers to other farm demands: "In the afternoon a gentleman came here in a sleigh and wanted to have some flower-books made for Valentine presents—to have them by Saturday noon—so I lost Mrs. Hosmer as she makes the covers from my groupe. & on cleaning day too" (qtd. in Garrison and Myerson 15). Curson takes pride in her dedication and ability to respond quickly to unexpected guests: "Then arrived a troop of visitors and beds to be made which kept me busy till late bed time" (qtd. in Garrison and Myerson 17). Throughout, her self-deprecating tone belies her desire to communicate the significance of her role, borrowing from the language of business: "In the evening I had my dormitory book to make out (you would be gratified to see poor old aunty cudgel her brains with the groupe accounts)" (qtd. in Garrison and Myerson 15).

In the same vein, Sophia Ripley writes as if reporting on a factory's production. In a letter to a former community member in 1842, she explains that "things are going on in every department better than ever before; more order prevails, & the wheels turn smoothly" (qtd. in Curtis 119). She records with pride her own role in the increased efficiency of the laundry:

> Sarah and I have taken the sole charge of affairs in the wash-room. Things were growing worse and worse there for want of a head. We knew how we thought it ought to be done & were willing to do it, so asked leave to take & make ourselves responsible for it. So far we have got along very well. Today (Weds) at noon we had finished off the washing

> entirely—the room was thoroughly clean & a good fire burning for the ironers, who had already done two forenoon's works. Two-thirds of the clothes were dried and folded & the rest entirely hung out. So we find that it was want of plan and not want of hands that prevented it from going on well before (qtd. in Curtis 119).

Ripley's emphasis on quantification and efficiency is emblematic of attempts to position domestic work as similar to managerial positions in the industrial workplace.[25]

The supervision of working-class recruits by middle-class founding members in the domestic departments at Brook Farm likely drew upon larger discourses linking women's class-based benevolence with management and industry. Housewives described the supervision of domestics as a form of benevolence, "home missionary work" extended "to the domestic and through her to all the poor" (Stansell 168; Dudden 166). At the same time, benevolence was a business: many middle- and upper-class women earned wages for charity work (Stanley 79). Similarly, in households with domestic servants, "supervision resulted in patterns of contest for control that were similar to and in some cases anticipated those of industry" (Dudden 173). Indeed, in Catharine Beecher's 1850 *Domestic Receipt-Book*, supervision looks a lot more like surveillance. For instance, Beecher insists that bread is central to the home, and that "the mistress of a family *must* take this care upon *herself*" (emphasis in original). Her elaboration of what taking it on herself entails is telling: "She must, if needful, stand by and see that the bread is wet right, that the yeast is good, that the bread is put where it is warm enough, that it does not rise too long. . . ." (*Domestic* 230). As Dudden intones, Sedgwick's 1837 novel, *Live and Let Live; or, Domestic Service Illustrated* might be more accurately titled, "Live Properly and Show Others How" (167). Middle- and upper-class women—whether as moral reformers or housewife-employers—framed their work and lives in a gendered discourse that had little to do with the lived experience of the more vulnerable women they purported to help. Whatever their intentions, "their sympathy for the collectivity of women, real indeed in some cases, took the form of an imagined womanhood which had little to do with the actual difficulties of laboring women and their working-class neighborhoods" (Stansell 75).

While women like Eastman did not have much choice in their roles at Brook Farm, middle-class women found rhetorical strategies for coping with their imagined or real association with housework. If they could not prioritize another form of work as their primary contribution and professional identity, they worked to position their domestic roles as managerial. While this analogy was often indirect, at times it surfaced explicitly: *Godey's Lady's Book* explained that systematization would help "the domestic mill" to run smoothly ("Maids" 286). In addition to defining themselves in opposition to the other women who did the dirty work, white middle-class housewives also asserted their value by defining their work to resemble the "rationalized, sublimated work" of business and management (Palmer 148). Thus middle- and upper-class women reframed the teleological imperatives of domesticity by positioning their supervision of domestics as both an extension of their domestic roles and as work analogous to masculine roles in the industrial economy. In these instances, we see the ethos of scientific rationality and businesslike efficiency applied to housework—a forerunner to later phenomena like home economics and domestic science. More broadly, what is striking about gendered labor in industrialization is not the gulf between housework and wage labor but how the reorganization of the two replicated each other.

Brook Farm argued that all work, including women's work, was of equal inherent worth, and many scholars have taken this philosophy as descriptive of life at Brook Farm. This chapter has interrogated this narrative. As Victor Vitanza frames it, the purpose of historiography is to seek the excluded "third man" that an existing narrative elides for the sake of coherence (181). In aiming to bridge the classes, Brook Farm neglected the gendered division of labor and excluded women's experience. Unsurprisingly, then, Brook Farm was unable to destabilize the hierarchy positioning women's domestic work as the lowest form of labor. And yet, as Michelle Ballif reminds us, we must also interrogate our own historiographic narratives, asking what silences they perpetuate in order to seek "the *new* Third Man—that which was excluded in order for *this* Third Man (or woman) to appear" (Ballif, "Victor" 340). In this case, giving voice to Brook Farm's women can obscure the role of class in the community's construction and practices of housework. While Brook Farm did grant some privileged women space to pursue work they found fulfilling and rewarding, that freedom required working-class women's further entrenchment in domestic labor. At Brook Farm, as has too often been the case, the struggle for white, middle-class women's rights turned upon the further objectification of working-class women and women of color.

THE RHETORICAL SIGNIFICANCE OF BROOK FARM

A contemporary visitor to Brook Farm would have found women engaged in nearly all aspects of the community's life—teaching, learning, farming, cooking, cleaning, attending meetings and lectures, performing in plays, hiking, swimming, and so on. On the landscape of nineteenth-century America,

Brook Farm was a space of comparative freedom for women. In contrast to the society at large, Brook Farm offered an attractive alternative for its white, middle-class female members. Marianne Dwight's letters express her appreciation: "I would not exchange this life for any I have ever led. I could not feel contented again with the life of isolated houses, and the conventions of civilization" (41). Brook Farm women appreciated the recognition of housework alongside all other forms of labor in the community. Further, they claimed the value of their work by completing labor for the market, such as Dwight's "fancy group," or by positioning their domestic roles as managerial. Dwight continues: "It certainly is very unusual for me, and I think it may be quite wrong, to look for less in the future than we have derived from the past, but it does seem as tho' in this wide waste of the world, life could not possibly be so rich as it has been here" (178). While not every woman at Brook Farm had these opportunities, from a distance the community did serve to challenge notions of women's work.

The middle-class women who broadened their horizons at Brook Farm went on to impact society at large. From the start, Emerson doubted that an insular community could have a significant impact: "Better that they should disperse and so leaven the whole lump of society" (qtd. in Sams 4). In one sense, that was just what happened. One writer described Brook Farm as "a seven years' course in a humanitarian college" from which its members "*graduated*, and went forth into the world carrying the principles of their *Alma Mater*" ("Brook Farm: Seven Golden Years" 186, emphasis in original). Brook Farm women in particular left their mark on the world after disbanding from West Roxbury. Mrs. Macdaniel, active in the domestic department, participated in "various social reform movements" after the community's demise (Whidden 902). Elizabeth Palmer Peabody—who directed the kindergarten at Brook Farm—went on to introduce the system more widely, founding the first U.S. English-language kindergarten in 1860 ("Brook Farm: A Social Enterprise" 102). Brook Farm women also forged notable careers as writers, editors, scholars, and critics: Georgiana Bruce Kirby wrote about women's health and motherhood; Anna Blackwell translated the works of Charles Fourier and Georges Sand and wrote for eleven newspapers in the United States, India, Australia, South Africa, and Canada; and Abby Morton Diaz became a lecturer and author of children's and adult books, championing women's education and cofounding the Women's Educational and Industrial Union in Boston.

Yet however meaningful Brook Farm was for its members, its attempt to level the status of all forms of labor did not—perhaps could not—succeed. As an experiment in gendered labor, Brook Farm served more to offer different methods of completing women's work than to challenge what counted as women's work in the first place. In the mid-nineteenth-century United States, the act of compensating middle-class women for housework—attending to their families' and neighbors' physical needs—asserted the value of women's labor. Certainly, the fact that the women who kept Brook Farm running were paid, enjoyed the company of coworkers, labored in public rather than private spaces, and specialized in certain areas is significant. On the other hand, the persistence of what Judith Butler calls the "already existing directives" associating domestic labor with women—the teleological rhetoric of housework—suggests that the understanding of women's work would not change as readily as the practices for completing it (526). Indeed, one reason for the celebration of housework at Brook Farm in media accounts was likely the fact that, at the end of the day, these innovations did not challenge the teleological understanding of housework as women's rightful purview.

Rhetorically, teleological understandings remove women's activities and work from debate by positioning them as immanent and intrinsic. Recall how Aristotle's conception unites origin, or cause, with end, or purpose: "Since nature is twofold, as matter and as form, the form is the end, and since all other things are for sake of the end, the form must be the cause in the sense of that for the sake of which" (*Phys.* 199a). Aristotle goes on to distinguish phenomena that happen by chance from those that happen for the sake of something, thus suggesting that widespread, predictable patterns—such as housework as women's work—must reflect natural purpose, not arbitrary chance. New materialists Diana Coole and Samantha Frost contrast teleological with aleatory principles, which disregard origins and ends in favor of contingency (35). They suggest that a better understanding of these logics can illuminate the "diverse temporalities" of ideological systems—"their more enduring structures and operations as well as their vulnerability to ruptures and transformation" (36). Teleological rhetorics create narratives of how women grow and develop toward particular ends. In such models, the presumed and desired end is the ideal Woman as wife and mother. Of course, in addition to its elision of women who fall outside (or age out of) this heterosexual ideal, this narrative is also classed and raced.

Teleological rhetorics of gender, with their accommodation of various stages in women's idealized life course, have proven remarkably flexible. Midcentury domestic texts illustrate the popularity and function of these rhetorics. As Catharine Sedgwick declares in *Live and Let Live: Domestic Service Illustrated*,

> Circumstances peculiar to our domestic life make it imperative upon American mothers to qualify their daughters to superintend their domestics, and to prepare the future housewife for the exigences that await her; as emergencies constantly occur where the *lady* must perform

> the primitive offices of woman, or her family must be comfortless (v, emphasis in original).

Teleology performs important work in such passages, suggesting that daughters will grow into housewives, a role entirely distinct from that of the female servant: daughters are future ladies, not future domestics. Sedgwick underscores the temporal nature of teleology in her discussion of emergencies where a lady must do the work of a woman, though that work is typically (and rightly) the lot of working-class women, not ladies. In this way, teleological rhetorics of domesticity exclude working-class women as a whole, whose actions and existence violate notions of woman's nature and woman's place.

One of the takeaways from Brook Farm is that women's work cannot be understood simply as a question of gender. Ideologically, women's work may be defined largely in opposition to men's work, but, in practice, divisions among women are just as significant. Middle-class white women at Brook Farm not only failed to understand the different situation facing working-class women like Sophia Eastman, they took advantage of less-privileged women in their efforts to change and claim recognition for their labor. In this light, Brook Farm redirects our attention from the gendered division of labor to the classed and raced division of labor in both the workplace and the home-as-workplace. I take up this theme in the following chapters, which explore women's supervision and surveillance of less powerful women in manufacturing and in religious hierarchies. As I will demonstrate, powerful women in these communities, whose privilege bestows some flexibility in gender roles, often use their positions to enforce compliance with dominant gender norms among more vulnerable women.

A second takeaway from Brook Farm leads directly to the focus of the next chapter. As I have argued here, midcentury housework may have been devalued more because of its perceived distance from the market than its unwaged status. On the whole, midcentury industrialization elevated productive market labor over reproductive or subsistence labor. Given this, what was the gendered status of women in professional and industrial labor? Chapter 3 pursues this question with continued attention to the dynamics among women as some women enter male-dominated professions and workspaces. Indeed, Brook Farm indicates that progress in terms of gender equality is often gained at the expense of alliances among women, as work with the least social value is reassigned along class lines.

3. PROFESSIONAL RHETORICS

Silk Raising in the Harmony Society

Active from 1785 to 1898, the Harmony Society, a pietist German community, was one of the longest-lived utopian communities of the nineteenth century.[1] The community's celibate lifestyle drew public attention and commentary, but the society also played a vital role in the economy and politics of the developing nation: the stone railroad station at the Harmonist settlement of Economy—a picturesque spot along the Ohio River eighteen miles northwest of Pittsburgh—was the most important stop between Pittsburgh and Chicago (Knoedler 103).[2] In a time when three-quarters of the Pittsburgh region lived in one-room log houses, Economy's neat rows of brick buildings—a portion of the two hundred buildings erected in an eighteen-month period from 1824 to 1825—were indeed something of a wonder (Ockershausen 22). Onlookers both near and far marveled at the community's industrial and material success. None other than Friedrich Engels pointed to the Harmony Society as a "completely successful" illustration that "the communal ownership of property is not impossible," as so many had claimed (qtd. in Arndt, *George Rapp's Years of Glory* 815). Much of the public's admiration focused on the community's many industries. As one visitor noted, "Their remarkable granaries, mills, and lumber mills . . . were driven by steam power. . . . Added to this the Economists, or Harmonists . . . also have an outstanding cottonmill, a woolenmill, a silk factory, a variety of weaving and dyeing establishments . . ." (Weil 10). One of these industries particularly inspired the American public: the silk business initiated and overseen by Gertrude Rapp, the granddaughter of the community's founder.[3]

In the mid-nineteenth century, Gertrude Rapp (1808–89) achieved minor celebrity status as a professional woman (fig. 3.1). She was publicly credited with the success of the Harmonist silk business, which operated from 1827 to the 1850s and was widely celebrated as the best source for quality silk in America. Visitors admired the mulberry trees—food for silkworms—lining Economy's central street and looked upon this unusual specimen of female professionalism with interest. One traveler described his encounter with Rapp as follows:

Fig. 3.1. *Gertrude Rapp.* Photo 660d, manuscript group 354, Old Economy Village Collection, Old Economy Village Archives, Pennsylvania Historical and Museum Commission, Ambridge, PA.

My friend Jacob, after leaving the church, took me to a building where in a small room were a few females cleaning damaged cocoons. One of these, who appeared somewhat turned of thirty, had a very pleasing countenance, with more character in it than the rest, but in her dress and manner did not differ from them. Jacob conversed with her more than with the others; but whilst I was in the room, I never suspected her to be Miss Gertrude. The idea I had formed of her was that of a maiden to be seen rather in the spacious dwelling-house of her grandfather, than of a woman dressed in a plain blue garment, with her hands in hot water,

> picking cocoons in a steam-house. I was therefore not a little surprised when Jacob told me it was Miss Gertrude he had been talking to, and who had been giving him such a cheerful and encouraging account of her branch of industry. (Featherstonhaugh 81)

This passage illustrates several recurring themes in the public's understanding of Rapp as a successful professional woman: her elevated status as the "first lady" of the community, her distinction from other working-class Harmonist women, and her humility and hard work. Unlike Brook Farm and Oneida, where individual women were relatively anonymous even as the *role of woman* was controversial, the German Harmony Society did have a female figurehead. In the public eye, Rapp functioned as an argument by example for the skilled professional woman.

Historical scholarship celebrates Gertrude Rapp's role as a female leader in industry, setting her up as an exceptional figure. The little extant scholarship on Rapp emphasizes her entrepreneurial leadership and the public recognition of her skill and ingenuity.[4] However, scholars have yet to examine what enabled Rapp to take on this unique role, a hybrid of scientist and businesswoman, much less what might have contributed to the American public's acceptance of this unlikely entrepreneur. This chapter takes up these concerns, asking: What does it mean to be a "professional woman" in the mid-nineteenth century? Who gets to be professional and under what circumstances? Equally important are the dynamics within the community, where Rapp enjoyed privileges available to no other Harmonist woman. Thus, this chapter investigates both Rapp's public positioning as a professional as well as the effects of her success for other Harmonist women. More broadly, I consider what Rapp's celebrity status indicates about the intersections of gender and professionalism during the age of industrialization. Indeed, for all the ways that Rapp was an exception to the average nineteenth-century woman—her class privilege and her education, not to mention her membership in a celibate, German, millennialist community—Rapp sheds important light on her contemporaries, other women who aspired to a professional status.

In taking up these questions, I join feminist rhetorical scholarship exploring women's professional rhetorics. As feminist rhetoricians have demonstrated, historical and contemporary women face the rhetorical challenge of demonstrating that it is possible to be at once a good woman and a successful professional (Skinner, "Purity" 105). To this end, women have deployed a variety of rhetorical strategies when entering professions traditionally gendered masculine: masquerade, which involves adopting a masculine voice or bearing; travesty, or subversion dressed as compliance to conventional gender roles (Wells 5–6);

collaboration with men as a means to increase access and influence (Moseley 359), and deployment of alternative professional genres (Applegarth, *Rhetoric*). Such studies often do the important work of recovering the rhetoric and labor of women who have been forgotten or cast as failures, illuminating the conditions for their acceptance or marginalization. However, scholars of gendered rhetorics are also interested in rhetorics of women's professional successes, gendered narratives that frame women's and men's accomplishments in "strikingly different ways" (Hallenbeck, "Inventing" 260). As this chapter will demonstrate, such success stories can function to disguise or reify the gendered dynamics that confront women in the actual spaces of their work. Thus, this analysis considers the role of the professional woman in the public eye and in the spaces of a specific profession, as both are significant for individual women and broader rhetorics of gender.

I argue that nineteenth-century understandings of professional women function through gendered rhetorics of *exceptionalism*, where narratives of individual success explain and excuse the relative absence of other members of a marginalized group. As Sarah Hallenbeck warns, "focusing exclusively on rhetorical successes in professional contexts" can promote "an 'exceptional woman' narrative that can actually militate against change within those contexts" ("Resituating" 71). This chapter takes up Hallenbeck's call to recognize that successes, as much as failures, emerge "from a constellation of material and rhetorical interactions" (82). In this light, my focus on exceptionalism addresses both contemporary exigencies surrounding women's work and calls for intersectionality in feminist scholarship. When prominent women are championed as evidence of women's equality in the workforce, how does this rhetoric function? Does their success "trickle down" to affect the working lives and opportunities of other women? Do these token women meaningfully shift broader rhetorics of gendered labor, or do they function to disarm feminist critique and resistance?

My consideration of Rapp as an exemplar of the "professional woman" echoes Rebecca Richards's concerns regarding the paradox of the "woman world leader." As Richards asks, "Does inserting the word 'woman' before 'leader' mean that this person will lead differently or provide a revolutionary or feminist model of leadership? Does 'woman leader' mitigate some of the negative connotations that one might associate with women? Or with leaders?" (17). Similarly, I ask, did women professionals change the nature of work or patterns of professionalization in burgeoning disciplines? Did "woman professional" mitigate negative cultural understandings of womanhood or of professionalism? I propose that, in the mid-nineteenth century, the term "professional woman" performed an anagrammatical function, scrambling the meanings of both "professional" and "woman."[5] Thus, while ostensibly acknowledging Rapp's success, the "professional woman" label—like "woman world leader"—indicates linguistically that the value of professional = man still holds true. Such anagrammatical terms simultaneously signify a break in logics of leadership or professionalism and reinscribe those same logics by marking the woman in question as an exception, disproving the wishful thinking of "trickle-down feminism," where one woman's success automatically improves the life chances of other women.

In this chapter, I explore the professional life of one woman not to suggest that Rapp can represent all women—reinscribing her as a token—but to inquire into the affordances and limitations of Rapp's professional success as an access point to larger rhetorics of gender. Understanding the public significance of women's work in the Harmony Society requires grappling with the persona of Gertrude Rapp, not only the most famous Harmonist woman by far but also a woman famous by virtue of her perceived professional success. If Rapp, a relatively privileged woman given contemporary standards, encountered these limitations, then how much more limited were the professional options of women with less privilege? In this respect, I hope to demonstrate that a focus on an individual woman rhetor need not prevent one from exploring broader ecologies of gender. This approach echoes Susan Wells, who writes of the female physicians in her study: "I am tempted to speculate that these women wrote an alternate medicine. . . . Instead, I advance a more modest claim: that women physicians did the work of medicine as it was understood in the last half of the nineteenth century, and that their writing can historicize and complicate our understanding of the relations among women and science, gender and knowledge" (5). In sum, this chapter approaches Rapp as a problematic figurehead: an example of discourses of gendered professionalism in the industrializing United States who was deployed by her contemporaries as an exemplar of the "professional woman."

To this end, I consider Rapp's business correspondence, preserved in the *Silk Letter Book* in the Old Economy Village Archives, alongside other remnants of women's lives from published sources, contemporary accounts, and archival materials. I argue that Rapp benefitted from several affordances that facilitated her success in the silk industry, affordances she seized through her business correspondence. These included the opportunity to position her work as patriotic through the rhetoric of the "Silk Cause," as well as new technologies and rhetorics of professionalism. At the same time, Rapp also illustrates encroaching limitations on women's access to professionalism as industrialization progressed: work with domestic associations, like silk raising, was increasingly feminized as amateur or as a hobby, and limits on Rapp's mobility combined with new spatial understandings of work further constrained her access to the spaces of the silk industry and the cultural capital of professionalism. Caught in the crosshairs of these affordances and limitations, Rapp—as individual or exemplar—proved unable to maintain her own professional standing while also advocating for increased recognition for the work of Harmonist women or for the professional capacities of American women writ large. Crucially, as a token "professional woman," Rapp's acclaim had little positive effect on the working-class Harmonist women whose work enabled her success, and her exceptional status as a member of this unique community prevented her from becoming a transferable demonstration of women's professional abilities. Thus, Rapp's case demonstrates a broader pattern whereby women's struggles to gain entry to professional communities led them to pursue "professional projects" that enhanced their own professional status by excluding others (Witz 675).

Before considering the affordances and limitations of Rapp's professionalism, I introduce the beliefs and practices that shaped women's work in the Harmony Society, drawing on their own tenets as well as impressions from contemporary accounts. Then, I move into a consideration of two factors that supported Rapp's career: the patriotic justification for her labor and the new technologies and rhetorics of professionalism deployed in her letters. Finally, I consider three factors that limited both Rapp's professional career and its effect on other women inside and outside Economy: the increasing feminization of the silk industry; spatial dynamics isolating Rapp from professional spaces and furthering the divide between home and work; and rhetorics of tokenism that elided other women's labor and prevented Rapp's achievements from disrupting broader rhetorics of gender and professionalism. I conclude by considering the liabilities of rhetorics of exceptionalism from a feminist standpoint.

SITUATING WOMEN'S WORK: PIETISTS, PEASANTS, AND CELIBATES

The Harmony Society's stance on gendered labor is bound up with its religious beliefs, sexual ideology, and working-class origins. George Rapp's leadership of the community was decidedly patriarchal, and conventional ideas regarding gender shaped the roles of men and women in the community's workforce. However, the doctrine of celibacy in some ways exempted Harmonist women from wider discourses of womanhood based in the *telos* of marriage, family, and motherhood. Moreover, as an agricultural community comprised largely of members of Germany's peasant class, the Harmony Society also exhibited fewer distinctions between men's and women's work, space, and roles than those espoused by the American middle class. That these irregularities stemmed more from class difference than an explicit political agenda made them no less surprising to American and European visitors. On the whole, though the Harmonists' policies and practices seem inspired as much by pragmatic as by spiritual concerns, the community engaged with the changing norms of gender and labor during industrialization.

The Harmony Society grew out of Rapp's participation in Separatist religious activity in the Württemberg region of Germany. These Separatists, or pietists—whose ideologies were based in the theosophic teachings of Jakob Böhme—questioned customs of baptism, communion, confirmation, and burial (Sargent, "Social and Political" 42). Pietists also shared millennial expectations, a tradition of authoritarian charismatic leadership by divinely inspired men, and an emphasis on active work over contemplation. Their absence from worship and refusal to send their children to "wordly" schools created conflict, but when they refused military service, the government joined religious leaders in actively opposing Separatist gatherings and organizations. In 1803, George Rapp, who had been a local leader in the movement since 1785, left for America to scout a likely spot for the three hundred followers who arrived on July 4, 1804 (Durnbaugh 80). The community remained in Harmony, Pennsylvania, until 1814, when they relocated to Harmony, Indiana. This chapter examines the community in their final settlement of Economy, Pennsylvania—on the Ohio River eighteen miles northwest of Pittsburgh—where the Harmonists lived and worked from 1825 to 1905.

Transplantation to the United States occasioned additional ideological and practical tenets for the German pietists. First, the need to adapt to an alien natural, political, and cultural environment made communalism pragmatically sensible. Religious communism, which had not been in practice in Germany, was established at Harmony in 1805. The Württemberg brand of Separatism also inspired other U.S. intentional communities such as the Blooming Grove Colony (Pennsylvania), Zoar Village (Ohio), and the Amana Society (Iowa), among others (Durnbaugh 79). These communities found religious backing for their communal lifestyle in the description of the disciples' living arrangements in Acts 2:44–45: "All that believed were together, and had all things common; And sold their possessions and goods, and parted them to all men, as every man had need" (qtd. in Kring, *Harmonists* 11). Second, a revivalist period in 1807 made celibacy the official, though not always observed or enforced, policy of the Harmonists. Though celibacy was advocated by Böhme, scholars have also suggested that the hardships of frontier life in America were a "predisposing cause" (Knoedler 10). Similarly, the pietist community of Zoar, in Ohio, adopted celibacy in its early years (while men and women were both needed to help clear the land), but renounced it once they were more settled (Kring, *Harmonists* 70).

Whatever the motivation for the Harmonist lifestyle, pragmatic or religious, the practice of sharing goods in common mounted an implicit critique of capitalist class relations in the industrializing United States. Pennsylvania industrialized rapidly in the nineteenth century, with workers in agriculture dropping from 68 to 17 percent between 1820 and 1900 (Greenwald 3). The Harmonists' return to Pennsylvania in 1825 coincided with the opening of the Erie Canal (Laurie 22). The state's transportation revolution continued throughout the 1830s, with the opening of the Pennsylvania Main Line (a system of canals and railroads between Philadelphia and Pittsburgh) in 1835 and the Ohio and Erie Canal (linking Cleveland and Portsmouth, Ohio) in 1836 (Laurie 22). The new transportation infrastructure supported the transition of textile production from the home to antebellum factories. In and beyond Harmony, women played a large role in the state's industrial growth, particularly in the textile industries.[6]

The decision to live in a community of shared goods implied a "spirit of true equality and brotherhood" as a component of the community's religious creed (Williams 49). Similarly, George Rapp's *Thoughts on the Destiny of Man*, a compilation of Harmonist commonplaces and beliefs, suggests that, as much as possible, the community treated all members equally: "Male and female, old and young, are usefully employed, according to their powers of mind and body; all contribute to the welfare of the whole and from the common stock all are supplied with all necessities of life" (Knoedler 74). The Harmonists' belief in the spiritual benefit of labor stems from Böhme specifically, but similar expressions across not only religious but also secular communities (like Brook Farm) suggest that a faith in the potential nobility of labor was widespread and attractive as industrialization threatened to degrade labor. The class implications of the Harmonists' successful implementation of communism were not lost on Engels, who explained:

> If this matter is important for all people, it is of special importance for the poor hired workers, who possess nothing, who tomorrow use up their pay which they earn today and any moment may become breadless through unforeseen accidents that are unavoidable. Hereby these are afforded a prospect for an independent, secure and carefree existence, on the basis of a complete equality with those, who at present because of their wealth, can make the hired worker their slave. (qtd. in Arndt, *George Rapp's Years of Glory* 815)

In a midcentury context, the Harmony Society's communal lifestyle might easily have been seen as joining reformers—such as the female labor organizers at the Lowell mills—in a larger "battle against the common evils of the new industrial economy" (Wan 29).

If communalism implied a sympathy for new ideas regarding labor and class relations, the justification and application of celibacy enabled a more independent role for women. On the whole, official Harmonist documents make little mention of women as a group, referring instead to the responsibilities of members, on the one hand, and of George Rapp and other community leaders, on the other.[7] This lack of a specific platform meant that, in many ways, the Harmony Society reproduced patriarchal attitudes.[8] However, the community's advocacy of a celibate lifestyle disrupted paternalistic structures that treated women primarily as the dependents of fathers and husbands.[9] Harmonist women were community members in their own right. For both the Harmonists and the Shakers, celibacy was based in the idea of the "dual Adam," the belief that God and Adam were androgynous, possessing both masculine and feminine qualities and natures (Durnbaugh 87; Kring, *Harmonists* 12). In this view, the religious fall resulted in the assignation of Adam's feminine qualities to Eve; in a perfect or heavenly state, that divided nature would be reunited. Thus, marriage and sexuality were understood as symptoms of the unnatural division of the sexes. This philosophy meant, in practice, that women were encouraged to seek out and express their oppressed masculine nature and men their oppressed feminine nature. This androgynous ideal had important consequences for the philosophy of work in Harmonist communities, as well as other communities that embraced celibacy through the ideology of the dual Adam.

As in Shaker communities, the Harmonist policy of celibacy was often practiced through a segregation of men's and women's working, spiritual, or social lives. Indeed, this division is evident in women's responsibility for the community's housework. This question came to the fore when the community was split during its relocation from the settlement of Harmony, Indiana, to Economy, Pennsylvania. George Rapp and a cohort of men formed the advance party, but the few women who accompanied them struggled to accomplish all the required tasks. As several women wrote to the Indiana branch, "we really are too few women for so many men" (Durrwachter and Weidenbach). Rapp himself describes the group's arrival in Economy, noting "what eyes my house girls made" when they realized the state of the new settlement and the uphill battle they would face over the coming months (qtd. in Arndt, *George Rapp's Harmony Society* 316). Even in this time of transition and hardship, it does not seem to have occurred to Rapp or the women that the men might help set up the household, grow and prepare food, and so on. There are also indications that men had an additional measure of agency in choosing their occupation.

While both sexes were educated up to age fourteen—attending school in the morning and working in the afternoon—their paths then diverged: "At 14 the male youths make choice of a profession and learn it where it is carried on in the society. The females, at the same age, are occupied in the usual branches of female labour" (Melish qtd. in Reibel 11). For visitors, then, the gendered working arrangements of the society, with its "house girls" and "branches of female labour," was likely quite comprehensible, however alien their other beliefs.

Despite this gendered division of labor, men's and women's work resembled each other's in some key ways. For instance, the structure of the workday was the same for men and women: "The bell rings for breakfast at half-past six A.M.: at seven they all go to their various avocations, and at twelve they are summoned to dinner. At one they resume their work. . . . At seven P.M. the labours of the day cease, and all retire" (qtd. in Arndt, *George Rapp's Years of Glory* 124–25). In addition, men and women did collaborate: both were involved in the community's textile businesses, with women predominating in the cotton factory and men in the wool factory, and both worked as weavers of silk and satin. Indeed, women participated in a variety of labor in the community. Writing from Indiana to the new Economy settlement, Gertrude Rapp describes the work she and other women have completed recently: "On August 6 we brought in all the oats. Yesterday we worked in the house, and today we husked corn" (Letter to Rosina Rapp). On the whole, women's work was shaped as much by community needs as by any strict confinement to "woman's sphere." To George Rapp and the other leaders fell the task of "classifying" the population and "assigning" them to whatever labor is needed, "for which they are most fit" (Buckingham qtd. in Arndt, *George Rapp's Years of Glory* 466). Both men and women were thus subject to the same authority when it came to their work assignments and were expected to have faith that their divinely inspired leaders knew best. As Rosina Rapp explains, Harmonist women's work kept them "busy in our usual beloved communal way."

That the gendered division of labor was less marked in the Harmony Society than we might expect reflects its character as a working-class community. Indeed, visitors who celebrated communal labor at Harmony sought not a model for their own lives but for society's "unfortunates."[10] Tourists accustomed to middle-class notions of women's work expressed surprise at what the Harmonist women were expected or able to accomplish. One bride on her honeymoon observed as "sixty or seventy women, wearing the large gypsy straw bonnet, with their rakes on their shoulders repaired to the field to perform their part of the labor," describing the occasion as "a novel and pleasing sight" ("Wedding Journal"; fig. 3.2). Another tourist noted that "women who are not otherwise employed often work in the field during harvest . . . with their sleeves rolled

Fig. 3.2. *Haymaking.* Photo 790, manuscript group 354, Old Economy Village Collection, Old Economy Village Archives, Pennsylvania Historical and Museum Commission, Ambridge, PA.

up, and broad rimmed bonnets," comprising "a very picturesque appearance" (Passavant qtd. in Arndt, *George Rapp's Years of Glory* 488). Still, not all visitors found the "novel" site of women working in the fields "pleasing" or "picturesque." Notably, one account in *Scribner's Monthly* scoffed at the notion that the rigorous labors of the Harmonists were motivated by George Rapp's religious zeal rather than his desire to accumulate wealth, asking, "Was it for their moral exaltation (!) that the society's younger females were frequently required to toil in the fields,—hoeing corn, raking hay, or burning brush?" (Nevin). The account continues, lamenting that the orderly and appealing grid of Harmonist fields, "which thus enchanted the spectator," was nothing but "the costly product of plodding, manual toil, perfected in its glory by old-fashioned, slavish drudgery." In such accounts, purported concern over protecting women ("younger females") masks a combination of class and ethnic prejudice ("plodding" Harmonists who are comparable to slaves) and an antiutopian unease with communal living.

As the first lady of the Harmony Society, Gertrude Rapp was both similar to and different from other Harmonist women. I argue that the key factors framing Rapp's emergence as a professional woman were her privilege as a member of the Harmonist leading class and the community's gender ideology as shaped by celibacy. As in Shaker communities, the segregation of men's and women's activities allowed some Harmonist women to move into leadership roles in the female domain. For the American public, Rapp was exceptional in at least two ways: her experience was unique within her own community, and her membership in this celibate, German community distinguished her from other American women. In these ways, Rapp's positioning shaped a success story more about personal qualities than structural affordances. The danger in such a view, as Barbara Biesecker explains, is that it locates women's successes or failures in "each individual woman's capacity to throw off the mantle of her own self-perpetuated oppression," and "deflect[s] critical attention away from those structures of oppression larger than individual consciousness and will" (342). In the sections that follow, I take up Biesecker's call to attend to the "conditions of possibility" that allowed Gertrude Rapp to emerge as a professional woman and limited her ability to sustain that role as industrialization progressed (350). These conditions—both affordances and constraints—shaped the "available means" for midcentury women who would be professionals.

JUSTIFYING WOMEN'S PROFESSIONAL WORK

The "conditions of possibility" that allowed Rapp's emergence as a female professional involve an intersecting network of material conditions and rhetorical strategies. The material conditions of silk raising as an untested and desirable industry for the new nation provided an opportunity for newcomers like Rapp and suggested that this work could be understood as patriotic rather than self-seeking. Similarly, the material conditions of industrialization—including new technologies and infrastructure, as well as new rhetorics of professionalism—provided crucial supports for Rapp's career. Rapp seized these affordances through her business correspondence, preserved in the *Silk Letter Book* in the community's archives.[11] By attending to these conditions of possibility, I avoid reiterating the heroic narrative of "woman-as-rhetor exercising deliberate, strategic agency *against* her world, rather than within it" (Hallenbeck, "Toward" 9). As I describe below, a mangle of material affordances and rhetorical maneuvers enabled Rapp to occupy the position of a woman and a professional simultaneously through rhetorics of patriotism and professionalism.[12]

As the remainder of this chapter draws largely on Rapp's professional writing, a few notes on those archival sources are in order. As business correspondence, the letters in the *Silk Letter Book* are in English. However, most of Rapp's personal writing—as well as the other private papers of Harmonist women—were written in German. Karl Arndt, the foremost historian of the Harmonists, has translated a good portion of the material in his series of documentary histories on the society. However, Arndt's focus on George

Rapp's leadership and the community's business dealings prevented him from devoting much time to translating materials pertinent to women's experience in the community (especially their own writing). Fortunately, the indefatigable Hilda Kring has devoted her own time and expertise to translate a body of archival materials relating to Harmonist women. In addition, in the 1990s, Old Economy Village participated in an NEH-funded project, "Raising Our Sites: Women's History in Pennsylvania," which worked to increase the representation of women's history in thirteen historic sites across the state. Despite these efforts, the lack of personal writing from Harmonist women, including Gertrude Rapp, remains a limitation of this project's scope.

Patriotism

From the early years of the republic, patriotism had served as a justification for women's public work. While not every industry is amenable to a patriotic lens, Gertrude Rapp's letters worked to advance this view of the nascent silk industry. Rapp contributed to the view of the silk industry as a national cause, a proof that American industry could produce goods equal or superior in quality to those of European markets. In her letters, Rapp positions the Harmony Society as a key player in an industry central to the international reputation of the nation. This approach allows her to explain or excuse her work while also positioning her unconventional German community as wholly American in their business acumen and pursuit of prosperity.

While silk raising in itself is not inherently patriotic—as, for example, war work would be understood in later eras—the industry was available for such a positioning.[13] Silk was a luxury good and in the early nineteenth century could only be acquired from Europe. To produce quality silk in America, then, would be an assertion of American independence: as George Rapp explained a decade into the Harmonists' silk endeavor, "A nation cannot be truly independent as long as it cannot produce its necessaries of life" (qtd. in Arndt, *George Rapp's Years of Glory* 385). Whereas in the colonial era raw materials from the colonies were sent to Europe and returned as finished goods, nineteenth-century America aspired to supply its own needs. In this regard, a successful silk industry would not only demonstrate that Americans were capable of providing these "necessaries" but also that they were self-reliant culturally, producing fine goods to equal those of Europe. Thus, silk growers shared notes on techniques, debated the government's role in the "silk cause," and petitioned states to bolster the industry by taxing foreign silk.

Rapp's letters seize the opportunity to promote silk raising as a patriotic endeavor. She refers to silk raising as a "new and most important branch of National Industry" and argues that ventures like that at Harmony must aim

> to convince every Patriot, that our own peoples hands themselves can produce and manufacture this so highly beloved article of luxury, with which we are so fond to adorn ourselves, and in a garment of which if thus obtained, one may justly feel a noble pride, but if the product of foreign hands, we have the best reason in the world, to feel a noble shame when we reflect, that by the way of obtaining it, we have so much and so unpatriotically contributed to squander our national treasure, burden our country with an enormous debt, and there by lay the sure foundation of ruin and misery. (qtd in Cannarella 43)

To acquire luxury items from abroad is here portrayed as an act of disloyalty. Thus, in producing quality silk, the Harmonists are not only acting in a patriotic spirit themselves but also facilitating the patriotic consumption of other Americans.

Patriotism helped Rapp address a key rhetorical challenge for professional women: the question of motivation. Indeed, feminist rhetoricians have noted that working women often need to defend their motives for working as communal or collective rather than individual. For instance, Hallenbeck describes how female inventors are situated by "gendered invention narratives" that define the spaces and motives of women's inventions as familial and domestic, part of their household duties ("Inventing" 261). Similarly, Jane Greer argues that framing her business as "a seemingly natural extension of her domestic desires and abilities, rather than articulating any financial ambitions or aptitude for business," helped Nell Donnelly Reed "sidestep resistance to female entrepreneurship" (160, 159). While Hallenbeck and Greer describe the domestic positioning of women's work, I suggest that patriotic positioning served a similar role, helping women to cultivate a nonthreatening professional identity. I agree with Anne Witz that "gendered actors engaged in professional projects as strategic courses of action will have differential access to the tactical means of achieving their aims in a patriarchal society within which male power is institutionalised and organized" (677). In this instance, patriotic professionalism was an attainable and effective rhetorical resource for Gertrude Rapp.

In her letters, Rapp positions Harmony as the central proof of the viability of American silk production, emphasizing her work as communal rather than individual and minimizing her role as a female entrepreneur. She writes, "There is not much doing in silk in this country except what is done by our society" ("To Layton Atkins," 3 Dec. 1842, *Silk Letter Book*). Perhaps the best evidence of this view is the letter accompanying Harmonist silk goods to the New York Fair and Exhibition:

> They with those from other sources will serve as fact by which all reasonable doubters may be conclusively convinced, that the production and manufacture of silk . . . is as possible and can be carried on . . . as fully in this country, as in any other on this globe. I have even the pleasure to be able to maintain that we can do here what . . . has never been done in any of the old silk growing countries, namely to go, in regular succession through the whole process of the silk business in one season, beginning with the raising . . . of the mulberry seed and ending with the manufacturing of the woven fabric. ("To Wakeman," 25 Sept. 1844, *Silk Letter Book*)

The Harmonists viewed their quality products as a decisive argument in support of the proposition that silk manufacture be pursued in America and thus perceived themselves as a vital part of this national endeavor.

Rapp also affected the material conditions of her industry by seeking and obtaining support from government leaders, a "legalistic tactic" for establishing professional status (Witz 676).[14] Through their advocacy of the cause, the Harmonists persuaded the Pennsylvania House of Representatives to adorn themselves with cravats and undergarments made of Harmonist silk, "so that in the next legislature every member should be able to attend wearing homemade garments, thus exhorting their fellow citizens to the support of domestic industry" (Farkas qtd. in Reibel 27). President Zachary Taylor visited the community in 1849 and received a gift of silk-velvet brocade for a dress for the first lady—a demonstration of the quality of Harmony goods and, indirectly, the need to tax foreign silk (Knoedler 122). Rapp also communicated with Pennsylvania governor Joseph Ritner, who wrote that Gertrude "will be glad to hear, that the Legislature . . . has done something to encourage the culture of silk for which her industry has accomplished so much" (qtd. in Arndt, *George Rapp's Years of Glory* 334).[15]

In addition to positioning her work as a defense of the nation—rather than a matter of personal ambition—Rapp's patriotic rhetoric also positioned the Harmonists as contributing members of American society. Harmony, composed of over 95 percent German-speaking immigrants, was subject to prejudice based on ethnicity. German immigrants as a group were seen as uncouth and uncivilized, attitudes due in large part to the impression that the majority came from the peasant class.[16] With the additional language barrier, German women struggled to compete with Irish immigrants for positions as domestic servants. Such prejudices echoed in visitors' accounts of Economy, which noted that the "foreign speech of the immigrants" set them apart (Nevin). Moreover, past actions and decisions had placed the Harmonists at odds with their neighbors.

The community refused to participate in the War of 1812 and was forced to relocate several times due to hostility from outsiders. In this light, the patriotic fervor of the silk letters worked not only to align the community with the silk cause but also to bridge the perceived distance between the German community and their American neighbors.

Indeed, though utopian communities are often imagined as nostalgic for an Edenic past, the Harmony Society embraced American notions of progress in the midcentury United States. In Indiana, Harmony owned the first steam engine in the region (Ockershausen 22). Mirroring a transition that would define nineteenth-century working patterns across the country, Harmony, "during its first decade, from 1804 to 1814 . . . began shifting from an agrarian and craft economy toward one based on manufacturing, and it created, among others, its own domestic cotton, linen, and wool industry" (Ockershausen 21–22). By linking its industrial development with patriotic rhetoric, the Harmony Society joined a larger discourse of producerism that held that "civic progress required industrial entrepreneurship" (Maddux 110). As Kristy Maddux explains, such rhetorics harnessed longstanding republican values "to the newer discourse of producerism—that is, a language that celebrated the virtues of the nation's producers, of both food and material goods" (120). The discourse of republicanism—in the form of republican motherhood—has long been understood as a rhetorical resource leveraged by women to justify their public activities. Here, without recourse to the powerful construct of the midcentury mother, Rapp nevertheless welds patriotism to her professional endeavors. The Harmonists' success in raising silk confirmed the community's reputation as entrepreneurs and innovators. If her grandfather was right that "only the control of money created respect for a man among American neighbors," then Gertrude Rapp was well positioned to garner that respect (qtd. in Arndt, *George Rapp's Harmony Society* 314).

The success of Rapp's appeals to patriotism is evident in the language others used to describe her accomplishments. An account of the venture in *The Silk Culturist* argues that the Harmonist "satins and cravats . . . are decidedly the best we have seen of American manufacture, and are pronounced by competent judges to be equal to foreign" (qtd. in Arndt, *George Rapp's Harmony Society* 580). Even the awarding of the gold medal from the 1844 Boston Fair took up the theme, declaring Rapp's "Figured Velvet Vesting . . . an elegant specimen of the success in manufacturing Silks in the US" (*Fourth* 58). Moreover, praise for Rapp's personal accomplishments went hand in hand with the understanding of the Harmonist silk business as a patriotic endeavor. As Gideon Smith maintained in the *Journal of the American Silk Society*,

> If every other establishment and person in the United States, had utterly failed in all their trials, the success of the enterprising, intelligent, and ingenious Miss Rapp, the head of the silk department of the society at Economy, would be sufficient evidence of the fact, that the business may be made profitable, and is practicable in this country. The fact that one has succeeded where a thousand have failed, only shews that the one has used more diligence, perseverance, and skill, than the others. (qtd. in Arndt, *George Rapp's Harmony Society* 583)

Such accounts illustrate how a patriotic lens explains and justifies the unusual sight of a professional woman exercising her intelligence, persistence, and skill. Yet the exceptionalist tone of this account ("one has succeeded where a thousand have failed") is clear. As we shall see, while such exceptionalism may be championed from a patriotic stance, it is less effective in elevating perceptions of the diligence, perseverance, or skill of women as a class.

Professionalism

Gertrude Rapp was able to achieve success and recognition in her professional role due to a confluence of factors that—with her privileged standing—allowed her to participate in the silk industry as an entrepreneur and business leader. Indeed, when Rapp took the helm of the Harmony Society's silk business in 1827, she found herself in a moment uniquely suited to support her professional aspirations. On the one hand, silk manufacturing in the United States was a new endeavor, and its professionalizing status created more opportunities for Rapp than a fully established industry would have offered. On the other hand, the understanding of professionalism was shifting in the early days of industrialization, a shift involving improved writing technologies and a new professional ethos. Attending to these aspects of midcentury life helps to relocate Rapp's success not in "the rhetor's body or mind, but within her material surround, conceived of as agential, emergent, and mutually constitutive" (Hallenbeck, "Resituating" 81). Like the women physicians in Susan Wells's groundbreaking study, Rapp's "strategies of gender performance" cannot be understood independently of the "emerging professional forms" they had to negotiate (13). Still, while Rapp was in some ways in the right business at the right time, her letters show that she seized the kairotic opportunities offered by this nascent industry on the eve of industrialization.

The forewoman of the Harmonist silk industry was granted the status of a professional. The society was well known as the American vanguard of experimentation with various means of producing quality silk, and Gertrude

Rapp received credit for much of this success. In her travel narrative, *Society in America*, Harriet Martineau dubs the Harmonists "the earliest silk weavers in the United States" (qtd. in Arndt, *George Rapp's Years of Glory* 197). Indeed, the community's silk business, which achieved "more than a local celebrity," was viewed as one of the "symbols of modern enterprise" in Economy, evidence that the Harmonists were not entirely antiquated (Nevin). Like other antebellum textile mills in the early years of the factory system, silk goods in Economy were created on-site from start to finish, from the purchase of silkworm eggs to the eventual sale of handkerchiefs, dresses, and cravats. Rapp's accomplishments were indeed noteworthy: in 1839, Economy produced 1,440 pounds of cocoons and 141 pounds of reeled silk, compared to 42.5 pounds of cocoons and 2 pounds, 6 ounces of reeled silk from the next highest producer in the state (Lapisardi 32–3).

Rapp's acceptance as a professional within the silk industry, on the other hand, appears to have been harder won. Leading silk grower Gideon B. Smith first addresses R. L. Baker, one of the Harmonist trustees, rather than writing to Rapp directly: "I presume I ought to address Miss Rapp, but not knowing exactly which is proper I have taken this course, and if wrong must beg your excuse" (qtd. in Arndt, *George Rapp's Years of Glory* 305). The male Harmonist leaders, however, were quick to settle any such confusion. When George Rapp responded to John Clarke's "several queries in relation to the Silk Business carried on at Economy," he clarified in no uncertain terms that this business was managed "under the exclusive superintendence of my Grand Daughter Gertrude Rapp" (qtd. in Arndt, *George Rapp's Years of Glory* 177). Before long, the other silk growers got the message, and Rapp was credited with the production and quality of Harmonist silk. Among other accolades, Rapp was awarded a gold medal from the Franklin Institute for the Promotion of Mechanic Arts for her silk velvet and fancy ribbons in 1838, two gold medals at the Boston Exhibition of the Charitable Mechanics Association in 1844, one at the exhibition of the American Institute in New York in the same year, and a silver medal from the American Institute in 1845 (Lapisardi 28).

In the midcentury United States, the silk industry was a new and unproven enterprise, one that had not yet established strict professional boundaries regarding training, expertise, certification, and so on. Though the colonial years witnessed several attempts to make silk one of the cash crops of the new world, these attempts were largely unsuccessful (Field et al. xx). In the mid-nineteenth century, there was renewed interest in producing American silk. The community of silk growers was united in person for perhaps the first time at the New York Convention of Silk Growers in October 1843, the source of the eventual publication: *The Silk Question Settled*. The convention itself is evidence of the un-institutionalized state of the field: those who couldn't attend in person sent written testimonials, demonstrating the community's willingness to communicate through texts (Field et al. 44–45).

The professionalizing status of silk manufacturing validated Gertrude Rapp's participation and the Harmony Society's success, and Gertrude Rapp's silk correspondence models how midcentury letters could and did function as professional rather than personal documents. For one thing, the dominance of print—which would limit women's access to professional outlets in the future—had not yet been fully achieved. Increased literacy facilitated the conduct of business through written correspondence, as "public and private affairs could rely on prose meant for silent reading only rather than as a script for oral performance" (Halloran 169). During industrialization, personal letters became "a flexible means of carrying out many kinds of business and other transactions" (Bazerman 18). As Charles Bazerman explains, conducting business in the new industrial economy "depended upon people believing in increasingly abstracted symbolic markers of value, removed from objects of concrete value and from personal trust of known individuals," and, in this context, "personal letters . . . can serve as tokens of reliability during the transition to abstract value" (22). Business letters provided an alternative to hiring an attorney, "represent[ing] the writer to a generally unknown party, one who may not be so easily forgiving with regard to the appropriateness of address" (Jeacle and Brown 39). The genre of the business letter eventually led to development of "printed forms, memos, reports, circulars, and other genres" (Bazerman 26). Finally, the flexibility of the genre may have made it especially useful for women, who adapted it to diverse ends such as political petitions and letters of recommendation; other midcentury women also deployed the epistolary genre "as a gender-appropriate vehicle for entering and persuading in the public realm" (Bordelon 87).[17]

The as yet unproven viability of domestic silk manufacture provided a relatively receptive audience for Rapp's silk letters. Indeed, Rapp's correspondents were among the predominant American specialists in silk production at the time. The proceedings of the inaugural New York Convention illustrate Rapp's standing: two keynote addresses were given by Gideon Smith, the corresponding secretary of the American Silk Society, and J. R. Barbour, a leading Massachusetts grower—both frequent correspondents of Rapp's (Field et al. 44). Moreover, the burgeoning state of the industry meant that these experts could acknowledge Rapp as an equal. For instance, Smith writes that he fears he is "carrying coals to Newcastle" in sharing his expertise with Rapp, as he is sure he is "telling you 'nothing new'" (qtd. in Arndt, *George Rapp's Years of Glory* 861).

To demonstrate her value to these esteemed colleagues, Rapp deployed the rhetorical tactics of the new culture of professionalism. In the evolving understanding of what it meant to be a professional, the citizen orator was replaced by the specialist, "whose service to society took the form of applying arcane, scientifically-based knowledge to 'the common purposes of life'" (Halloran 168). As fields (both academic and commercial) professionalized, they "worked urgently to distinguish themselves from one another and to distinguish professional research from work undertaken by amateurs" (Applegarth, *Rhetoric* 2). This boundary-drawing work mobilized "discourses of insularity, objectivity, and gender neutrality" (8). Texts were treated as knowledge-bearing objects, means of making professional expertise available for use and replication—in this sense, the period witnessed a convergence between discourses of professionalism in scientific and business communities. Jeacle and Brown's description of the criteria for a credible business letter might also have described the desired ethos of scientific writing: a recognizable format, a "plain and simple" writing style, and the adoption of the "neutral tone favored within professional networks" (40–41). The convergence of science and commerce was particularly salient for the silk industry, given the technical intricacies involved in "raising" silk from silkworm eggs and mulberry trees to finished consumer products.[18]

Rapp's letters deploy this new professional rhetoric, including the scientific vocabulary of experimentation. She addresses silk grower H. P. Byram as a fellow scientist: "We have been very successfull in retarding the hatching, we adhere to your plan, and always meet with good success, but it will give us pleasure to hear, that you have still improved on it" ("To H. P. Byram," 14 Feb. 1842, *Silk Letter Book*).[19] Rapp also shares her own methods and invites others to replicate her techniques. To this end, the letters are crammed with detail, as in this description of the society's spinning process: "Shelfs upon which the straws are placed for spinning are best to be 3 feet wide 16 inches apart, as many above one another as the highth of the room will allow. Two rows of straw bunches of 15 to 25 straws each tied below, are first placed in the middle, length way in the shelf" ("To H. P. Byram," 18 Feb. 1843, *Silk Letter Book*). Many letters respond to queries about Rapp's processes, experiments, and insights. Correspondents were especially interested in Rapp's technique for using floss silk, often discarded as unusable, to produce serviceable everyday garments ("To Clinton S. Fay," 8 Mar. 1843; "To Layton Y. Atkins," 21 Oct. 1845; "To J. R. Barbour," 30 Aug. 1844, *Silk Letter Book*). Other notable innovations included producing the first American-made silk velvet (Lapisardi 28) and developing methods that used multiple spinning wheels simultaneously ("To C. L. Fay," 4 Oct. 1844, *Silk Letter Book*).

Another dominant trope of the new professional-scientific rhetoric is research, a stated purpose of many of the letters. As Bazerman has demonstrated, letters played a crucial role in the development of many emergent genres, such as the first scientific journal, which began as the publication of the correspondence of Henry Oldenburg (15). Successful silk growers had to determine which species of mulberry tree would fare well in their respective climates, what kind of silkworm eggs to buy, and what means of temperature control would keep the eggs cool and the cocoon-spinning worms warm, among other details (fig. 3.3). Rapp's letters investigate these and other concerns, as this passage demonstrates:

> My object in writing to you now is to enquire how you and some of your neighboring silk growers succeeded after the 11 of July last year, date of your last letter, and also this season? How did your worms and cocoons compare this year, as to health, weight and etc to the last? How many pounds did you raise? Which variety or kind of worm suits your climate best? How do the multicaulis trees seem to be adapted to your climate? ("To Edwin P. Lord," 30 Oct. 1845, *Silk Letter Book*)

Rapp's use of scientific tropes as a female entrepreneur is particularly crucial—women in other fields, most notably dressmaking, were finding their craft traditions undermined by more overtly "scientific" methods made and marketed by men (Gamber 128).

Fig. 3.3. *Silk Mill Cocoonery.* Photo 436a, manuscript group 354, Old Economy Village Collection, Old Economy Village Archives, Pennsylvania Historical and Museum Commission, Ambridge, PA.

Professionalism during industrialization also shifted to become less about one's personal connections and more about the circulation of texts. Halloran notes that one often-overlooked consequence of the industrial revolution was an advance in writing technologies, as pens, ink, and paper became superior and cheaper. The U.S. Postal Service, dating from 1775, also underwent many improvements in the first half of the nineteenth century (Halloran 169). These material conditions allowed for the development of professional communities through networks of correspondents, as Charles Bazerman and James Paradis explain: "Out of provisional clusterings of people, activities, and language emerge highly organized professions of great social consequence. Once established, professions maintain their organization, power, and activity in large part through networks of texts" (4). Applegarth stresses the importance of "citational uptakes" in establishing the professional and generic "status of both the text that is *citing* and the one that is *cited*" (*Rhetoric* 179). Such developments allowed similarly engaged individuals across the country to find one another, share notes, and begin establishing professional norms and expectations.

Through her letters, Rapp promotes the circulation of her knowledge as part of the professionalizing network of silk growers. For example, she asks her correspondents to share her processes and views with others in what Applegarth might call a "contrived" uptake (*Rhetoric* 180). When Barbour inquires about the Harmonists' floss silk, Rapp chooses to "make my communication of all points verbally to our mutual friend Mr. O'Hara of Sharpsburgh" ("To J. R. Barbour," 30 Aug. 1844, *Silk Letter Book*) and thus "to give you through him the particulars about the floss silk manufacture" ("To J. R. Barbour," 1 Oct. 1844, *Silk Letter Book*). She additionally directs Barbour to ask their mutual friend Wakeman for one of her letters ("To J. R. Barbour," 1 Oct. 1844, *Silk Letter Book*). The postal service also allowed Rapp to circulate published texts and material goods. Texts circulated from Economy to interested silk amateurs and aficionados include the proceedings of the New York Convention, *The Silk Question Settled*, and a book by the U.S. secretary of the treasury on the topic. Moreover, *Poulson's American Daily Advertiser* described the Harmonists as "able to supply plans and eggs to all who may desire them" (qtd. in Arndt, *George Rapp's Harmony Society* 392). Most significantly, Rapp's renown grew through her practice of sending silk goods to fairs and conventions. In this way, developments in technology and infrastructure enabled Rapp to conduct her business through the circulation of publications, letters, and goods among her professional network.

The material-discursive construction of professionalism and patriotism were two primary affordances that permitted Rapp's emergence as a female professional.

The "silk cause" gave Rapp the opportunity to position her work as patriotic, part of "a model of economic citizenship in which women contribute to the nation through production and financial leadership" (Maddux 112). As an alternative to suffrage, advocacy for women's rights based in women's work mobilized "material displays"—like the circulation of Rapp's silk goods at silk fairs and exhibitions—as a demonstration of "women's capacity to contribute to the nation's industrial production of goods" (Maddux 112). Similarly, the nascent status of the silk industry gave Rapp access to the field, just as other women found it easier to break into "masculine" disciplines that had not yet professionalized.[20] And yet new rhetorics of professionalism demanded that Rapp participate on masculine terms. Indeed, many women gained access to masculine work not by resisting but by consenting to the gendered understanding of that work. As Pierre Bourdieu explains, "Social categories disadvantaged by the symbolic order, such as women and the young, cannot but recognize the legitimacy of the dominant classification in the very fact that their only chance of neutralizing those of its effects most contrary to their own interests lies in submitting to them in order to make use of them" (164–65). In this light, as the following sections will show, gendered notions of professionalism hindered Rapp's ability to positively impact other women workers in and beyond Economy.

LIMITS ON WOMEN'S PROFESSIONAL WORK

While the previous section explored the "conditions of possibility" for Rapp's emergence as a female professional, this section considers three limits on her professionalism. These limits stem from larger discourses and material conditions of gender, industry, and professionalism at the time. That Rapp herself perceived these limits is evident in her letters as they work to combat restrictions on her professionalism and career. The first limiting factor is the growing view of silk raising as an amateur project, a hobby for women of the leisure class. In response, Rapp's letters insist upon her status as expert, not amateur, unwittingly furthering the divide between her work and that of other women in domestic industries. The second limiting factor is the spatial dynamics that both isolated Rapp in the Harmony Society and designated domestic industries like Rapp's as outside the purview of real work. Rapp's letters betray the frustrations borne of having to operate her business at one remove from the central spaces of her field. The third limitation is Rapp's tokenism as a professional woman, a designation that furthered her division from other women in the Harmony Society differentiated by class or race and that prevented her from advocating for women's professional capacities writ large. Throughout this section, these limitations on women's professionalism circumvent potential alliances among women; as Rapp attempts to minimize the damage to her own career, she is left with few rhetorical resources to combat larger rhetorics of gendered labor.

Feminization

Rapp's management of the Harmony Society's silk industry was not without its challenges. One such challenge involved the increasing understanding of silk as a female hobby rather than a national industry as the century progressed, threatening Rapp's status as a professional. Intriguingly, Rapp's letters are notably silent on the subject of gender—either her own standing as a professional woman or the gender of the Harmony silk workers. This stance was likely a response to the threat of being labeled a dabbler or an amateur, a threat bolstered by the close association of silk raising with sewing, weaving, and other "women's work." Indeed, professional women in a variety of industries faced the same double bind: the domestic associations of particular kinds of work helped them gain access to professional positions, but maintaining those positions required differentiating their labor from amateur women's work. When professions or occupations attempt to bar women "as a class of ineligibles," strategies of usurpation seek to "replace gendered collectivist criteria of exclusion with non-gendered individualist criteria of inclusion" (Witz 680). In this way, struggles for inclusion often invoke individualist rhetorics that reinforce exceptionalism. As Rapp's case illustrates, maintaining one's status as a professional woman requires, to some extent, distancing oneself from ideas about women's work and from other women.

As industrialization progressed, Rapp faced seemingly inevitable changes as the silk industry was pulled in two contrary and, for Rapp, undesirable directions. Shortly after the high point of the Harmony Society's silk production in the 1840s, the national production of silk would become, on the one hand, a mechanized, factory-based operation, and on the other hand, a leisure-time activity and hobby for middle- and upper-class "ladies." Women were barred from the silk profession through a process of exclusionary closure, which "serves to create women as a class of ineligibles" (Witz 680). In the public eye, silk raising transitioned from a serious industry to a do-it-yourself fad, including a feature on the subject in the November 1854 edition of *Godey's Lady's Book.* This professional hurdle affected women differently than men, just as discussions of reproduction uniquely undermined the professional ethos of the "woman physician" (Skinner, "Purity" 105). While it was the large-scale mechanized production of silk that would ultimately drive the Harmonists out of business, this transition was accompanied by definitions of silk raising as a female hobby and representations of women's labor in such work as natural rather than skilled.

Unsurprisingly, Rapp resisted the perceived feminizing of the silk industry, adopting the masculine writing style that Wells terms "masquerade" (5). Her letters are unambiguous in their claims that the silk industry is a professional, not an amateur, venture. As Applegarth notes, "The categories *amateur* and *professional* were in many ways mutually constitutive" (*Rhetoric* 2). Over the years covered by the *Silk Letter Book*, Rapp moves from willingness to educate anyone about the production of silk to annoyance with dilettante growers. As one letter explains,

> I am sorry to have to share: that we have for many years devoted a great deal of time to give answers to a large number of letters on the subject of silk, but have effected very little. We have therefore come to the conclusion to discontinue any correspondence on that point. We have always been, and still are, willing to give verbal instructions to *practical* silk growers or manufacturers. ("To Mr. Van Epps," 25 Sept. 1847, *Silk Letter Book*, emphasis added)

Rapp's annoyance with amateurs is common among female professionals at the time, especially in fields that might be deemed domestic and thus natural work for women. As Ava Baron explains, "Abilities that women acquire informally in the home or in such 'women's jobs' as sewing and typing often are defined as unskilled and go unrewarded by promotion or wages" (14). In this light, avoiding mention of gender and other personal concerns was both a marker of the new disembodied, professional ethos and a means of designating silk raising as a serious business, not a woman's hobby.

Rapp's adoption of an impersonal, disengaged persona may have enhanced her professional ethos, but it also performed important boundary work. As she fought to maintain her own professional standing and ward off encroaching amateurs, her efforts, like other female professional projects, were characterized by "the two-way exercise of power" (Witz 685). As the Harmonist silk industry grew in renown, visitors sought an introduction to the business from Gertrude Rapp herself. Yet Rapp remained aloof from the general public, as this letter from a close friend suggests:

> In a few days a family by name of Rutherford who had been our neighbors will come to visit Economy. They are asking from me an "Introduction note to you" which I did not give them because I know that you do not care to mix with strangers and besides Mrs. Rutherford is somewhat pushy and nosey. I told her that she would find everyone in Economy very friendly and helpful and that I would write a general letter asking to show her the silk industry. (N. Ott)

Having achieved the public status of a professional woman, Rapp could afford to be aloof—or, more precisely, could not risk being familiar.

The conspicuous absence of any mention of gender in Rapp's letters is an implicit argument against depictions of silk raising as women's work. Rapp's letters avoid *identity statements*, "in which a writer explicitly refers to some facet of her self-identity as a person affiliated with a particular place or community, saying in effect, 'I am a ——'" (Christoph 670). Rapp avoids identifying herself as a woman professional—or even a woman—betraying a profound *somatophobia* or fear of the body as a danger to reason and objectivity (Grosz 5–6). Even when her correspondents explicitly raise the question of women's role in the industry, Rapp eschews the subject. For instance, Ephraim Bacon writes to ask whether his daughter might come to Harmony to learn the silk business from Rapp. Her response contains a good deal of practical advice but declines taking his daughter on ("To Ephraim Bacon," 14 Feb. 1842, *Silk Letter Book*). A more pointed example comes from H. P. Schetterly, founder of an intentional community in Michigan. Schetterly seeks Rapp's opinion of his plan to employ women and children "for whom we can not now furnish suitable employment" in growing and manufacturing silk. Schetterly goes on to ask about the number of workers needed: "Will you please inform us, how many men we must employ, and how long, to do it, provided we employ children between the ages of 1 and 15 years old, and women? How many such women and children it will take, to do it with the least necessary number of men?" He stresses that his community has "no experience in the silk business" and does "not propose to go into manufacturing." Nevertheless, he notes, "It seems to us we could make the raising of cocoons profitable by employing our women and children" ("To Gertrude Rapp," undated letter, *Silk Letter Book*). By positioning silk raising not as a business venture but as an occupation for women and children, Schetterly explicitly defines the undertaking as feminine rather than professional.[21]

Rapp's reply frustrates Schetterly's aims, declining to discuss the gender of the workers either at Harmony or in his community. She emphasizes that silk raising is not merely an employment for idle women and children, as "a great number of persons in different parts of the United States have turned their attention to it with good results" ("To H. R. Schetterly," 26 Sept. 1845, *Silk Letter Book*). At no point does she answer his questions regarding the working abilities of women and children, contrasted with men. In fact, though textile work was broadly associated with women throughout the nation, the work engaged Harmonists of both sexes: female adolescents cared for the worms, children harvested mulberry leaves after school, adult men and women wove silk and satin, and Harmony trustee Jacob Henrici worked in the silk house and cared for the silkworms when Gertrude was away (Lapisardi 29). The implication that Rapp does not know the composition and hours of her workforce seems especially unlikely given the incredible detail in other letters as to how many times the silk eggs are turned in the night, among other minutiae ("To William Hickman," 14 Feb. 1842, *Silk Letter Book*). Rapp further counters the feminization of silk raising by mentioning two prominent male growers—Bynam and Barbour—and directing Schetterly to the silk journals. Finally, she claims scientific disinterest, arguing that the Harmonist silk business derives not "from a motive of mere gain" but from "a desire to Experiment" ("To H. R. Schetterly," 26 Sept. 1845, *Silk Letter Book*). While Schetterly addresses her as a fellow member of an intentional community and a female leader of a domestic industry, she responds by bringing out the big guns: the male experts, the publications, and scientific objectivity. As Grosz explains, once knowledge—professional or philosophical—is seen as purely conceptual, "its relation to bodies, the corporeality of both knowers and texts, and the ways these materialities interact, must become obscure" (4).

While avoiding the topic of gender may have emphasized Rapp's own professional standing as well as that of the silk industry, this strategy has more ambivalent implications for rhetorics of women's work. Most directly, Rapp's refusal to discuss the silk workers at Harmony prevented her from celebrating and crediting the work of the Harmonist women who did the bulk of the silk reeling, dyeing, and so on. Indeed, there is archival evidence that these women took a good deal of pride in their work: when Gertrude is away, the girls in the silk business write to report on their progress and seem "deeply devoted to the work of making silk" (Arndt, *George Rapp's Harmony Society* 552). On another occasion, three Harmonist girls competed with three girls at a nearby factory to see who could produce the most yardage in one month (Arndt, *George Rapp's Harmony Society* 381). While Frederick Rapp interprets this as evidence of the superiority of Harmonist industry, such accounts, absent in the writings of Gertrude Rapp, also inadvertently demonstrate and celebrate the capacities of female workers. Rapp's reticence also did not help Harmonist women relegated to other feminized work in the community, such as teaching or housework. Indeed, when a friend sent his daughter to stay with the Harmonists and learn from Rapp, rather than introducing this would-be mentee to her professional labor, Rapp showed her "how to make wax fruit and wax flowers . . . a good and pleasant employment for females" (qtd. in Arndt, *George Rapp's Years of Glory* 259). From all indications, Rapp maintained a fairly strict divide between her professional work and the work of other women in Economy.

Why did Rapp insist on distancing herself from femininity and contemporary understandings of women's work? Her choice, while not unique, was not the only option available to midcentury working women. In this regard, it is useful to contrast Rapp's rhetorical strategies with those of other women in the textile industries, especially the "operatives"—women who operated machines—at New England textile mills. These "factory girls," romanticized in public accounts of the 1830s and 1840s, fought for better working conditions by "cultivat[ing] questions about industry's effect on their femininity" and highlighting their "gender, religiosity, and native-born status" (Wan 18–19). These appeals to understandings of women as a protected class were effective reform strategies for women labor organizers. However, Rapp was not fighting for better working conditions for all women but rather for her own professional standing. In addition, the rhetorical resources of "gender, religiosity, and native-born status" were largely unavailable for Rapp due to her celibacy, membership in an unusual religious community, and German ethnicity. While the mill girls were imagined as temporary workers intended (*telos*, again) for marriage and motherhood, Rapp would never marry or bear children. Like rhetorics of professionalism, the mill girls' reform tactics excluded other groups and classes of women, using their "status as white Yankee women (a status not available to the Irish mill girls of the 1850s) to argue publicly for labor reform" (Wan 23).[22] In this regard, while Rapp's rhetorical strategies are more difficult to align with contemporary feminist ideals, they may have been no more or less exclusive than other midcentury rhetorics of gendered labor.

Gertrude Rapp did not write a strong defense of the idea that silk production could be associated with both serious industry and women simultaneously, even as her own career was an implicit argument against the opposition of gender and professionalism. Indeed, Rapp left unquestioned professional-scientific rhetorics that aligned "objectivity, technical rationality, gender neutrality, and expertise" (Jack, *Science* 6). In this light, the absence of gender in Rapp's letters suggests a missed opportunity to support other women in and beyond Economy who strove to make the leap from amateur to professional status. Unlike the anthropologists in Applegarth's meticulous study, Rapp did not "question the discourses of insularity, objectivity, and gender neutrality" of scientific professionalization or "reinscrib[e] gendered embodiment into [her] acts of knowledge production" (*Rhetoric* 8, 13). Rapp was aware that fields or industries seen as welcoming to women and amateurs are likely to be viewed as unscientific and unprofessional. And nineteenth-century women's work, particularly in the textile industries, was seen as essentially domestic, even when women learned their trades in the workshop. The few women who did achieve professional status thus felt themselves "increasingly vulnerable to amateurs who believed that their domestic skills qualified them for the marketplace" (Gamber 128). In this way, norms of gender and professionalism colluded to impede women's professional alliances.

Space

Industrialization's impact on the silk industry had a second consequence for Rapp as the century continued. As silk rearing calcified as a factory industry or a domestic hobby, Rapp had to struggle against not only the feminization of her work but also new spatial dynamics asserting an increasingly rigid divide between home and work. While Rapp was able to participate remotely in her profession, her participation was limited by her inability to travel away from Harmony. As an example of a professional woman, Rapp's experience is a microcosm of the growing spatial and cultural divide between home and work. This divide placed women like Rapp in a double bind: on the one hand, gender norms limited their mobility, particularly their movement into conventionally masculine public spaces, and, on the other hand, their association with domestic spaces disqualified their labor as "real work." More broadly, Rapp's physical absence from the spaces of the silk industry did little to challenge larger views of women's professional capacities.

Industrialization furthered the ideological divide between home and work—as well as the association of women with the former and men with the latter. The typical narrative explains that, as industrialization drew work out of the home, nineteenth-century urban patterns separated domestic spaces from workplaces, increasing the isolation of domestic work and quite literally dividing work in the home from "real work" in urban workspaces. However, as Amy Dru Stanley argues, "separate spheres" was never a reality but rather a coping strategy used "to contain the contradictions and ambiguities of market society" (76). As Stanley explains, this construct began as a description of northern middle-class housewives but became "a tidy shorthand for summing up the entire history of women and gender from the early national era through the Gilded Age" (78). The outcome, in Boydston's words, was that the workplace was gendered male in spite of women's constant participation: "Femaleness had been defined successfully as absence from the work place. Of course women remained in the labor force, but always on the terms of outsiders having to make anew the case for their seriousness, their respectability, and their economic contribution" ("Woman" 206).

At the same time, the midcentury rhetoric of separate spheres also represented material changes in women's employment. The swell of antebellum immigration was unprecedented: in 1846–47, "the number of immigrants rose from 82,000 to over 142,000 and climbed steadily thereafter, reaching the antebellum high of 267,000 in 1851" (Laurie 26). As immigrant men and women provided a new source of cheap labor, white women who had seized new opportunities in manufacturing and other areas returned to the home. Industries once populated largely by women that came to be dominated by immigrant men and women included cotton and other textiles, boot and shoemaking, cigar making, and sewing (Abbott 86). As the proportion of women operatives in manufacturing decreased in the second half of the century (Abbott 361), public commentary about factory girls shifted from the picturesque descriptions of the Lowell girls to immigrant and working-class factory women who represented "a more disturbing kind of female independence" (Stansell 125). As white middle-class women withdrew from, or were replaced in, a number of industries, women's work became less visible, reinforcing the myth of separate spheres.

Though the Harmonist silk business was in many ways similar to the New England mill towns and early factories central to the textile industry, the space of the Harmonist industry would likely have been perceived as more domestic than professional. Mill towns arose in the spirit of a *deus ex machina*:

> The combination of absentee ownership and workers largely recruited from afar meant that the mills and mill towns often had few local roots. Industrial capitalism—which in the United States, as in England, had the textile industry at its lead—did not develop organically out of existing communities but was implanted, fully formed, by outside merchant capital. (Freeman 56)

In contrast, the Harmonist silk industry was a communal endeavor accomplished in spaces neither fully public nor private. The fields of mulberry trees, hatcheries, and cocooneries were steps from the Harmonists' residential buildings, and weaving and sewing transpired in the homes as well as in the factory. Unlike the highly regimented work of factory girls, women in the Harmonists' silk industry had no set hours and slipped easily between home and work. The local and domestic flavor of Economy's silk business would have clearly differentiated it from other industrial centers. As feminist geographers Mona Domosh and Joni Seager remind us, "*Where* work occurs has considerable influence on whether it is considered to be 'work' or not and on whether it is counted as work or not" (37, emphasis in original).

Gertrude Rapp's professional career took shape within a midcentury culture that associated women with—and at times confined them to—domestic spaces. Indeed, despite her many privileges as the first lady of the Harmony Society, Rapp was seemingly unable to travel in support of her silk business. In this regard, her leadership role in the community was strikingly gendered: when she did travel, it was under the direction and supervision of her male elders, not at her own behest (Kring, *Harmonists* 36). Notably, she did not travel away from Economy to promote her silk business at all during the years covered by the *Silk Letter Book* (Lapisardi 28). The silk business was clearly a source of pride to the community, but there appears to have been a stated or unstated understanding that silk rearing should not interfere with Rapp's other duties or take her away from her rightful place—at "home."

Rapp's inability to travel away from Economy directly impacted her ability to participate in the profession. First, her limited mobility meant that Rapp's silk business was dependent on the cooperation, honesty, and promptness of her male correspondents and colleagues. For instance, at one point Rapp hoped to import French silk worm eggs, which she planned to acquire through A. Fombelle, who would get them in turn from his friend La Forte ("To A Fombelle," 12 Oct. 1844, *Silk Letter Book*). After numerous follow-up letters, the below was sent to Mr. Fombelle one year after the initial inquiry.

> In case you have not heard from [La Forte] yet, I wish to know whether you will write to him soon and whether you think it worth while, to renew to him my desire of obtaining the articles above named. *I am determined* to procure them through some person or other from France. . . . If therefore from the tenor of his letter you would judge that it is not convenient, or he shows any kind of reluctance to fill this order I would thank you to inform me *frankly* that I may know what to do. ("To Alexander Fombelle," 20 Sept. 1845, *Silk Letter Book*, emphasis in original)

This letter is signed "George Rapp," and, whether Rapp wrote in her grandfather's name or asked him to write on her behalf, the fact that she stood behind the Harmonist patriarch rather than writing herself betrays her dependence and frustration. Other female entrepreneurs were similarly forced to rely on male allies: fashion magnate Nell Donnelly required the support of her "primary male ally" in order to respond to combative union tactics (Greer 168). Tellingly, the authorship of Donnelly's statement responding to the organizers was also in question—the public was told that she merely signed a statement written by her husband (170). Though Rapp finally received the French eggs six months later, the incident shows that her long-distance participation materially hindered her industry ("To H. P. Byram," 24 Mar. 1846, *Silk Letter Book*).

Rapp's lack of mobility also limited her participation in the very fairs and conventions most crucial to her success: the Boston and New York fairs of 1844. First, Rapp's inability to attend the fairs in person meant that, for a good while, no one at Harmony knew of her success. By the middle of November, one or two months after both fairs, Rapp had heard nothing ("To J. R. Barbour," 19 Nov. 1844, *Silk Letter Book*). She did not learn the good news until January: "Mr. Wells has informed us that a Gold Medal has been awarded me at Boston, and . . . a Gold medal as a special award has been granted to me at NY. In both cities therefore our silks have met the approbation of the public . . ." ("To J. R.

Barbour," 15 Jan. 1845, *Silk Letter Book*). Moreover, the material evidence of her success—the medals and payment for or return of the silk goods—was even more elusive. Rapp requested that Barbour sell the remaining goods or return them with the medals to Economy once "spring navigations shall have fully opened" ("To J. R. Barbour," 15 Jan. 1845, *Silk Letter Book*). Nevertheless, the location and possession of the medals remained unclear. Seven months later, the leader of the Boston fair had not rendered the silk goods or payment, though Gertrude had received "the beautifull and valuable gold medal" ("To Charles Wells," 20 Oct. 1845, *Silk Letter Book*). Overall, it took Rapp three months to learn of her success at the fairs, another three to receive her medals, and at least a year to recover her goods or the appropriate compensation. In contrast to attending the fairs in person, these circumstances show that Rapp's participation was highly mediated and not nearly as straightforward as the acclaim signified by the awards might suggest.

From the standpoint of rhetorics of women's work, attendance at the fairs would have afforded Rapp the opportunity to participate in embodying her profession. If we think of a professional community as a kind of public, the central role of space and the physical circulation of bodies becomes clear. David Fleming describes the spaces necessary to public formation as a modern-day *agora*, where strangers circulate, meet, and engage in casual conversation about shared concerns (153–54). Similarly, Applegarth describes the processes of professionalization as shaped by "the rhetorical and physical mobility of writers and readers, who shift across professional, personal, and public contexts" (*Rhetoric* 18). Nineteenth-century silk conferences, exhibitions, and fairs provided this space for the new profession, encouraging talk among strangers united by professional interests. Attendees would have witnessed the same exhibits, making observations to fellow viewers or asking questions of presenters. While Rapp's materials circulated at these events, she was not able to participate in this physical manifestation of the profession. Though the profession in theory included as one of its foremost growers a female member of a utopian community in Pennsylvania, it did not incorporate her as a full-fledged participant, an anonymous woman walking among her colleagues, potentially overhearing their comments or interjecting her own views. This missed opportunity is highlighted by Applegarth's study of women in anthropology, where the very presence of "women's bodies . . . disrupted the ostensibly gender-free practices of field research" (*Rhetoric* 24).

Ironically, Rapp's lack of mobility may also have promoted public acceptance of her entrepreneurship. Had Rapp traveled in person to the silk growers' conventions and fairs, her gender and old-fashioned Harmony dress would have marked her as distinctive—if not abnormal—among the participants. While

Rapp's correspondents knew she was a woman, her physical presence would have made her gender undeniable. Indeed, "widespread gender and race-based inequities, often materialized in a writer's institutional location," influence how an individual's contributions are "integrated into or isolated from mainstream disciplinary practice" (Applegarth, *Rhetoric* 176). Thus, it is possible that her long-distance participation made Rapp less threatening as a female business and scientific leader for some of the same reasons that most colleges and universities welcomed women in correspondence courses before opening their campuses and classrooms to women. Professions may be largely constructed through the circulation of texts, but they are also formed through the circulation of bodies in physical spaces, spaces to which Gertrude Rapp and other nineteenth-century professional women had limited access. From the standpoint of larger rhetorics of gender, Rapp's absence from the silk fairs and exhibitions did little to challenge prevailing assumptions about women, women's work, and professionalism.

Tokenism

In this final section, I consider Gertrude Rapp as an example of the dangers of tokenism, defined by Adrienne Rich as a rhetorical mechanism through which "the power withheld from the vast majority of women is offered to few, so that it may appear that any truly qualified woman can gain access to leadership, recognition, and reward" (qtd. in Biesecker 338). Though in some ways embraced as a model of the professional woman, Rapp is not a typical Harmonist, let alone a typical midcentury American woman. Within Economy, Rapp's labor is defined over and against the labor of other less-remarked-upon women. In other words, we need to understand Rapp's construction, like the construction of Woman, "not just in terms of gender, but also in terms of class and race," by articulating "the specificity of certain gendered, classed and raced constructs" rather than "fundamentalising (i.e. arguing that one element is the fundamental oppression)" (Smart 10–11). These anonymous women, divided from Rapp by class standing or their status as hired maids or indentured servants, form the invisible backdrop of Rapp's success and acclaim. Outside Economy, Rapp's exceptionalism as a member of a celibate, German community also set her apart from other aspiring entrepreneurs. These factors did not necessarily limit Rapp's own success as a businesswoman, but they limited the effect she could have on other women inside and outside Economy as a token of the "professional woman."

Within Economy, Rapp's leadership and class standing distinguished her from other women. Visitors and neighbors noticed class distinctions in the Harmony Society and whispered that there was "no equality in [the] community, saying that some have much, and some have little" (Pfeffer). Indeed, the community's class structure was inscribed in its architecture:

> The town has beautiful houses—in the first row where the privileged persons live, the houses are of brick, in the second, the residences of the middle class, there are well-painted frame houses, and in the third, the abodes of the lower classes, there are log cabins. In the middle, toward the river, Rapp lives enthroned in a palace. (Liszt qtd. in Arndt, *George Rapp's Years of Glory* 60)[23]

As a resident of George Rapp's "palace," Gertrude Rapp was among the community's elite. By the time she reached adulthood, she was also a communal leader, as illustrated by her handling of a group of deserters from the community.[24] When one of the defectors wrote seeking forgiveness, Rapp's response—noting that "we have as little in common with you as Christ with Belial"—imperiously refused (Letter to Christopher Müller). Of course, the most consequential sign of Rapp's influence and authority was the nineteen-year-old's initiation of the silk business. Unlike her response to the deserters, this role demonstrated that Rapp's authority extended beyond spiritual matters. Finally, a degree of fame had begun to be attached to her name outside the community, as well. Rapp's membership in the local aristocracy beyond Economy is designated by her invitation to and attendance at a ball on May 25, 1825, as part of General Lafayette's triumphal return tour of the United States (Knoedler 23–24).

Yet Rapp's social standing and acclaim as a professional woman do not appear to have changed the public's view of other Harmonist women, who are nearly absent from both internal and external accounts. When visitors do describe these women, they are represented as nearly indistinguishable—nameless, faceless drones. Their uniformity in dress is read as indicative of their lack of individuality and spirit: the *Atlantic* noted that the dress itself was "not unpicturesque" but that the women's "faces were alike faded and tired; . . . each had a curious vacancy" (Davis). In addition, the labor of these women does not appear to have been elevated by Rapp's status as a professional woman. As Harmonist scholar and translator Hilda Kring quipped, "There are no gold medals for doing the daily chores" ("Getting to Know" 1).

In particular, it is worth comparing the celebration of Rapp as a female professional with public representations of the anonymous Harmonist women who worked in the silk industry. The silk business was framed from the beginning in terms of women's work. As one community descendant recalled, "silk manufacturing was begun when a few silk worms were sent to Father Rapp from China. . . . It afforded easy employment for the older women" (May 11). This account not only suggests that the beginning of the industry was more serendipitous than planned but also that silk raising was work suited to elderly women.[25] Visitors' accounts confirmed the association of the community's textile businesses with unskilled women's work:

> In the wool-loft, eight or ten women were employed in teasing and sorting the wool for the carding machine. . . . From thence the roves are brought to the spinning-house in the town, where we found two roving billies and six spinning jennies at work. They were principally wrought by young girls, and they appeared perfectly happy, singing church music most melodiously. (Melish qtd. in Reibel 6)

The working girls here are depicted as thoughtless and carefree, not specialized and skilled. The sense of this work as physical rather than mental surfaces repeatedly as visitors marvel at the "strong, healthy, and robust" appearance of the Harmonist women (Buckingham qtd. in Arndt, *George Rapp's Years of Glory* 465). In addition, unlike factory girls elsewhere, silk workers at Economy would not have experienced the freedom of living independently of their families.[26] Silk work at Harmony was likely more similar to the system of outwork, which reinforced women's ties to the family and inscribed familial gender relations into manufacturing (Stansell 116).

Rapp's labor was defined against and supported by not only the labor of other Harmonist women but also hired workers, servants, and indentures. Indeed, the Harmonists relied on German maids—mostly new immigrants—for menial labor (fig. 3.4).[27] In 1855, 14 percent of domestic servants in New York City were German, working primarily in German households (Stansell 157). Harmonist trustee R. L. Baker writes that he is seeking "hard-working white-persons who will work for wages," and feels that "it is better to get them from afar. That way we are not constantly bothered with visiting relatives." The idea of securing maids new to the country and isolated from friends and family is clearly exploitative, if not unusual; indeed, the community engaged in something of a trade in menial female labor, exchanging servants and maids with a number of correspondents.[28] Finally, Harmony housed an even less visible class of worker: indentured servants, including Hannah, "a woman of colour of full age," who put her mark to a contract promising to be "a good and faithful Servant" for the term of forty years ("Certificate"). Without these laborers, Harmonist women were forced to assume roles they found distasteful. As Sarah Ott wrote to a friend in Zoar, "The maid from not around here who worked at the inn has left. Now Lois is supposed to work at the inn and I should help Christiana. But . . . I don't want to be her servant, nor do I want to go to the inn." The presence of these women—working-class immigrants and African Americans—lightened the duties of Harmonist women and formed the silent backdrop for Gertrude Rapp's professional success. As Adrienne Rich writes,

Fig. 3.4. *Unidentified Woman Doing Laundry.* Photo 1051, manuscript group 354, Old Economy Village Collection, Old Economy Village Archives, Pennsylvania Historical and Museum Commission, Ambridge, PA.

"The token woman is encouraged to see herself as different from most other women . . . and to separate herself from the wider female condition; and she is perceived by 'ordinary' women as separate also" (qtd. in Biesecker 338).

More broadly, the effect of Rapp's success on professional women beyond Economy was likely circumscribed by her exceptionalism as a member of a celibate German community. Celibacy was the Harmony Society's most remarked-upon characteristic, and public views of the practice ranged from perplexity to hostility.[29] The idea that a woman's body would never be used for procreative purposes disqualified her from contemporary gender ideals.[30] Despite new options for women in the form of paid labor, clubs, and benevolence, "popular imagery persisted in equating praiseworthy womanhood and the maternal role" (Apple 165). In this vein, Rebecca Harding Davis describes Harmonist women as pathetic shadows of what they were meant to be—that is, mothers. They are depicted as "dried-up," "withered," and "shriveled," and Davis laments that "none of them could ever hold a baby on her lap, and call it hers." Though such views were obviously problematic, Rapp's celibacy may have freed her from some of the attitudes opposing womanhood and professionalism. Americans continued to think of work outside the home in teleological terms, as something women did prior to marriage; indeed, across the century, 95 percent of married women remained outside the paid labor force (D. Smith 122). Since Rapp would never be a wife and mother, her work could not "unfit" her for those roles. Thus, Rapp's work could be understood as the entrepreneurial output of a "female man" or as a substitute for the family she would never have. At the same time, however, Rapp's exceptionalism prevented her from serving as an example of the professional capacities of American women writ large.

Feminization of the silk industry, spatial dynamics, and rhetorics of tokenism constrained Rapp's access to professionalism. The fear of feminization functions as a threat that, as Applegarth has explored, circumvents alliances among women and promotes "masculinized" discursive and professional practices ("Field Guides" 194). Spatial divides between home and work uniquely disadvantage women by discounting work done in the home and discounting women as workers by means of their association with domesticity. Finally, tokenism elides differences among women even as one woman is taken as a representative of many. All three dynamics intervened in Rapp's career and complicated her ability—as individual or exemplar—to positively impact other working women or challenge larger rhetorics of gendered labor.

THE RHETORICAL SIGNIFICANCE OF THE HARMONY SOCIETY

The public acclaim for Gertrude Rapp's leadership and ingenuity in the Harmony Society's silk industry set her up as an exemplar of the midcentury professional woman. Yet a focus on Rapp's personal qualities misses much of what endorsed and allowed her professional success. As Applegarth cautions, we must craft histories of women's work "without rendering the author as a rhetorical hero, dramatically altering her profession through her choices" (*Rhetoric* 179). Specifically, new technologies and infrastructures such as the U.S. Postal Service allowed Rapp to conduct her business by mail, the nascent state of the silk industry facilitated her participation alongside men, and new professional rhetorics offered a means of positioning herself as an expert pursuing scientific experimentation. In addition, the view of the "silk cause" as a patriotic endeavor created the opportunity to frame her work as serving a larger good rather than as personal gain or unwomanly ambition. While it is tempting to celebrate, as her contemporaries did, Rapp's skill, self-education, and persistence, we must at the same time acknowledge that these material affordances positioned Rapp such that her personal strengths could surface and prevail—at least for a time. Moreover, even while public responses championed Rapp as a professional woman, it is worth paying attention to the way her accomplishments were framed, as Hallenbeck notes in her study of female inventors, in "strikingly different ways" from the accomplishments of men ("Inventing" 260).

The triumphal narrative of Rapp as professional woman also masks the hurdles she faced as she navigated the seeming contradictions of femininity and professionalism in midcentury America. In particular, Rapp struggled to maintain her professional identity as a woman in an industry increasingly associated with women's leisure and hobbies. By the end of the 1850s, silk production at Harmony was over, a fate shared by many home- and community-based businesses due to the combined pressures of an 1840s blight that devastated mulberry orchards and American silk factories' preference for cheap supplies of imported raw silk. As the transition to the large-scale factory continued, Rapp's home-based endeavor was excluded by new understandings of work as opposed to domestic spaces. Indeed, this pattern was repeated across professions: "Although professionalization seemed to offer clearer paths into the discipline for white women and for people of color, it also masked ongoing discrimination based on gender and race" (Applegarth, *Rhetoric* 4). In addition, Rapp's isolation in Economy prevented her from inhabiting the spaces where the silk industry was embodying itself as a profession. In other words, while the nascent, unformed state of the silk industry in the early nineteenth century created opportunities for female entrepreneurs, the spread of industrialization and professionalization in the mid- and late-nineteenth century shouldered those women aside.

As an individualist discourse, rhetorics of exceptionalism obscure the larger situational constraints and affordances that re/produce women's professional successes and failures. While professional success stories sometimes serve feminist aims by representing certain professions as welcoming to women, Rapp's case suggests that they can also elide both the affordances that support and the obstacles that circumscribe women's careers.[31] In this way, such success stories imply that women who fail to achieve professional standing lack the skill or talent of these exemplars, reflecting "western and masculinist" attitudes "that privilege personal agency and [workers'] unique abilities above structural factors such as race, class, education, and ethnicity" (Dingo, "Foreword" xi). Just as feminist scholars should "resist viewing historical erasures as markers of merit, or as evidence confirming the limited roles women have played" in professional settings, we should likewise avoid viewing historical successes as evidence of women's widespread access to particular professional roles (Applegarth, *Rhetoric* 181). Instead, we need layered narratives that do not isolate gender as the primary determinant of women's professional activities. As Hallenbeck suggests, we should craft histories where "gender is no longer a blanket explanation, but a factor that influences the specific interactions of which the confluence is composed and out of which emerges the success or failure of [women's] activities" ("Resituating" 82).

In this manner, Rapp's case also suggests a second shortcoming of exceptionalist narratives of women's professional achievements insofar as they reinforce the myth of "trickle-down feminism," the notion that one woman's success automatically improves the life chances of other women. There is reason to be skeptical of such attitudes: as Lindal Buchanan shows in the case of the Navy, rhetoric emphasizing new work opportunities for women often obscures the reality that only a few privileged women are positioned to seize these opportunities ("Few Good" 44–45). In Rapp's case, public acclaim functioned more as a token of the American public's willingness to accept women in the professional realm than a transferable example of women's professional capacities. As a member of a religious, celibate, German community, Rapp was decidedly *not* representative of U.S. women as a whole. In addition, internal Harmonist sources refute the notion that Rapp's professional status trickled down to other women in the community or that Rapp's professional writing defended other women's work in or beyond Economy. Indeed, it seems likely that Rapp's tenuous grasp on the professional moniker discouraged her from drawing further attention to her gender when communicating with other silk experts or the public. As Rebecca Richards argues, the struggle to achieve and maintain professional standing often makes women "complicit" in "patriarchal constructions" of leadership or professionalism, leading women in marginal positions to strive for a kind of "becoming-imperceptible" to preserve their limited political or professional capital (138, 154).[32]

Finally, exceptionalist narratives all too often celebrate womanpower without recognizing how that power is buttressed by economic privilege and whiteness. A primary challenge facing feminist scholars is the conundrum whereby women are both powerful and powerless—commonly referred to as "intersectionality." As feminist historian Carol Smart explains, we have tended to resolve these seeming contradictions by separating them:

> By this I mean that we have argued, for example, that white women are powerful when compared to black women, but are powerless when compared to white men. . . . In doing this we have operated with a concept of power as a material possession which is held or withheld as we move from one situation to another. . . . When this construct, Woman, is challenged, we have simply sought to add class and gender as *variables* but at a completely different level of conceptualization. Thus class and race, and we might add religion, are prefixed to the dominant

> theoretical categorization. Hence we have working-class women, black women, muslim women. This formulation, of course, retains the un derlying assumption that they are all Woman, that their 'Womanness' is held fast in some way. (9)

Intersectional approaches thus often turn on strategies listing variables that are added to an otherwise unquestioned and indifferent category of woman. Yet the interactions among the variables we so often list—race, class, gender, sexuality, (dis)ability, ethnicity, education, age, marital status, maternity, nationality, citizenship, religion—do not function *additively*. As this chapter shows, the anagrammatical term "woman professional" scrambles the meaning of its component parts: a woman professional is neither a real woman nor a real professional. Similarly, Christina Sharpe notes the anagrammatical functioning of "black girl," where blackness modifies girlhood in a cultural view of black girls as "boyishly aggressive" (122). And these anagrammatical interactions are equally operative in pairings where gender takes a backseat to other identity formations: Tobin Siebers highlights the historically unthinkable pairing of disability and sexuality that undergirds compulsory sterilization and other modern horrors (298–302).

While this chapter illustrates the dominance of exceptionalism in rhetorics of women's professional work, professionalism also participates in the temporal rhetorics discussed in chapter 2. Teleological rhetorics of gender may insistently position women in relation to (moving toward or away from) the home, but teleology also participates in rhetorics of professionalism. As Applegarth notes, "Professional science is already shot through with teleological ideas, with the sense that professionalization naturally follows a course toward greater exclusivity, greater rigor, and better science" (*Rhetoric* 182). Narratives of inevitable professional progress endorse exclusive practices that disproportionately disadvantage women and other marginalized groups. Progress narratives also intervene in narratives of success and failure by suggesting that professional and entrepreneurial ventures that fall by the wayside did not merit further attention, that they were "relics, quirks, or nonfunctional adaptations" (Applegarth, *Rhetoric* 183). One of the ironies of contemporary teleological rhetorics is the seemingly peaceful coexistence of progress narratives of professional development (professions as increasingly exclusive and rigorous) alongside progress narratives of gender (women moving steadily out of the home into more and more powerful professional roles), narratives that history suggests may be at odds with one another.

Teleological rhetorics frame women's gender in relation to the space of the home as well as their embodied, reproductive capacities. In this chapter,

I speculate on the effects of Rapp's celibacy on her professional stature and success. In the nineteenth century as in the present, a celibate or childless state intervenes in understandings of women's gender identity and affects women's access to professional identities. I take up the interconnections of women's reproductive and professional roles in chapter 4, as I consider how innovations in birth control and shared childrearing affected the re/production of women's work in the Oneida Community.

4. REPRODUCTIVE RHETORICS

The Work of Motherhood at Oneida

Few utopian communities drew the ire of the American public quite like the Oneida Community (1848–81), located in the "burned-over" district of upstate New York—an area particularly active in the fiery religious revivals of the Second Great Awakening, as well as abolition, women's rights, and utopian experimentation.[1] The community of perfectionists was threatened with lawsuits and civil unrest both in their early years in Putney, Vermont, and in their permanent home in Oneida, New York.[2] In almost every aspect, and particularly when it came to gender, the beliefs of the Oneida Community ran counter to dominant nineteenth-century norms. In its moment, as Lawrence Foster explains, Oneida can be understood as a strategy for coping with "the crisis of transition from pre-industrial to more modern forms of family and social life" (*Religion* 4). Led by the charismatic and authoritarian religious leader John Humphrey Noyes, Oneidans practiced "complex marriage," an unconventional system where each adult male was considered married to each adult female—a system often misleadingly represented as "free love." An 1852 article in the *New York Observer* condemned the society as follows: "All the laws, both human and divine, that are designed to regulate the marriage relation, are set aside and denounced, while the unrestrained indulgence of the human passions is practiced, not merely as the means to present enjoyment, but as means of grace or helps to holiness" ("Perfectionism and Polygamy").

Yet on the whole, the public's concerns regarding Oneida fixated on the figure of woman. One representative article from the *New York Observer and Chronicle* notes, "We have been furnished with a large number of certificates signed by females of this community, stating that at first they were fearful they were not doing right, but the longer they have practiced on the system here pursued, the holier they are sure they grow" ("Perfectionism and Polygamy"). Despite the testimony of the community's women, the article's author remains troubled, identifying their short dress as "the germ of *Bloomerism*" and illustrating the common linkage of Oneida's gender reforms with the specter of women's rights and the new woman (fig. 4.1). As physical evidence of their deviance from midcentury gender norms, Oneida women not only wore an early form of the Bloomer costume but also cut their hair short.[3] But perhaps the most shocking aspect of Oneida for contemporary observers was their rejection of traditional family ideals, especially norms of motherhood. Indeed, the Oneidans practiced an early form of birth control called "male continence" and averred that woman was not meant to drudge away her life as "a mere wife and mother" (qtd. in Dalsimer 80). Motherhood at Oneida was to be planned and desired, and the community's children were to be raised communally rather than under the primary care of biological parents.

Fig. 4.1. *Rustic Summer House with Group of Community Members.* Photo 10, Oneida Community Collection, Special Collections Research Center, Syracuse University Libraries; courtesy of the Oneida Community Mansion House.

Given these complexities, historians have struggled to fairly represent this long-lived and unusual community. As Lawrence Foster explains, many have treated the Oneidans as "colorful freaks in a circus sideshow or strange natives in some primitive tribe. The dominant tone has been unsympathetic and voyeuristic" (*Women* 3–4).[4] And scholars have been especially divided about the question of women's roles in Oneida. On the one hand, the community's system of complex marriage and birth control prefigured later movements for sexual liberation and women's rights: Oneida aimed to free women from an unending cycle of pregnancy and childcare and allowed their participation in the work and social life of the community. As Noyes espoused, "When the partition between the sexes is taken away, and man ceases to make woman a propagative drudge, when love takes the place of shame, and fashion follows nature in dress and business, men and women will mingle in all their employments" (qtd. in Dalsimer 243). Such statements support Foster's contention that "few societies in human history have done more to break down arbitrary distinctions between the sexes than did Oneida" ("Free Love" 175). On the other hand, Noyes unambiguously declared women's inferiority to men, an underlying ideology that undercut the community's superficially egalitarian practices. Indeed, at times Noyes seems to embrace a single sex standard, arguing that his communal structure will allow "woman [to become] what she ought to be, a *female man*, (like the Son in the Godhead)" (*First Annual Report* 41, emphasis in original). In this light, Noyes's goal of elevating Oneida women above the degraded status of their contemporaries may not have extended to asserting women's equality with men. As Louis Kern concludes, Noyes's approach to women's rights involved "reform mainly *of* the female, only secondarily *for* her, and very seldom *by* her" (273).

Methodologically, the debate over the fundamental feminism or misogyny of Oneida seeks answers in Noyes's beliefs and intentions. Given Noyes's authoritarian leadership, this makes a certain sense: Noyes himself advised visitors or potential members to read up on his theories before coming to Oneida, as he was "its central mind" (*Second Annual Report* 31). But this insistence on understanding Oneida "in terms of its own goals"—typically conflated with Noyes's goals—has overlooked the fact that members had their own goals for and views of the community (Foster, "Rise and Fall" 3). As one physician who visited Oneida in the 1880s noted, we must look beyond the perspective of the community's male founder: "It is necessary to say something upon the other side. The illumination must be direct and oblique to give us the lights and shadows. . . . There are no persons so well qualified to give the subject this oblique illumination as the women themselves" (Van de Warker 788). This chapter offers this oblique illumination through a rhetorical approach that echoes rhetoricians of science who examine reproductive rhetorics surrounding abortion or infertility as "a way of orienting struggle around new ways of living" that involve "diverse and competing variables related not just to rhetoric but also to material, social, cultural, and legal spheres" (Stormer 4; Jensen 12). In other words, I first avoid the presumption that Noyes's ideology deterministically shaped women's experience and, second, consider Oneida's innovations in relation to broader ecologies of motherhood and women's work.

The Oneida experiment offers a unique opportunity to study the construction of motherhood in a community that made a direct, intentional attempt to reconfigure norms and practices of motherhood. If we hope to productively intervene in contemporary rhetorics of motherhood, we must inquire into the differential power of individuals and institutions to negotiate these constructions, and we must address the capacity and limitations of such efforts to contest or buttress larger gendered ecologies. Scholars from communication and rhetorical studies have examined "mothering rhetorics" in a variety of "historical and contemporary permutations," including the mid-nineteenth century (O'Brien Hallstein 2).[5] At this time, the ideology of domesticity encouraged women to delegate their housework so they might pursue higher callings such as church and benevolence work, supervision of domestics, social standards for décor and dress, and—above all—motherhood. Catharine Beecher's 1841 *Treatise on Domestic Economy* encouraged women to adopt a scientific approach to motherhood: "Just as men studied and trained for their profession, so women must educate themselves for their life's work, mothering" (Apple 166). When the *Ladies Home Journal* proclaimed in 1899, "If maternity is an instinct, motherhood is a profession," it expressed a commonplace forged in the midcentury United States (qtd. in Apple 166). Even as the elevated status of motherhood provided a means to argue for new rights and opportunities, women also felt—or were made to feel—society's judgment of them as mothers.[6] In an 1851 diary entry, one mother describes sewing as a "confinement of my energies," concluding that such tasks are "really unjust to [the children] and I won't be guilty of it anymore" (qtd. in Dudden 147). These judgments had particular consequences for poor women, as, after 1820, charitable aid often depended on assessments of how they were raising their children (Stansell 73). By encouraging women to train and study for motherhood, midcentury domestic experts and popular discourse represented motherhood as woman's true vocation.

By making motherhood into a profession, such midcentury rhetorics designated the idea of the working mother as either redundant—motherhood was her work—or internally unstable—how could one be employed *and* be a mother? As industrialization offered increasing opportunities for women's work outside the home, such rhetorics suggested either that women's work should end when motherhood began or that women who continued to work were not "true" mothers. This framework operates through a *rhetoric of choice*, suggesting that women can be either mothers or workers, not both. Thus, Lindal Buchanan articulates motherhood's "paradoxical impact" on nineteenth-century women, where motherhood "afford[ed] them potent persuasive means while also constraining them in public life and cultural memory" (*Rhetorics* xix). For Buchanan, rhetorics of motherhood "not only benefit women, giving them authority and credibility, but also impede them, always/already positioning them disadvantageously within the gendered status quo" (*Rhetorics* 5). Of course, some women had little choice whether to combine work and motherhood. Outwork, perhaps the most exploitative industrial occupation, thrived in part due to its mediation of familial and manufacturer demands on poor women: most outworkers were married women. Outwork allowed mothers to earn a living without leaving the tenements, providing "a viable way of working a double shift as housewife/mother and wageworker" (Stansell 106). In this light, as Greta Gaard has argued, "the rhetoric of 'choice' appeals only to those who have options, but is meaningless to those who do not, and thus it politically divides women by race and economic class, since these factors circumscribe women's choices" (107). Thus, one of the central aims of this chapter is to consider whether Oneida's redefinition of motherhood helped women avoid the rhetorical double bind of the working mother.

In this light, this chapter probes the rhetorical force of motherhood—and its relative adaptability or intransigence. Indeed, the Oneida Community's experiment shows that to challenge norms of motherhood is to challenge gender ideology writ large. As Buchanan observes, "The code of motherhood functions as 'an abbreviated version of the entire system' of gender" (*Rhetorics* 6). I extend existing scholarship on rhetorics of motherhood to show how, even as contemporary discourses opposed motherhood to women's work, these same reproductive rhetorics had persuasive effects far beyond women's biological roles and the nuclear home—with important consequences for understandings of women's work. To this end, I take up Lynn O'Brien Hallstein's two-part definition of mothering rhetorics as including both "rhetorics of reproduction (rhetorics about the reproductive function of women/mothers)" and "reproducing rhetorics (the rhetorical reproduction of ideological systems and logics of contemporary culture)" (2). While my analysis begins with Oneida's *rhetorics of reproduction*—its ideology and practices of motherhood—I extend that analysis to the *reproducing rhetorics* that link ideologies of motherhood to women's ostensibly nonbiological, nondomestic roles in the workplace. Thus, this chapter addresses women's work on two fronts: first, the redistribution of the work of motherhood, and second, the implications of this redistribution for women's work outside the home. I maintain that to fully understand the lives and work of women in the Oneida Community—or to fully understand the implications of rhetorics of motherhood in any time and place—we must consider the labor of reproduction and production together.[7]

On its face, the philosophy of John Humphrey Noyes appears as an all-out rejection of contemporary norms and practices of motherhood. Noyes trumpeted the cost of unwanted pregnancy on women's health and well-being and encouraged women to seek fulfillment through work and spirituality rather than service to husbands and children. And, indeed, liberation from maternal roles freed Oneida women to work in conventionally masculine industries such as the steel-trap shop. However, this liberation narrative seems overstated insofar as the Oneida women who were able to pursue careers of their choosing were buttressed by the mechanization of domestic labor and hired help. Moreover, despite Noyes's aim of freeing women from biological motherhood, the ideology of cultural motherhood—the increasingly essentialized view of woman-as-mother—was harder to shake. Indeed, despite new options in paid labor, clubs, and so on, "popular imagery persisted in equating praiseworthy womanhood and the maternal role" (Apple 165). This ideology reasserted itself in Oneida women's resistance to being denied the role of mother and in their workplace association with industries or tasks involving care, detail, and support—"motherly" skills. In the end, Noyes's vision served more to substitute the communal for the nuclear family. Specifically, familial terminology and logics framed expectations that women would perform after-hours "mothering work" and endorsed a hierarchy where elite women—the community's "aunts" and "mothers"—exerted authority over less privileged women. On the whole, Oneida's rejection of motherhood left the binary opposition of work and motherhood intact, a shortcoming characteristic of feminist choice rhetorics in the past and present.

In what follows, I begin by providing an introduction to Noyes's views on motherhood alongside the material spaces and practices of motherhood at Oneida. Next, I consider the accounts of women as well as internal records and outside perspectives to reveal the reproductive and reproducing rhetorics in operation at Oneida: the rejection of motherhood and cultivation of women's sense of vocation and access to masculine work; the division of the work of motherhood whereby childcare is valued and housework is shunted off to machines and hired workers; the persistence of cultural motherhood via women's resistance to surrendering maternal roles and the penetration of the workplace by views of women as essentially "motherly"; and lingering familial vocabularies and logics that justify women's after-hours work and undermine alliances among women through a social and religious hierarchy or caste system. The surveillance of less privileged women by elite women in Oneida echoes widespread midcentury class and gender dynamics where housewives were encouraged to view supervision—and surveillance—of domestic servants as a form of cultural missionary work, preaching the gospel of white middle-class womanhood. I conclude by considering the material-rhetorical effects of Oneida's reliance on rhetorics of choice, including associations between birth control and eugenics and zero-sum rhetorics of work and motherhood.

MATERIALIZING MOTHERHOOD: COMPLEX MARRIAGE, MALE CONTINENCE, AND WOMEN'S LIBERATION

John Humphrey Noyes's revision of contemporary ideals of motherhood was based in his theology and composed of three main facets: the institution of complex marriage, the practice of male continence, and the goal of women's liberation. While Noyes's aims in many ways replicated the logic of historical and contemporary feminist efforts (particularly the view of women's biological and reproductive roles as the root of gender inequality), the materialization of his philosophy at Oneida showed that, in practice, efforts for women's liberation can serve to reinforce gendered hierarchies and undermine women's agency. While we might be tempted to speculate about the sincerity of Noyes's protofeminist rhetoric, we do not need this verdict to consider the impacts of Oneida's gender reforms on the community's women. Here, I argue that the material-rhetorical implementation of complex marriage, male continence, motherhood, and women's work at Oneida reinforced notions of male spiritual superiority and compromised women's sexual and maternal autonomy—showing the significant constraints that shaped women's choices in the community.

Noyes's ideas about gender stemmed from his religious beliefs. Noyes held that humans had suffered a breach with God, for which they were punished with the following consequences: a disruption between the sexes, involving the curse of excessive and painful childbearing on women; a corresponding curse of oppressive labor bearing especially on men; and death itself (*First Annual Report* 27). Thus, Noyes felt that the nuclear family unnecessarily exacerbated arbitrary distinctions between the sexes. As he explained, "The restoration of true relations between the sexes, is a matter second in importance only to the reconciliation of man to God" (*First Annual Report* 27). Believing that the second coming of Christ had already occurred, Noyes held that it was possible to live in a sin-free state (a doctrine known as perfectionism), a possibility he hoped to demonstrate by overcoming the aforementioned negative consequences in the Oneida Community. For Noyes, a truly holy society would be marked by fewer distinctions between men and women—a sinless state would heal the breach between the sexes imposed as part of the fall.

Noyes's intervention into motherhood began by replacing conventional marriage with complex marriage, a system where each adult male was considered heterosexually married to each adult female. Insisting that conventional marriage made women men's property, Noyes joined other cultural observers who increasingly connected the sufferings of women with slavery (Kern 57).[8] As Noyes explained in the community's *Third Annual Report*, "Precisely the same principles are involved in the two cases; and the controversy which is bringing out the horrible character of negro slavery, is but furnishing principles to mirror forth the exceeding iniquity of marriage slavery" (27). Yet Noyes chose to reform rather than abolish marriage. Among other means, complex marriage was instituted through spatial arrangements that defied the norms of the nuclear household. Men and women had separate sleeping quarters in segregated dormitories; even men and women who joined as married couples lived separately.

Complex marriage also involved a large degree of surveillance and control that distinguished it from other models of free love. Members were encouraged to love all their husbands and wives equally, and "any exclusive monogamous attachments to the opposite sex were broken up as antisocial behavior inimical to group order" (Foster, "Sex and Conflict" 35). These norms were enforced through the practice of "mutual criticism," where members were publicly evaluated in terms of their compliance with communal ideals.[9] The community also enforced a complicated caste system of ascending and descending fellowship, a practice of religious "leveling" where younger members were paired with older, more spiritually mature partners. Despite the common association of complex marriage with free love, the emphasis on control in Noyes's system bore little resemblance to the tenets of actual free lovers such as Stephen Pearl Andrews and Josiah Warren (Klaw 175). For instance, in Warren's model of "Individual Sovereignty," practiced at the socialistic experiment Modern Times in Long Island, members were entrusted with managing their own sexual relations in accordance with their own attractions and affinities, guided from within rather than without.

Unsurprisingly, the realities of complex marriage were not universally appealing, particularly for women. New converts in particular struggled to adjust. For instance, the "Family Register" describes the conversion of Polly Hotchkiss as follows: "Received the truth about the same time as her husband, but was never satisfied with her own experience, or in full sympathy with his feelings till within two months. Within that time she has lost some of the repugnance she felt to Association." Without knowing how Hotchkiss overcame her "repugnance," we do know that she was not alone in her struggles. Harriet Worden recalls "the Holmeses, a family of five, who made only a short trial, on account of the discontent of Mrs. Holmes" (70). Similarly, twenty-six-year-old Emma Campbell joined in 1847 but "soon after revolted, abandoned the fellowship of believers, and continued in opposition till Jan 1850" ("Family Register"). Though the reasons for women's displeasure are not recorded, the expectation of sexual availability to multiple partners was likely shocking, at the least. Indeed, while rhetorically Oneida espoused a philosophy of sexual consent, there is reason to believe that this right was severely compromised.[10] As generations of scholars have noted, "free love at Oneida was anything but free" (Vickers 6).

While complex marriage was intended to free women from the position of property, Noyes's most significant innovation in women's lives was liberating them from unwanted pregnancy, the dangers of childbirth, and toilsome childcare. Pregnancy was no longer meant to be an accident of nature, a recurring inconvenience attendant upon the condition of marriage. Inspired by Malthusian arguments and rudimentary methods promoted by Charles Knowlton and Robert Dale Owen, Noyes discovered his own method of birth control: male continence, a practice where men avoided ejaculation during intercourse. Noyes hoped male continence would prevent the mental and physical drain of unwanted pregnancy, a cost he knew first—or, rather, second—hand. As he explains, his discovery:

> was occasioned and even forced upon me by very sorrowful experience. In the course of six years my wife went through the agonies of five births. Four of them were premature. Only one child lived. . . . After our last disappointment, I pledged my word to my wife that I would never again expose her to such fruitless suffering. (*Male Continence* 10–11)

While Noyes held that children taxed both parents, he believed women's sacrifice was greater. Thus, he aimed to "enforce the rule that women shall bear children only when they choose. They have the principal burdens of breeding to bear, and they rather than men should have their choice of time and circumstances, at least till science takes charge of the business" (*Male Continence* 15). Given the community's later foray into eugenics, Noyes's stipulation that women's choice was only necessary until "science" took charge was prescient.

The existing records suggest that male continence did successfully reduce unplanned pregnancies. In all, 135 children were born in or brought to Oneida before 1869, and there were few accidental births (Klee-Hartzell 190). While the general fertility rate in the United States dropped from 48.3 annual births per 1,000 women in 1840 to 38.3 in 1870 (Haines), the estimated birth rate for Oneida women between 1848 and 1869 was 17.1 (Carden 51).[11] Yet despite Noyes's concern for women's health, there were other practical motivations for establishing a system of birth control. For one, complex marriage without birth control would be practically untenable: as Noyes admitted, "The Oneida Community in an important sense owed its existence to the discovery of Male Continence" (*Male Continence* 17).[12] Furthermore, the emphasis on male self-control, evident in both the name and practice of male continence, undermines Noyes's rhetoric of restoring women's reproductive autonomy. As he explains, intercourse has a beginning, a middle, and an end, and "this whole process, up to the very moment of emission, is *voluntary*, entirely under the control of the moral faculty, and *can be stopped at any point*" (*Male Continence* 7, emphasis in original). Male continence thus required a significant degree of self-control from the male partner, rendering it compatible with Noyes's patriarchal religious beliefs. By fetishizing the male will, male continence joins other discourses of "willed pregnancy," which tend "ineluctably to lead to a disdain for and even fear of women's bodies and reproductive functions" (Ruhl 642). Women's reproductive capacities, in this view, make them inherently disorderly, a disorder that can only be neutralized by male self-mastery.

Noyes's revision to contemporary norms of motherhood didn't stop at the notion that children should be planned and wanted; it also targeted the emotional tie between parent and child. As a document about the Oneida Children's House declared, "The essence of our principles is, that children cease to be private property and become property of the Association; and the true way to manage them is, as soon as nature allows, to place them under a system of general control" (qtd. in Noyes and Foster 54). Noyes felt that society encouraged women to form obsessive attachments to their children—a distortion of the motherly instinct that he referred to as "philoprogenitiveness." Glossing over women's concerns about surrendering their children to the care of others, Noyes insisted that "the wounds of philoprogenitiveness" healed quickly: "The mothers soon learned to value their own freedom and opportunity of education, and the improved condition of their children, more than the luxury of a sickly maternal tenderness" (*First Annual Report* 6–7). Importantly, there was no discussion of male philoprogenitiveness; men, it seemed, did not suffer this particular affliction.

Oneida's practices of motherhood and childcare aimed to combat maternal fixation by replacing a child's biological parents with communal caregivers. An infant remained with his or her mother only "until the weaning . . . at nine months" (T. Miller, "Parentage"). After this point, the child attended the "first department" of the Children's House from eight in the morning until five in the afternoon, returning to its mother overnight. Children from one and a half to three years old—the "second department"—slept with their peers in the Children's House (T. Miller, "Parentage"). As with the division of married couples, separate sleeping quarters for children and parents physically reinforced the community's aversion to familial attachments. The practice of taking meals communally rather than in more intimate groups also helped overthrow the spatial practices of the nuclear home. After graduating from the Children's House at puberty, adolescents were assigned a special guardian to help them transition to full adult membership in the community. As with complex marriage, compliance with emotional norms of motherhood was enforced through sanctions and punishments, contributing to the overarching atmosphere of surveillance and discipline.

The presumed goal of Noyes's revision to the family system was the liberation of women, and one facet of this liberation was women's full participation in economic labor. Noyes urged both men and women to engage in "vital labor" and to take pride in their work and contributions. Indeed, Noyes specifically attacked the gendered division of labor: "The present division of labor between the sexes separates them entirely. The woman keeps house, and the man labors abroad. . . . Instead of this, in vital society men and women will mingle in both of their peculiar departments of work" (qtd. in Dalsimer 243). Freed from unwanted pregnancy and burdensome childcare, women at Oneida were thus theoretically welcome to participate in nearly any aspect of the community's work. Noyes challenged his followers to shun the gendered conventions of the time and "to end all sexual distinctions in economic life that were not intrinsic" (Foster, *Women* 228). Furthermore, Noyes felt that Oneida would be more productive as men and women worked alongside one another, arguing that "loving companionship in labor, and especially the mingling of the sexes, makes labor attractive" (*First Annual Report* 40).

In practice, men and women did "mingle" in labor at Oneida. Perhaps the most celebrated example was the tradition of holding "bees" for particularly burdensome or time-sensitive tasks (fig. 4.2). Some bees tackled domestic tasks, such as oiling or waxing the floors (Dalsimer 249). Others involved farming or other community industries: culling, husking, shucking, or paring fruit and vegetables; sewing pre-cut carpetbags; setting type; and folding newspapers (Leonard 17). The Oneida women speak fondly of these occasions. Jessie Kinsley reminisced, "How well I remember being awakened by the shouting cry—'A pea bee!'"

Yet working alongside men also came with its complications. Because Noyes was the ultimate arbiter of women's sexual, professional, and religious lives in the community, the experience of women's work at Oneida—particularly in male-dominated industries—was undoubtedly colored by the presence of men with whom they were expected to have sexual relations. Girls were introduced to the community's sexual activities at or even before puberty, traditionally by Noyes himself—a practice euphemistically referred to as "Noyes's prerogative."

Fig. 4.2. *Community Bee to Clear the Lawn.* Photo 112, Oneida Community Collection, Special Collections Research Center, Syracuse University Libraries; courtesy of the Oneida Community Mansion House.

But Noyes was not the only sexual aggressor that Oneida women had to contend with. Susan Worden warned her brother that the women "are very much annoyed by the habit you have of catching hold of them when in your company." The predatory culture is further illustrated by a letter from Noyes to several male members urging them "to be liberal and diffusive in our love and attention to the other sex" and to "consider whether we may not do good, get good, and feel good by drawing nearer than we have to certain worthy young ladies whose charms have not yet been fully appreciated, such as L. B. R. and N." (qtd. in Noyes and Foster 26). Indeed, Noyes himself routinely engaged as sexual partners young women who worked alongside him in the trap shop.

As with many leaders of utopian communities, Noyes's attempt to materialize his vision produced many unintended consequences. Understanding the rhetoric of motherhood at Oneida requires grappling with not only Noyes's ideals but also, as Jenny Edbauer (Rice) reminds us, "the *processes* that both comprise and extend the rhetorics" (Edbauer 19). In what follows, I explore the tension between Noyes's ideals and the material realities of life at Oneida in greater depth, considering how Oneida's rhetoric of motherhood reproduced rhetorics of gendered labor. Caught in a system in some ways preferable to and in some ways more restricted than the larger society's construction of motherhood, Oneida women operated in between midcentury norms of cultural motherhood and Noyes's redefinition. As they grappled with these layers of institutional motherhood, Oneida women struggled to enact their own goals and choices for their personal and professional lives. Like many women caught between competing rhetorics of motherhood and gendered labor in contemporary society, Oneida women found that, regardless of their own reproductive status, the rhetorical resources of gender and motherhood at times empowered and at other times constrained their ability to make and enact choices in their working lives.

RHETORICS OF MOTHERHOOD AND THE REPRODUCTION OF GENDERED LABOR

What did motherhood mean for women in Oneida? Contemporary scholarship follows Adrienne Rich in distinguishing between "two meanings of motherhood, one superimposed on the other: the *potential relationship* of any woman to her powers of reproduction and to children; and the *institution*, which aims at ensuring that that potential—and all women—shall remain under male control" (13, emphasis in original). In other words, while Noyes's beliefs and the community's material practices comprise the institution of motherhood at Oneida, the experience of motherhood—the potential significance of motherhood for individual women—is also shaped by individual women's choices and perceptions. As Rich explains, despite the often masculinist, oppressive nature of institutions of motherhood, the *experience* of mothering is potentially empowering for women and children. So, what did it mean to be a woman (or a mother) in a community attempting to cleave the associations of motherhood from those of womanhood? How did this attempted separation of woman and mother play out across the lived experience of gender, especially women's work, at Oneida?

As the following analysis draws largely on firsthand accounts of Oneida women, it is important to consider the material and social conditions that produced these documents. Methodologically, while of course any account is partial, there are particular reasons to be cautious in assessing accounts of life at Oneida. For one thing, with their history of persecution, the Oneida perfectionists embraced a rhetorical practice called "Bible Secretiveness," which amounted to using code language to avoid revealing salacious details to a hostile public (Foster, "Rise and Fall" 8). Structural and editorial elements of the women's journals also indicate a degree of self-censorship. For instance, Charlotte Leonard's description of a mutual criticism session on February 13, 1876, suggests a writer laboring to edit her raw reaction into an acceptable response:

> Offered myself to the committee for criticism to-day, and received a very sincere criticism, more so I think than any I ever had before. No more sincere than I wanted however—though of course such criticisms are mortifying and cutting—but it is just what I have needed and knew would come sometime, and I am glad it has come. Some particular points I might mention as not being really true, but I do not care to dwell on them as they probably hit a spirit. [There follows four and a half lines which have been erased]. (14)

A month later, Leonard more directly censors herself, erasing two entire entries for March 18 and 19, leaving only the fragment: "[I] confess my union with them both and believe that earnestness can accomplish unity" (18). Leonard's self-censorship likely attempts to conceal jealousy, as such emotions were seen as dividing members of the community and disrupting the unity of the extended family. Besides women's overt or unconscious suppression, our access to life at Oneida is also shaped by later generations who purged controversial documents. In Oneida's second life as a corporation, the community's radical origins were carefully concealed.[13] Maren Carden laments that "the present community decided to destroy the greater part of these official records and personal accounts. 'Half a room full' of paper was burned" (xviii). Indeed, the Oneida Community Collection at Syracuse Library, which forms the basis of this chapter, was completely restricted until 1991, with additional restrictions lifted in January 2007. As Royster and Kirsch discuss, feminist rhetoricians must rely on inquiry tools such as critical imagination, an awareness of presence and absence, "taking into account the murky and mysterious as well as that which is easier to document and know" (20). Due to the significant likelihood that the extant evidence offers an unusually limited picture, I engage in some necessary speculation as I trace the contours of work and motherhood at Oneida.

In the following sections, I consider the intersection of motherhood and women's work in two respects: first, the (re)distribution of work conventionally associated with motherhood (largely childcare and domestic work), and second, the implications of views of motherhood for women's work outside the domestic realm. I find that the rejection of motherhood as the primary *telos* of women's lives opened the door for Oneida women to pursue a sense of vocation in a variety of industries, even as this rhetoric maintained the cultural opposition between motherhood and work. At the same time, the labor associated with motherhood became divided: while the more valued part of a mother's role (childcare) was elevated to the status of "real work," housework and other subsistence labor was separated from the work of motherhood and increasingly delegated to machines and hired workers. Further, despite the community's disavowals, the ideology of cultural motherhood persisted, as evidenced both by women's resistance to giving up the identity of mother and the assignation of women to "feminine" tasks and industries in the workforce. In the end, Oneida did not so much replace traditional family roles with a more egalitarian model as replace the nuclear family with a larger, communal family, as is borne out by the continued expectation that women complete after-hours "mothering work" and the undermining of female solidarity through a caste system that placed privileged women in positions of authority (and surveillance) over their less fortunate compatriots. Throughout this analysis, rhetorics of choice are shown to be something of an illusion, especially for women who lack privilege and elite status in the community.

Rejecting the Code of Motherhood

One of the Oneida Community's most progressive impulses was to challenge the contemporary understanding that women's primary role and end in life was motherhood. As one woman claimed in the *Circular*, the community "emancipates [woman] from the slavery and corroding cares of a mere wife and mother" (qtd. in Dalsimer 80). Indeed, Oneida challenged not only the use of women's time and energies but also the very understanding of what it was to be a woman. As Linda Gordon explains, the nineteenth-century cult of motherhood promoted "the extension of motherliness to the very definition of femininity" (20). Thus, rejecting teleological rhetorics of motherhood opened the door for Oneida women to pursue other goals and aims, like participating in masculine industries, experimenting with diverse forms of labor, and pursuing a sense of vocation. And, indeed, Oneida women seized and benefited from these opportunities. Yet despite these innovations, Oneida women were encouraged to identify as workers, not mothers, through a rhetoric of gender that maintained the cultural opposition between work and motherhood. In other words, while the Oneida Community did demonstrate women's capacity for all kinds of "masculine" work, it did so without reconciling the perceived incompatibility—and women's need to choose—between such work and maternal roles.

The accounts of Oneida women show that, to a large extent, their experience confirmed the community's claims of liberation from the degrading and toilsome nature of contemporary motherhood. Indeed, many women articulated remarkably modern critiques of the cult of motherhood. As one member wrote in the *Circular*, "This propensity in woman to have pets and worship them, seems barbarous to me now. It belittles her, distracts from her charms, her power of usefulness, and above all is an abuse of God" (qtd. in Dalsimer 173). In addition, the benefits of communal childcare were seen as involving women's work as well as their intellectual and spiritual lives: "The old way of each mother caring for her own child . . . in many ways tends to degrade woman. . . . I appreciate the opportunity [communal childcare] affords me of not only joining in public work but of self-improvement and 'going-home' to God every day" (qtd. in Dalsimer 172–73). For some women, then, the community's approach to childcare and motherhood was a liberating force that fostered self-improvement and self-definition.

The rejection of the code of motherhood was part and parcel of a larger directive encouraging Oneida women to challenge the conventional femininity of their time—a stance with important consequences for women's work.[14] Overall, Oneida aimed to avoid any sexed distinctions that were not intrinsic. In fact, Noyes went further, arguing that woman should be "a *female man*, (like the Son in the Godhead)" (*First Annual Report* 41, emphasis in original). Noyes was particularly interested in overcoming unnecessary restrictions for women's work and, especially in times of financial duress, prodded women to engage in labor traditionally understood as masculine. Especially in its early years, when finances were tight, the Oneida Community maintained that men and women should share in the work of running the farm.[15] The mostly working-class recruits brought useful skills: they were "neither poets nor political anarchists, but farmers and mechanics who knew how to run a mill, plow a field, and lay a foundation" (Fogarty, "Oneida" 206). And resolutions in the *Circular* urged that Oneida "women should not let a day pass without engaging in manly work" (qtd. in Fogarty, "Oneida" 218). Over the years, Oneida's men and women commenced and abandoned a number of enterprises, manufacturing palm leaf hats, gold chain, brooms, collars, flour, beehives, mop-wringers, and rustic seats (Noyes and Foster 286). The first permanently profitable industry was making steel animal traps, the forerunner of the silver tableware for which Oneida is known today (McClymond 221).[16] The community also operated a machine shop, peddled their goods, manufactured traveling bags, and completed printing jobs.

From the beginning, women's participation in outdoor labor corroborated Noyes's vision of mingling the sexes in labor and involving women in masculine work. The first Mansion House was built entirely by community members, including two leading women:

> Harriet Noyes and Mary Cragin toiled from two to four hours every day, handling trowels, small stone and mortar, with a dexterity equal to that of most men. This work was not drudgery, but a thrilling pastime. . . . Fresh air, manual exercise, free and easy mingling of the sexes, and the consciousness of rendering public service, all contributed to a novel sense of freedom. (R. Parker 172)

On the whole, existing accounts suggest that the women enjoyed their physical labor. Harriet Matthews speaks proudly of having "worked all day in the garden with the men" and enjoys the challenge and camaraderie of farming: "Worked out nearly all day. We ate supper under the tree and then marched round and round the yard and flower garden" (26, 29). Manual labor offered a broader scope for women's abilities and contributions. As Harriet Noyes testified in the *First Annual Report*, "At Oneida my employment has chiefly been sport. I have taken pleasure in conquering difficulties—in doing things which once would have appeared impossible for me" (55).

Women's participation in the trap shop also confirmed the community's ethos of "mingling" men and women in labor as well as women's capacity for conventionally masculine work. One male mechanist noted in a work log his appreciation for "the presence of the women in the shop" (qtd. in H. Worden 51). While this gratitude for women's "presence" feels strongly gendered, the rest of the mechanic's account confirms that Oneida's shop girls managed to strike the difficult balance of displaying "an acceptable combination of femininity and . . . expertise" (Skinner "Purity" 105). He continues: "I have been led to notice the mechanical judgment and skill some of them display. Let them have good opportunities, and they will become very efficient" (qtd. in H. Worden 51). Women valued their work in the trap shop and articulated such work as preferable to the lot of women in larger society. As one woman wrote,

> Factory work gives us women a chance . . . to taste of the pleasures of <u>production</u>. This is a pleasure that most women are debarred from. The wives, daughters and sisters of men in good circumstances, are forbidden by fashion to do anything with their hands, beyond the lighter chores of housekeeping and making some of their own and their children's clothes. . . . Women become first-rate consumers—trained and confined as most of them are by custom to that profession—but it is a miserable, self-absorbing profession, taken alone. . . . It is more blessed to be producers than consumers. (qtd. in Dalsimer 266–67, emphasis in original)

Though the cult of domesticity described women's roles largely in terms of consumerism, clearly women at Oneida (like those at Brook Farm) ascribed to the larger market logic that elevated "producing commodities for exchange in the marketplace" above "the making of goods for immediate use" (Laurie 15). Indeed, such accounts suggest that Oneida women were not only capable of doing productive masculine work but found it preferable to subsistence domestic roles. As Harriet Matthews writes, "One change we see is that it has come to be a permanent, easy & natural thing for the women to engage freely in all manner of outdoor labor and in the labors of all the different shops" (9). Indeed, the

Oneida Community provided embodied testimony that there was no inherent incompatibility between feminity and mechanical or technical work.

In addition to engaging in masculine work, women at Oneida also benefited from the community's practice of rotating jobs. Communal childcare meant that women were less bound to the home, and, as the *Circular* explained, job rotation ensured that "all have a variety of occupations, and an opportunity to find out what each one is best adapted to" (qtd. in Fogarty, "Oneida" 216). For instance, one man was a blacksmith in 1850, a machinist in 1870, and a dentist in 1880 (Fogarty, "Oneida" 217). Oneida women seized their work assignments as opportunities for personal growth and exploration. Harriet Matthews, for instance, was assigned to the school, a post she found challenging but was determined to grow from. In August 1855, she noted, "I have commenced teaching school again. I find it quite a stretch of my faith, patience & good nature" (6). These sentiments persisted into late September: "It is only by faith that I am able to occupy that post for it is a place where I feel my own weakness very much & therefore my experience there has been very profitable" (11). A month later, Matthews's perseverance paid off: "I am thankful for prosperity & good experience in school—it is more satisfactory to me than ever before" (12).

On the other hand, the practice of rotation was complemented by a rhetoric of vocation: once an individual found their "calling," they might stay in that position. As Jessie Kinsley noted,

> Many of the girls of my class . . . were learning to set-type in the printing office—but sedentary work was not thought best for me. . . . When book-keeping or type-setting proved to be someone's <u>special province</u>, or gardening and the care of plants seemed someone's <u>positive gift</u>, or business-leadership or other leadership was unmistakably evident, then such people, so gifted, were left to use their highest, best talents, but the usual plan was a changing round of duties, and I took the circuit year by year.

One's vocation was based in individual preferences and skills and might involve manual labor as well as business or leadership roles. For instance, Jerusha Thomas was known as the "presiding genius of the dairy"; Oneida children marveled that she was "strong as a man" (Dalsimer 267). Indeed, despite her assignment—and achievement—in the school, Harriet Matthews also invokes a calling as a writer. She prods herself: "I criticise myself for neglecting my journal, for lack of faith about writing for the paper, & for not having more of a spirit of improvement" (11). Having rejected the code of motherhood, which elevated childrearing "to the status of a profession," Oneida women explored alternative professional identities by embracing new experiences and cultivating an awareness of their passions and enthusiasms (Apple 166).

Even as Oneida's rejection of the contemporary code of motherhood provided women with diverse work and a sense of calling, it failed to provide a model of working motherhood. Because it rejected motherhood in favor of women working "like men," the rhetoric of gender in Oneida upheld the cultural opposition between work and motherhood. This opposition is evident in the women's accounts as a tension between their roles as mothers and workers. For instance, in her autobiography, Noyes's wife Harriet expresses this conflict in the early days of communal life at Putney, Vermont. Recording her experience in the third person, she recalls,

> Mary Ann nursed her baby and left him three hours with one of the women whose turn it was to stay at home, she only staying with him when it was her turn. She baked, washed, and etc afternoons while Fanny and Caroline worked in the printing office. . . . Now, a temptation assailed her that when she was merely taking care of her baby, she was misemploying her time and that she ought to be working on the paper. (*History of M.A.H.*)

Decades later, in Oneida, Charlotte Leonard confessed the same experience: "I often feel as though I were wasting my time. I know my children often take up my time and attention when it is unnecessary. What a distraction they are to us if we are not very earnest" (34). Such accounts suggest that Oneida women felt insufficient as workers when they took up their roles as mothers. As one new mother wrote, "Of course I shall have to write about babytending, for what else do I know? I used to think I was busy in the old reporting time at [the Wallingford community]; and I thought my time quite fully occupied when we worked on the paper: and I certainly thought I wasted but few moments when engaged in book-keeping . . ." (T. Miller, "To Mary," 23 Feb. 1871). Though outwardly commenting upon the significant labor of caring for a child, this letter also expresses a longing for and continued identification with former professional roles. Such accounts show women's appreciation for their work and the difficulty of reconciling that enjoyment with culturally ingrained views of motherhood. For, as Catherine Sedgwick instructed the readers of *Ladies Magazine* in 1835, a mother had "no right to seek her own pleasure more than that of her children, or her own improvement more than theirs" ("Plea for Children" 96–97).

Lindal Buchanan cautions that rhetorics of motherhood both benefit and impede women—and, as this section shows, the same is true of Oneida's rejection of the cult of motherhood (*Rhetorics* 5). On the one hand, this rejection helped Oneida women pursue forms of work that other midcentury women could access only with difficulty, if at all. On the other hand, to the extent that Oneida women still were (or wanted to be) mothers, taking up maternal roles diminished that newfound professional ambition and autonomy. Then as now, models of working motherhood that do not assume a zero-sum tradeoff between familial and professional roles and identities are hard to come by. Seemingly progressive rhetorics of choice leave this opposition intact: "having it all" largely means taking on public, professional roles in addition to women's conventional responsibilities for reproduction and childcare, rather than renegotiating them.

Dividing the Work of Motherhood

Naturally, the rhetorical disidentification of womanhood with motherhood raised some practical questions. If women are meant to stop identifying as mothers, to think of themselves as "female men," then what happens to the labor that traditionally accompanied that role? At Oneida, these challenges were met by dividing the work of motherhood: while childcare was elevated to the status of work, housework and traditional domestic labor were increasingly delegated to machines and hired workers as the community became more prosperous. This bifurcation of the role of mother and housewife echoed a national trend. For more affluent, white families, the mid-nineteenth century effected the separation of idealized motherhood from devalued subsistence labor. Lydia Sigourney's 1838 *Letters to Mothers* advised that a woman should "provide herself with competent assistance, in the sphere of manual labor, that she may be enabled to become the constant directress of her children and be happy in their companionship" (86). The cultural understanding of a mother's work shifted from subsistence tasks to increasingly demanding childcare and the supervision of domestics. That is, the cult of motherhood was accompanied by a trend that divorced motherhood from housework—for those who could afford it. The rhetoric of choice in this instance—choosing the role of "directress" and "companion" to one's children rather than "the sphere of manual labor"—is clearly only operable for women of means. In this regard, rhetorics of choice simultaneously made true motherhood the domain of privileged white women and relegated other women to menial labor.

With the exception of a male supervisor in the Children's House, the work of childcare in the Oneida Community continued to belong primarily to women. In contrast to dominant imagery, however, the women who cared for children were not necessarily their own biological mothers or even relatives. Though Oneida emphasized its distance from sentimental contemporary rhetorics of motherhood, the involvement of unrelated women in the care of children was hardly a new invention. Wet-nursing was a common practice in middle- and upper-class households, and in the mid-nineteenth century it followed the same pattern as the transition from "help" to "domestic" in domestic service more broadly. That is, wet-nursing in midcentury America shifted "from informal temporary arrangements to the practice of hiring wet nurses to live with a family for extended periods" (Golden 73). In this regard, the practice of communal childrearing at Oneida may have been less strange at the time than we might imagine in hindsight. On the whole, American mothers "could and did delegate much of child care to servants but generally escaped censure so long as they did not contest the principles of motherhood's sacred responsibilities" (Dudden 156). What was unique at Oneida was the openness with which the community asserted that biological parents should not bear all the responsibility for raising a child, a forthrightness that also circumvented the growing class estrangement in conduct literature's opposition of the nurturing working-class mother and the threatening lower-class nurse (Golden 77).

The idea of children being raised collectively by the community rather than by individual mothers rhetorically elevated childcare to a skill rather than a biological imperative or feminine instinct. Indeed, midcentury discourses of motherhood were conflicted about whether good mothers were born or made: "Were women born to be mothers, or was it an office that was to be achieved? Were women suited as they were, or did they have to be changed?" (Lewis 62). While some viewed motherhood as women's natural calling, an emotion and practice welling up from within, others thought mothers needed to cultivate their skills and self-discipline. For its part, Oneida participated in the new midcentury discourse of "scientific motherhood," which devalued instinct and traditional knowledge, insisting instead "that women require expert scientific and medical advice to raise their children healthfully" (Apple 161). As Tirzah Miller explained, childcare at Oneida was seen as something one might specialize in: "We have found that the more carefully any one function, like that of child-training, can be differentiated, the more economical will be the workings of the institution" ("Parentage"). This view of childcare as a profession, not something inevitably following the biological processes of conception and childbirth, was also seen as a boon to communal life and an economical savings. The community's *First Annual Report* declared, "It was found to be altogether a more comfortable task to take care of six [children] in the new way, than it had been to wait on one in ordinary circumstances" (6). In this respect, Oneida's system acknowledged childcare not only as a vocation that might not suit every biological mother but also as a skill that could be honed and handled more efficiently and beneficially as a community than in separate nuclear households.

Of course, childcare was not the only work traditionally apportioned to wives and mothers: the Oneida Community's stance against conventional motherhood also raised questions about how members' domestic needs would be met. Indeed, domestic labor at the Oneida Community—and in the nineteenth century generally—was a rigorous affair. Among other challenges, Oneida women recalled the hardships of the upstate New York climate: "My business is in the washing department, having the care of it, and with the thermometer from 20 to 26 degrees below zero, as it has been most of the time for a week or two past, it is quite a trying place for good nature" (Matthews 33). While this work still fell primarily to the women, it was improved by communal methods. Working alongside other women offered a pleasure denied to isolated housewives: "My first remembered work was sweeping a flight of stairs with my mate Edith Waters. With small brooms, with great glee, with much haste, we raced the sweeping and Edith won. . . . We did our work together often, we girls" (Kinsley, emphasis in original). Because the women supervised the domestic departments, they were able to devise systems to avoid overtaxing any individual. For instance, women rotated through the position of planning and preparing the community's meals:

> Of all the offices that relieve us of burden, that of superintending the kitchen is the one most appreciated. . . . [Excepting the two women in charge] all the others go to the table entirely free from the loss of appetite occasioned by the responsibility and planning, and the anxiety of preparing the food. No wonder we women of 30 are mistaken for Misses when we are saved from so much care and vexation. (qtd. in Dalsimer 247–48)

Such job-sharing arrangements were planned at regular "Ladies Meetings," where "the thousand and one matters which the single housekeeper has to meet and sink under alone are talked over and settled by the united strength and wisdom of over 100 women" (qtd. in Dalsimer 218).

Yet as time passed the novelty of this communal work ethic faltered, and Oneida women began to seek ways of lessening their housework so they might pursue other forms of work. As the community opened to the public in 1850, the increased traffic of visitors multiplied the necessary cooking and cleaning: in 1866 alone, four thousand people signed the visitors' book (Carden 81). This increased workload was, for the most part, not relieved by the assistance of Oneida's men. Though mutual criticism sessions hinted at an androgynous ideal and encouraged some men to explore and express their feminine side, men's work in the domestic realm was limited to particular tasks seen as requiring manly qualities. As Dalsimer explains, "Women performed most of the menial work associated with feeding the Oneida family; men worked in the kitchen either as supervisors, as in the case of the head baker, or as those performing tasks which required unusual muscular strength" (248–49). In the end, Oneida women's freedom to work outside the domestic realm and control their own professional destiny was dependent upon much more than their skill and talent. Importantly, women's professional opportunities at Oneida were bolstered more by increased mechanization and hired help than by the willingness of men to share in this necessary work.

Unlike childcare, the domestic labor of cooking and cleaning continued to be perceived as menial. Thus, Oneida invested in mechanical innovations to diminish women's domestic labor (fig. 4.3). Over time, the community adopted many steam-operated laborsaving devices, often operated by men, who were purported to have a natural aptitude for mechanical work (Kern 259, 262). Jessie Kinsley remarked on the change, "Before school there were two or three hundred knives and forks for us to scour. . . . Later some one invented a machine to scour our knives and forks." Despite the community's insistence that, in a vital society, there is no "unattractive labor," Oneida women were

Fig. 4.3. *Vegetable Washer Invented by John Leonard.* Photo 150, Oneida Community Collection, Special Collections Research Center, Syracuse University Libraries; courtesy of the Oneida Community Mansion House.

grateful to be relieved of the burden and monotony of domestic labor (qtd. in Noyes and Foster 204). As Harriet Worden wrote of the new washing machine, the women "were glad when the release came and gave us a chance to devote ourselves to education and industries more profitable and better adapted to our tastes" (qtd. in Dalsimer 250–51). The community's rhetoric of vocation allowed women like Worden to express their dissatisfaction with housework in communally sanctioned terms.

As the community became more prosperous, Oneida women were additionally relieved by hired workers. When the community's industries outstripped the labor members could supply, hiring outside workers was framed as inevitable. Francis Wayland-Smith explains, "The manufactures grew and it became necessary to hire outside help, first in the Trap Shop, then on the farm, then in the laundry, and at length in the kitchen" (8–9). This practice further undermined the notion that all work was equally attractive; as at Brook Farm, the challenge of distributing the most unpleasant labor was circumvented through hired labor. Over time, Oneida men and women worked fewer hours and left "the most menial, exhausting, and boring jobs to outside workers" (Klaw 89). Though the community was a fair employer, providing housing, transportation, and generous wages, the use of hired labor undermined their claim that "neither in theory or practice do we recognize a 'laboring class'" (*Second Annual Report* 12).

The Oneida Community laundry provides one telling instance of the community's management of less desirable duties. The women, recognizing that "an immense weekly washing was inevitable," began the process as "a committee of the whole" (H. Worden 26). Before long, however, material improvements were made: "A large cistern was built, a copper boiler purchased, and two long wooden boxes made, at each of which twelve persons could work at a time" (26). Soon thereafter, the community received a washing machine as a gift. As the process became mechanized, men were brought in to manage the machines, which were continually improved (H. Worden 27). But even these improvements could not overcome the stigma associated with working in the laundry. As Harriet Worden explains, "Hired help was introduced, as our own people were required in various increasing businesses. Since that time . . . the family generally have been discharged from washing" (28). As Worden acknowledges, there is a direct relationship between the relegation of domestic duties to hired women—such as the two African American laundresses who worked two to three days a week—and Oneida women's professional advancement in white-collar work. Like their middle-class counterparts outside the community, Oneida women's use of hired labor freed them from housework so that they might pursue more fulfilling pursuits. While domestic service liberated wealthy, white American women at large to pursue the profession of motherhood, hired women at Oneida facilitated other women's participation in "various increasing businesses."

Oneida's revision of motherhood involved a bifurcation of labor traditionally associated with maternity. While the community's women retained the more valued parts of the work of motherhood, tasks such as cooking and cleaning were increasingly delegated to machines and hired workers. In a new materialist sense, the "translation" or "delegation" of this work to machines or hired workers functions in much the same way, regardless of whether those "actants" are human or nonhuman (Latour, "Mixing" 299–300). But from a feminist perspective, the instrumentalization of nonhuman machines and the bodies of women and people of color is a crucial corrective to the narrative of how the Oneida Community liberated women to work like men. In Jennifer Bay's language, the delegation of menial labor indiscriminately across machine and human bodies participates in "the complex material-discursive process by which bodies become things" (Walsh et al. 446). Too often, the poverty of choice for women balancing work and domestic duties results in the reassignment (or delegation) of less-valued work along race and class lines while leaving the gendered division of labor largely intact.

Cultural Motherhood and Feminine Industry

Despite the Oneida Community's opposition to the nineteenth-century cult of motherhood, the notion of woman-as-mother was not so easily unseated. As we will see, larger connotations of women as "motherly" were difficult to overcome, even in a community where the labor associated with biological motherhood—pregnancy, childbirth, and childcare—was differently distributed than in midcentury society at large. This difficulty is evident in women's resistance to giving up their identities as mothers as well as the steps taken to discipline errant Oneida mothers. Moreover, the associations of women with "motherliness" followed women into their working lives: Oneida women were allocated feminine tasks in male-dominated jobs and assigned to feminine industries such as domestic manufacture and white-collar work. On the whole, both inside and outside the Oneida Community, the social construct of woman-as-mother shaped women's work-related choices far beyond the domestic sphere.

One sign of the intransigence of cultural motherhood is the resistance of Oneida women to surrendering the care of their children and the social value accorded them as mothers. Indeed, many Oneida women struggled internally with the community's stance on motherhood. Charlotte Leonard's journal entries show her efforts to govern her feelings: "I believe the Community is the best mother a child can have, and I confess my confidence in it. . . . I pray God to help me do right about [Humphrey] that I may please God and Mr.

Noyes about it" (1). Failing to please Mr. Noyes could have dire consequences: Leonard's son was removed from her care when she was deemed too attached to him.[17] Cultivating emotional distance from one's child was challenging in a society that declared, in the words of Reverend John Todd in *The Mother's Magazine* in 1839, "God planted this *deep,* this *unquenchable* love for her offspring, in the mother's heart" (qtd. in Lewis 52, emphasis in original). Leonard continued to work to discipline her own affections to avoid punishment in the future:

> [Noyes] said he thought that I had a weaned love for Humphrey now, and he thought I was ready to take him back again. . . . I feel like taking care of Humphrey as one of God's little children, and not as though he was mine. I do not feel at all like claiming him, for he belongs to God and the Community, and I am only appointed to take care of him for them. (2)

Despite her efforts, Leonard's journal entries continue to revolve around her son—she routinely writes on the eighteenth of most months, the anniversary of her son's birth. Yet Leonard's struggle to govern her emotions was also echoed in maternal literature: *The Mother's Magazine* cautioned mothers not to "permit the anxieties of your mind to mantle your countenance with forbidding gravity or gloom," to "always be dignified calm, consistent with herself. . . . She must never be observed to betray a weakness, changeableness, or vascillation of character'" (qtd. in Lewis 61). At Oneida, mutual criticism sessions, where community members assessed an individual's strengths and weaknesses, provided an opportunity for reinforcing the struggle against philoprogenitiveness.[18] For instance, a criticism of Mary Prindle noted approvingly, "She seems to have overcome the desire to have children herself and has got to be considerably free in enjoying other folks' children—is apparently as much pleased as she would be with children of her own. . . . That is the kind of love we have got to cultivate" ("Criticism of ML Prindle"). Like Leonard, many of the community's women found it difficult to redirect their attachment from their children to the entire community.

Oneida women's struggles with philoprogenitiveness are suggestive as to the consequences of the rhetorical and literal distancing of women from traditional motherhood. In direct contrast to Buchanan's "code of motherhood," which upheld a distinction between "the sainted mother or selfish career woman," the rhetoric of philoprogenitiveness portrayed the career woman as unselfish and community-minded and the doting mother as self-absorbed (*Rhetorics* 9). Moreover, given the cultural authority and ethos that women could access through rhetorics of motherhood, it is perhaps unsurprising that at least some Oneida women resisted their "liberation" from this role. In the nineteenth century, a woman's failure "to desire maternity, to become mothers, or to 'manifest the qualities required by mothering'" marked her "as 'deviant or deficient,'" aligning her with "others who likewise strayed from the code—by exhibiting sexual interest or pleasure, by pursuing their own ambitions, by focusing on a career, by entering the public sphere—and came to inhabit the devalued position of Woman, the antithesis of the Mother" (Buchanan, *Rhetorics* 19). The growing association of motherhood with moral leadership and piety likely made this role particularly attractive for religious Oneida women (see Blackwell). Rejecting the code of motherhood also involved class implications, as the ability to engage in full-time mothering was a marker of privilege and whiteness. In a time when a civilized society was marked by women's luxury to focus on domestic concerns—motherhood foremost among them—the ideological consequences of eschewing motherhood were severe.

Oneida's women and mothers were not the only ones who struggled to shed conventional views of women as motherly and nurturing. Despite the community's promise that "men and women will mingle in all their employments," gendered notions of men's and women's abilities and rightful or natural occupations persisted (*First Annual Report* 40). As Noyes wrote in the *First Annual Report*, "The constitutional distinctions and offices of the sexes belong to their original paradisaical state . . . so the sexes, though one, in their innermost life, as members of Christ, yet retain their constitutional distinctions" (19). Noyes's religious ideology held that men and women were united before the fall and thus that they should strive as far as possible to reunite their natures. Of course, since the fall did happen, the sexes could never be completely united, and so distinctions between men and women were inescapable. Ideologically, this meant that women at Oneida faced a double bind: they *should* be more like men, but they would inevitably fail to achieve this. In this manner, Noyes's ostensibly egalitarian ideology preserved a useful notion of feminine capacities and limitations that played out in women's work, as in larger labor rhetorics that mobilized "vulnerable" women workers to agitate for shorter hours (Margo 25).[19]

Indeed, there are strong indications that Oneida women's "mingling" in masculine industries was driven more by economic necessity than progressive gender ideology. Women were most involved in trap making during the economically turbulent 1850s, when the business was first established, and from 1863 to 1865, when the community was flooded with orders (Dalsimer 264). Similarly, women were most active in farming and other outdoor labor when seasonal demand required their assistance, and they retired to more conventionally feminine duties for the remainder of the year. Indeed, broader shifts in women's access to male-dominated professions often correlate more with economic necessity than ideological progress, as feminist scholars have demonstrated.[20] Moreover, access to conventionally male occupations does not in itself dislodge persistent understandings of gender difference or gendered labor. As Jordynn Jack illustrates of women's work in World War II, women's presence in wartime factories did not overturn essentialist notions of women as homemakers ("Acts" 285).

In Oneida as elsewhere, the rhetorical salience of women's presence in male-dominated realms was circumscribed by a continued reliance on rhetorics of gender difference.[21] When women at Oneida did participate in masculine industries, they primarily performed simple, repetitive tasks deemed suited to their "constitutional distinctions" as women. For instance, in trap making, women were confined to assembling the chains for the traps—work that children did in "boom" times (Kern 261). Indeed, women were seen as uniquely adapted to such tedious tasks, as one *Circular* article noted: "Almost every kind of manufacture in iron, steel, and brass has parts adapted to feminine fingers. Woman's patience with details, and long-suffering routine, fits her for many monotonous operations on the lathe" (qtd. in Dalsimer 265). Women's shopwork at Oneida thus foreshadowed women's role in wartime factories, where "women's entry into technical spheres was accomplished by defining specifically feminine attributes that could be useful for war production and by shifting workplace arrangements accordingly" (Jack, "Acts" 286). Moreover, this understanding of femininity was part and parcel of the nineteenth-century cult of motherhood, according to which "capacities for tenderness, self-control and patience, tolerance for tedium and detail, emotional supportiveness, dependability and warmth—were not only instinctive but sex-linked" (Gordon 113). When women mingled with men in these industries, they were cast in the role of helpmate or assistant rather than equal, indicating "the power of family patterns as a model for women's proper role in industrial development" (Stansell 116).

Just as some industrial roles were seen as particularly suited to women, some entire industries were perceived as feminine, in both Oneida and U.S. society at large. Though it is true that there were "almost no formal institutional blocks" to women participating in particular industries at Oneida, gendered patterns soon emerged (Foster, *Women* 266 n18). Oneida women dominated as workers and supervisors in the fruit- and jelly-canning factory, the laundry, and the satchel factory—industrial extensions of the domestic realms of cooking, washing, and sewing. Similarly, one roster of community members and professions lists Harriet Joslyn and Julia Wightman as the Consulting Superintendent and Forewoman of the Silk Department, respectively ("Roster"). Women's role in the community's silk industry may have been inspired by the famous New England textile mills, which extended the association of women with textiles from the home to the factory. In contrast, the animal trap shop, machine shop, and dairy were supervised by men with only a few women workers. Finally, women were absent from heavy farm work, carpentry, milling, lumbering, and sales (Dalsimer 246). Overall, men dominated, "as workers and supervisors, the income-producing labor activities of the community" (Klee-Hartzell 183).

Despite these limitations, Oneida women did take advantage of their opportunities, leveraging their role as helpmates to achieve greater access to particular trades. Indeed, Sarah Moseley has demonstrated that women's participation in "overlooked, feminized, supportive work" often functions "as a bridge to more visible productive work" (350). As in the machine and trap shops, women's first roles in the Oneida printing office were repetitive and menial. Jessie Kinsley recalled, "I kept the sheets of paper smooth as they fell down from the press, and bronzed hand-bills, or pamphlet covers (work done for merchants and others in near-by cities)- when bronzing was needed."[22] But the women soon moved beyond these secondary roles: "Type-setting in the office of *The Circular* has long been monopolized by girls, and there is danger of their meddling with the editorship one of these days; for printers are very apt to grow into editors" (qtd. in Dalsimer 262). Indeed, as printing operations nationwide began to employ steam-driven presses, the "art of book publishing" was divided into smaller and smaller tasks, with the "precision work" of female compositors representing "the last vestige of the trade as it once was" (Laurie 38). Before long, the women had more or less taken over Oneida's printing office, as this account suggests:

> Leonora is feeding the Campbell press; two or three girls are bronzing for George Henry, and a company of six are taking out papers from the press. . . . Here in the composing-room you will find Marion and Charlotte at work upon a catalogue; Annie Kelly is over in the corner, and by the case in front of her stands Miss Harriet Allen, who frequently comes up from the silk-room to help. Mrs. Noyes, with a handful of type, is going from case to case distributing. ("History of the Printing Business of the O.C.")

Over time, Oneida women took on significant leadership roles at the press: Harriet H. Skinner was a prominent author and served as "editress" of the *Circular* in 1850, and later editors and publishers included Tirzah Miller, Mary Prindle, Augusta Hamilton, and Harriet Worden.

On the whole, Oneida women who worked outside the domestic sphere were likely engaged in white-collar rather than manual labor. The number of women reporting a nondomestic occupation rose from 13 percent in early years to 41 percent in 1867, and half of the members employed in business or office positions were women (Kern 261). Though there were always more women in housekeeping than any other category, the community's business and professional women worked in the counting room, store, silk factory, dentistry, bag shop, school, and library, as well as the printing office (Dalsimer 272–73). Women at Oneida were especially gifted bookkeepers: six women handled the entirety of the community's accounts by 1866 (Dalsimer 262). As the *Circular* crowed, "For the encouragement of those who wish for women equal freedom with men to engage in trades and professions, we can say that the Oneida Community women make excellent accountants; they are quick to comprehend, prompt in execution, patient, faithful, and accurate in details" (qtd. in Dalsimer 263).[23] As in Oneida women's machine shop work, such accounts justify and circumscribe women's participation in conventionally masculine work through rhetorics of difference.

The Oneida Community's experiment with birth control and childcare shows that changing the material practices of motherhood couldn't unseat ideas of women as, essentially, motherly. What should we make of the fact that the Oneida Community encouraged women to be "female men" while at the same time perpetuating gendered (and maternal) notions that limited women's work? The tension here is the tension between equality and difference that, as Joan Scott explains, has haunted feminism: "When equality and difference are paired dichotomously, they structure an impossible choice. If one opts for equality, one is forced to accept the notion that difference is antithetical to it. If one opts for difference, one admits that equality is unattainable" (43). To the extent that Noyes's vision of "female men" is a vision of equality, it is a vision of equality grounded in sameness. Granted this starting point, any acknowledged difference between men and women undermines the possibility for equality. Woman *should be* a female man, but to the extent that she's not, she can't be treated equally. This rhetorical sleight of hand first blames women for not being more like men and then resigns them to traditional roles with a reluctance that belies the ways this system benefits men. Men in the Oneida Community benefited from the lingering association of maternal qualities with women outside the domestic realm. This articulation of motherhood thus served conventional power relations even as it ostensibly challenged them, driving home Jordynn Jack's points that the "arrangements of space, time, bodies, and dress" fostered by rhetorics of gender are "not separate or arbitrary" as they re/produce gender difference ("Acts" 288–89). Denied the social status aligned with the role of mother, Oneida women nonetheless found themselves confined by workplace notions of where motherly bodies belonged.

Communal Mothers and Hierarchies among Women

Despite its aim to dismantle the traditional family, Oneida did not so much replace family roles with a more egalitarian model as replace the nuclear family with the larger, communal family. Women were still expected to take on mothering roles in the community, yet much of this "mothering work" was unacknowledged and unaccounted for. Moreover, within the community, a religious caste system elevating some women as community "mothers" and "aunts" fostered divisions among women. Women with more education, from more well-to-do families, or with ties to Noyes were viewed as natural community leaders, while other women were seen as objects of discipline. The power of these leading women over other female members betrays a lack of solidarity among Oneida women and a sense that, for some women to access a wider array of choices, other women must lose a measure of autonomy. On the whole, the continuing deployment of rhetorics and vocabularies of motherhood at Oneida functioned to justify women's after-hours work and elevate some women above others.

While the Oneida Community's women were encouraged to eschew their maternal instinct vis-à-vis their own offspring, they were nevertheless expected to perform maternal duties for the entire community as a kind of extended family.[24] While the percentage of women engaged in household duties fluctuated throughout the communal period, these duties remained the primary responsibility of women. "Even at the height of female employment in areas removed from the domestic sphere, no less than half the total number of women remained 'communal housewives,'" a term suggestive of the limits of Oneida's domestic revolution (Kern 258). In addition, despite the community's practice of rotating jobs, women at Oneida tended to rotate mainly from one realm of women's work to another (Dalsimer 275). As Polly Hayes Noyes, John Humphrey Noyes's mother, protested,

> I observe the young men in the Community are called out in various ways to new businesses and positions . . . and I ask, is there anything like this for the girls? Is not the range of their operations very uniform and the extent of their opportunity for display of talent and genius too much confined? (qtd. in Dalsimer 213)

While workers often did rotate jobs, the degree to which one rotated, the positions one was able to hold, and the agency one had over such decisions was shaped by one's gender, as well as other predisposing factors.

In this way, the emergent structure of women's work undermined Oneida's explicit critique of woman-as-mother. Familial terminology pervaded the community's lexicon. As Jessie Kinsley explained, "To work in the Children's House was almost like being an older sister to a great family of brothers and sisters." In addition, women regularly played the role of "mother" to children who slept with them when they were too young to stay at the Children's House. Harriet Matthews wrote: "Little Harriet loves me like a daughter & she seems to fill that place in my heart so that I cannot feel childless" (10–11). In this light, rather than demolishing familial roles, Oneida substituted a larger, communal family for the smaller, nuclear unit. Even as it eschewed the code of motherhood, Oneida embraced larger views of motherhood, "now specifically linked to piety," as "a social role played out in churches and voluntary associations" (Blackwell 32).

Significantly, much of the "mothering work" performed by women in the community was not accounted for as part of their official work. In this sense, women in Oneida had a second shift by virtue of their supposedly natural roles as nurturers and caregivers. Thus, these motherly duties take on additional import if we accept Jordynn Jack's invitation to attend to how time structures women's work ("Acts" 287). While a tailor's shop made the men's clothes, women were expected to design and make their own clothes in their leisure time. In addition, women were assigned the role of "mother" to one child and one or more men, for the purpose of mending their clothes: "Each week the men would collect their freshly laundried clothes from the Distributing Room in the cellar, take them to the room of the woman appointed and, receive in return a pile of nicely mended garments" (qtd. in Dalsimer 253). This mending also fell outside women's official work assignments and needed to be fit into the evening hours. Though the women officially worked less than men—six hours and forty minutes compared to men's seven hours—these after-hours responsibilities belied this twenty-minute concession to women's supposedly weaker constitutions (Dalsimer 272). These arrangements and expectations show that in Oneida, as in midcentury society at large, "motherhood was no longer an intrafamily ideology; it now had important ideological functions for the whole society" (Gordon 21). Regardless of whether women were biological *mothers*, the expectation of women as *motherly* followed them to work.[25]

The lingering power of family association continued in the labeling of women leaders as "aunts" and "mothers." Privileged women such as Harriet Noyes, Mary Cragin, Harriet Noyes Skinner, and Charlotte Noyes Miller had authority over other members, especially women, and functioned as intermediaries "whose task it was to interpret Noyes's ideology and decisions to the Oneida women and to secure female obedience" (Klee-Hartzell 183). In this way, Oneida's "Aunts" functioned much like those in the dystopian Gilead in Margaret Atwood's *The Handmaid's Tale*. These women were offered a role in the patriarchal leadership of the community, contradicting the professed deviation from the hierarchical power relations of the traditional nuclear family. While ostensibly they had earned this authority through their spirituality, they were also distinguished from other Oneida women through class and education, and most were direct relatives of Noyes. These women served as mediators for sexual relationships, approaching the woman in question, seeking her consent, and recording her liaisons (E. Wayland-Smith 19). Through their surveillance, "central authorities were pretty well informed as to what was going on and the general trend of every individual" (La Moy and Cragin 131). Importantly, the same women were the arbiters of women's work assignments.

This internal caste system meant that work looked very different for some Oneida women than it did for others. Indeed, the leading women were routinely exempted from more mundane community work assignments, a privilege that was not extended to all female members, much less those who came to Oneida as hired domestics (Klee-Hartzell 183). As Faye Dudden explains, hiring domestics made domesticity more flexible, "accommodating roles of authority and activity rather than passivity and isolation." Indeed, "supervising domestics . . . helped to effect the transition into leisure and consumption since the same domestics who secured a woman some ease also demanded of her a work role similar to that of entrepreneurial men" (7). Many of the women in leading professional positions were also those designated by Noyes as spiritual models. Just as pious middle- and upper-class women outside the community were encouraged to view supervision of domestics as a form of benevolence or missionary work, elite women in Oneida were charged with supervising and surveilling less privileged or "wayward" women.[26] Thus, while the rhetoric of Oneida's leaders emphasized the community's opportunities for women, those opportunities were doled out along an unwritten but powerful social and religious caste system. As in contemporary discourses that trumpet the presence of a few women in leadership positions while leaving the rank and file largely untouched, hierarchies of class, education, and race—like Oneida's internal hierarchy—complicate optimistic narratives of women's entry into previously restricted roles (Buchanan, "A Few" 45).

Women further down in the community's caste system lacked the agency to control their work assignments and claim a vocation, and noncompliance with the community's gendered expectations could negatively impact women's work assignments. Charlotte Leonard's experience provides one glimpse of this power structure in action. Leonard speaks to "Aunt" Anne Dunn about her social experience, possibly on the occasion of a man propositioning her through Dunn. As Leonard wrote in her journal, "My great trouble about it is a lack of interest or appetite. I am not only lacking in enthusiasm, but it has sometimes seemed positively distasteful to me. I have wanted to do the right thing, and yet I can not bear to make up a part—I had rather have nothing to do with it" (22). After confessing her decision to go to her "Shaker" (read: celibate) life, Leonard finds that Dunn has given her a new work assignment:

> Mrs. Dunn has lately spoken to me about taking the business of waiting on company this summer! I could not express my astonishment at the idea, and my feeling of utter inability to take such a post. But, no, she was sure I could do it, and would be a good one, and c. . . . I always thought people who had that business had a disagreeable post, and needed the support of the family. (27)

While it may be a coincidence that Leonard's decision to be abstinent was so closely followed by her reassignment to a less agreeable work post, the timing is certainly suggestive. Other accounts confirm that the power of sexual and professional supervisors was subject to abuse. As one former member attested, if a woman refused a sexual proposition from one of the leading men, "she was just as likely to be taken out of any responsible position she held at the time, and not be allowed to do anything until it was thought she had a good spirit and was humble" (qtd. in Van de Warker 790). The notion that a woman who declined sexual activity would suffer a demotion at work is a clear instance of the predatory nature of Oneida's system of complex marriage and the crucial role of powerful women in policing and enforcing it.[27]

While the Oneida Community successfully altered some aspects of women's paid work, women's unpaid work was not meaningfully revised. Oneida women still had maternal duties to perform, duties excluded from the category of "real work." Such invisible work, justified through familial terminology, was likely more difficult for women to resist or critique than their official work assignments. In this regard, Oneida women's agency was curtailed by the larger structures that render the work of motherhood invisible and unaccounted for. As Oneida substituted the communal for the nuclear family, some leading women were invited into the patriarchal leadership structure and offered personal and professional opportunities denied less-privileged women. Thus, the Oneida women who did take steps to level the playing field with men did so by joining men in the existing caste structure rather than elevating women as a group. In this light, as in the case of women's redelegation of domestic labor, women's agency along the axis of gender seems to come at the cost of reinforcing divides among women.

THE RHETORICAL SIGNIFICANCE OF ONEIDA

Life for women at Oneida did in some ways differ dramatically from the circumstances of women in mid-nineteenth-century America at large. Oneida's revisions to what Lindal Buchanan has called the "code of motherhood" altered the daily rhythms and opportunities of women's lives. Rather than working in isolated homes, Oneida women worked as a team—sometimes alongside men—to complete necessary tasks. They worked on behalf of their community rather than the nuclear household. But Oneida also participated in broader trends: though fertility was much lower in Oneida than in America writ large, American women's fertility steadily dropped over the course of the century.[28] Similarly, while childcare at Oneida was granted more professional status, childcare was also paid labor for many women beyond the community. On the whole, the promise that Oneida "emancipates [woman] from the slavery and corroding cares of a mere wife and mother" held true (qtd. in Dalsimer 80). Whether all women desired this emancipation is a more complex question.

Diminishing the expectation that women's primary role in life was that of wife and mother did free Oneida women to participate in a wider variety of work. Census information from 1855, 1865, and 1875 gives a sense of the diverse professions the community's women occupied: tailors, shoe binders, printers, hat braiders, teachers, editors, bag makers, reporters, florists, silk manufacturers, bookkeepers, stenographers, and compositors (Myers 198–210). Moreover, the women articulated an increased sense of self-worth and value: "Gradually, as by natural growth the Community women have risen to a position where, in labor, in mind, and in heart, they have all and more than all that is claimed by the women who are so loudly asserting their rights" (qtd. in Dalsimer 80–81). Such reflections suggest, as Kristy Maddux has intimated, that "economic participation" could function "as a substitute or alternative for the political enfranchisement that other women were promoting" (123).

Yet while men and women at Oneida may have "mingled" in labor to some extent, important rhetorical and practical distinctions between masculine and feminine work remained. These distinctions were based in the persistence of familial and maternal terms and roles, as this extended recollection suggests:

> The Trap Shop was then where the old Silk Mill is now, and some of the women worked in the Trap Shop regularly, drilling holes in the pans and pan posts, blowing bellows for the men who worked at forges, painting the trap springs, and performing other light duties. . . . All the housework, laundry work, sewing, etc, was done by our own people, and in those days the women made all their own underclothing as well as their dresses, hats and coats. . . . In addition to all this the women worked in the Trap Shop, attended bees for picking peas and strawberries, cutting corn, and did the typesetting and other things. The men did all the farm and shop work, and all the building and painting, and helped the women in the housework. (F. Wayland-Smith, 5–6)

In this passage, the trap shop is clearly a masculine space, despite the presence of women who perform "light duties" "for the men"; similarly, housework belongs to the women, even though men occasionally "helped." In this light, Oneida didn't so much overturn traditional family roles as substitute the larger, communal family for the nuclear family, as is borne out by the continued expectation that women will complete mothering work above and beyond their official assignments. Finally, the elevation of some women to leadership positions was afforded by increasing divisions among women: the labor of motherhood was divided into the more valued work of childcare and the drudgery of housework (delegated to machines and hired workers), and female solidarity was further undermined by a hierarchical arrangement through which privileged women surveilled their lower-caste counterparts.

Oneida's birth control experiment also underscores the close rhetorical association of choice and control. In its later years, the community's innovative system of birth control morphed into something more ominous—a eugenics experiment. This development is less surprising given the leaders' close involvement in members' social relations from the start. The eugenic program at Oneida reinforced hierarchies among women: women higher in the community's caste system were deemed better candidates for motherhood. Importantly, Oneida was not the only place where birth control furthered eugenic rhetorics and practices. As Leslie Ruhl notes, the evolution of Margaret Sanger's thought from "arguments rooted in women's autonomy to eugenic arguments about using birth control to 'improve' the race is a necessary reminder of the slipperiness of attaching a notion of control to processes of conception" (660). At Oneida, as in the larger society, eugenics and birth control were closely linked—birth control offered autonomy to some women while limiting the choices of others deemed less fit by eugenic standards.[29] As Greta Gaard has noted, historic and contemporary advances in contraception unfold along race and class lines, such that "first-world, economically-privileged white women" are offered "technologies with least harm and most freedom of control (i.e., condoms, the diaphragm, the sponge, the cervical cap, the pill)," while "third-world, economically disadvantaged women of color" are offered or coerced to employ "technologies . . . with the least safety and freedoms (i.e., sterilization, hysterectomy, Depo-Provera, Norplant)" (111). Too often, rhetorics of motherhood—often truly rhetorics of white, middle-class motherhood—gloss over the ways that reproductive choices differentially affect diverse populations of women. And the illusion of free choice further obscures the significant constraints that unevenly frame women's choices.

Rhetorics of choice also continue the cultural opposition of work and motherhood. While the midcentury "code of motherhood" encouraged women to see themselves as mothers rather than workers, Oneida reversed this logic and asked women to identify primarily as workers rather than mothers. In this way, Oneida failed to offer a model of working motherhood and reinforced the notion that women must, in the end, choose between career and family. A similar zero-sum logic underlies contemporary rhetorics of choice surrounding work and motherhood. Such rhetorics ostensibly offer women autonomy while surreptitiously engaging in "a form of victim-blaming by attributing rising infertility rates to middle-class women who delay childbearing while struggling to launch careers in a working environment constructed to suit the lives of married heterosexual males with stay-at-home wives" (Gaard 105). Oneida's seemingly progressive eschewal of the nineteenth-century code of motherhood proved limited insofar as the predominant work associated with motherhood (childcare and housework) remained the province of women. Contemporary feminist rhetorics of choice thus can be understood as a form of egalitarian feminism, where the specificities of the body are seen as something that must be overcome or denied in order for women to gain the rights and privileges of men. As Elizabeth Grosz explains, "Many feminists within this category see a conflict between the role of mother and that of political or civic being" (15). Too often, discussions of birth control as "liberating women" perpetuate this narrative of women's embodiment and reproductive capacities as weakness, implying that "women's oppression is, at least to some extent, biologically justified" (16).

Rhetorics of choice operate alongside teleological rhetorics in shaping women's relation to work inside and outside the home. Returning to the example of housework at Brook Farm, the teleological insistence that women's activities be framed in relation to the home subtly undermines the community's well-intentioned rhetoric of choice regarding members' work tasks. As my analysis in chapter 2 demonstrates, women's continued sense of responsibility for "indoor duties" in the community compromised the notion that they were free to choose any form of labor they felt drawn to. Similarly, Oneida's opposition of work and motherhood suggested that women workers needed to eschew motherhood biologically and emotionally, a sacrifice that was felt keenly in part due to the prevalent teleological view of motherhood as the end and goal—the "final cause," "that for the sake of which"—of women's lives.

Rhetorics of choice also extend the exceptionalist, anagrammatical logics of the "professional women" to the "working mother." Just as Gertrude Rapp's gendered status was threatened both by her celibacy (her childlessness) and her professional activities (as shown in chapter 3), Oneida women found they were unable to combine their own vision of motherhood with their community's demands on them as workers. At the same time, the cultural insistence on the opposition between domestic and professional roles is belied by the feminization of the silk industry through its association with women's work in textiles and the predominance of Oneida women in feminized industrial roles.[30] In the enduring understanding of work and motherhood as a zero-sum relation, the working mother finds that her authenticity in both realms is up for debate. In the next chapter, I consider the contemporary effects of the idea that working mothers are insufficient both as workers and as mothers, as well as other modern-day vestiges of the ecologies of gendered labor explored in these communities.

5. ARGUMENTS ON THE LANDSCAPE

Rhetorics of Gendered Labor Now and Then

If the field of feminist rhetorics is to continue in the direction of pursuing "rhetorics of genders" (Rawson 49), "the rhetorical history of gender" (Jack, "Acts" 299), and "rhetorics of gendering" (Hallenbeck, "Toward" 14), we will need ecological methodological approaches such as those explored and embodied in this study. Such approaches help us to consider gender as produced by interactions between humans and nonhumans rather than by the conscious, willful interventions of specific individuals and groups. An ecological stance views gender as a lived phenomenon produced and reproduced not only through texts and discourse but also through space, time, bodies, dress, images, objects, institutions, and networks. In this light, feminist rhetoricians exploring ecologies of gender join material rhetoricians in a methodological reversal of figure and ground, where what was once the background or context becomes the focus of our research. Moreover, an ecological approach situates gender among intersecting valences such as class, race, ethnicity, nationality, religion, and education. Without surrendering all hope for conscious gender reform, feminist rhetoricians taking an ecological approach assume that well-intended interventions often have undesirable consequences and that practices and policies implemented to reify or celebrate conventional gender norms may produce unforeseen, even liberating, effects. Whether applied to historical or contemporary cases, an ecological framework thus embraces a radical sense of contingency, an attunement to ways things could be otherwise.

In its own consideration of the "otherwise" that the things of gendered labor might have been or might yet be, this book foregrounds the emergence of three recurring tropes in rhetorics of gendered labor. The first is the power of *teleological* rhetorics that position women's work in relation to presumed domestic trajectories. As the construction of housework at Brook Farm illustrates, the temporal framings of these teleological rhetorics prove remarkably recalcitrant and resilient in the face of material innovations and reforms. Second, rhetorics of *exceptionalism* contain the potential impact of individual workers' achievements for women as a class. As in the Harmony Society, the celebration of one woman's professional status often mystifies and reifies structural inequities and masks the boundary drawing essential to professional rhetorical projects. Finally, rhetorics of *choice* are disclosed as something of a mirage, blurring both the institutional and material conditions that frame individual choices and the punitive consequences that often accompany unsanctioned choices. As in the Oneida Community, contemporary rhetorics of choice continue to oppose women's reproductive and productive labor, thereby underscoring zero-sum logics positing work and family as irreconcilable. By articulating work as a crucial node in the rhetorical construction of gender, I identify rhetorics of teleology, exceptionalism, and choice as central to historical and contemporary ecologies of gender. I anticipate future scholarship that deepens, complicates, and adds to these themes as feminist scholars continue to interrogate the re/production of gendered labor.

Beyond the subject of gendered labor, this study has impressed upon me the need to adapt feminist rhetorical vocabularies to new ecological frameworks, and I would like to offer two suggestions along these lines. First, I advocate a shift from intersectionality to interactionality. As Elizabeth Grosz has maintained, our understanding of the interlocking of gender with race, culture, and class "cannot occur by way of intersection (the gridlike model presumed by structural analysis, in which the axes of class, race, and sex are conceived as autonomous structures which then require external connections with the other structures) but by way of mutual constitution" (20). Throughout this book, rhetorics of teleology, exceptionalism, and choice are permeated by myriad identities that *interact* with gender. The teleological pull of home and family operates differently for the working-class women, like Sophia Eastman of Brook Farm, who were expected to spend their lives caring for the homes of other women rather than retiring from public space to preside over their own. In the same vein, if the Harmony Society silk industry enabled one woman to pursue an entrepreneurial role, her exceptionalism only provided a starker contrast to the indentured servant memorialized only as "Hannah, a woman of colour." And the rhetorics of choice that shaped pregnancy and motherhood in the Oneida Community no doubt rang hollow for the generations of teenage girls forcibly inducted into the sexual practices of the community by John Humphrey Noyes and other religious elders. As these instances show, class, race, age, ethnicity, and religion do not so much *intersect* with or *add on* to gender norms as *interact* with them. A model of interactionality, rather than intersectionality, highlights how anagrammatical pairings—black woman, poor woman, young woman ("girl"), old woman ("crone"), unmarried woman ("spinster"), impious or unchristian woman ("infidel"), sexual woman ("harlot")—function in less linear or gridlike ways than intersectionality might suggest, sometimes disqualifying individuals from the identity of Woman and other times reinscribing an abnormal, deviant, troubling femininity.

Second, given the shortcomings of feminist choice rhetorics in and beyond discussions of women's work, I suggest that we reconsider "choice" as a central terministic screen for describing and analyzing women's rhetorical action. A vocabulary of choice risks reifying an unrealistic and punitive view of individual agency. As Butler cautions regarding what she sees as misunderstandings of gender performativity, "This is not freedom, but a question of how to work the trap one is inevitably in" (83–84). Joining Julie Nelson Christoph, I suggest that "strategy" may be a more helpful term for describing individuals' rhetorical negotiations. As Christoph elaborates, because "strategies exist within specific historical moments and may change from moment to moment," this term acknowledges "the material constraints of a writer's physical space and geography" as well as "the means by which individuals are 'managed' by larger, bureaucratic entities" (669). In this sense, strategy designates "a force through which an individual both *acts* and is *acted upon*" (670, emphasis in original). As opposed to a discourse of women making choices in a situation comprised of constraints and affordances, a vocabulary of strategy clarifies that the strategy isn't enacted *in a context* of beneficial and harmful elements but is itself *bound up with* those elements. Admittedly, "strategy" can still connote an ethos of individual agency, but, as compared to "choice," it better frames individual decisions and actions as always already reactive. Perhaps there are still better options out there. For instance, "practices" also has appeal for describing the rhetoricity of our research subjects, in addition to our own scholarly moves (Royster and Kirsch). Regardless of the terms we deploy, I view undermining the illusion of free choice as a vital feminist project.

In the remainder of this chapter, I suggest that feminist rhetoricians continue to examine work as a crucial node in the production and reproduction of gender. I also return to the overarching theme of this study—*utopia*—as a key component of contemporary rhetorics of gendered labor and gender reform in the workplace. I conclude by offering some final thoughts on the dream called utopia and its place in our shared past, present, and future.

WHY STUDY RHETORICS OF GENDERED LABOR?

While rhetorics of gendered labor are in some regard a natural extension of earlier feminist rhetorical projects, this research focus offers several specific benefits. Specifically, studies of gendered labor help feminist rhetoricians to move beyond a sometimes limiting preoccupation with civic and political rhetorics.

In addition, by turning our attention to rhetorics of gendered labor, we can attune to the concerns of our historical subjects, provide compelling analyses and interventions into contemporary rhetorics of gender, and strengthen our disciplinary efforts toward intersectionality and interactionality.

First, rhetorics of gendered labor offer an alternative to the civic orientation of much of the field. Historically, feminist rhetoricians have largely marshaled their energies to recover, recuperate, and retheorize women's public and civic rhetorics. Bonnie J. Dow observes that Karlyn Kohrs Campbell's chronology of women's rhetorics "has a *telos:* to account for the development of rhetorical strategies that contributed to the passage of the 19th amendment in 1920" (322).[1] Indeed, nineteenth-century women's rhetorics in particular have been validated by virtue of their participation in broader discourses of citizenship, nationhood, and political agency, as well as suffrage specifically (Logan; Johnson; Gere). Yet arguments that align women's private activities with political activism can echo the logic of Republican Motherhood, elevating some women rhetorically while denying them actual political power and eliding the experience of poor, immigrant, African American, and indigenous women. Moreover, reading women's rights through the lens of citizenship endorses an idealistic view of the nation, a problematic stance in light of the history of exclusion, domination, and persecution of women, racial and religious minorities, immigrants, and other marginalized groups in the name of nationhood. Undeniably, women have sometimes been complicit in these national projects, but at other times femininity and gender have functioned rhetorically to enforce problematic norms without the consent of individual women.

Second, attending to rhetorics of women's work helps us to better grapple with the lives and concerns of our historical subjects. For instance, rhetorics of domesticity augur economic as well as political consequences. Defining woman in terms of her potential roles as wife and mother justifies her economic oppression and treatment as a "permanent dependent" (Norton 4). Historically and in the present, as Alice Kessler-Harris explains, "positioning women (even those with neither husbands nor children) as family members" contributes to many aspects of gendered economic inequality: "the sexual division of labor; disparate wages for male and female jobs; the feminization of poverty; protective labor legislation for women only; women's dependence on government welfare" (3). Even within the political realm, many early women's rights efforts focused as much or more on economic as political rights. For instance, nineteenth-century activists fought for married women's rights to wages and property, humane working conditions for women in both homes and factories, and access to education and male-dominated careers, as documents like the Declaration of Sentiments attest.[2] Such concerns foreshadowed later arguments by economically attuned feminists like Charlotte Perkins Gilman, who protested that sex was, for women, a means not just of attracting a mate but of getting her livelihood, "as is the case with no other creature under heaven" (39). We ought to seek a better understanding of the interactions of political and economic agency rather than imposing anachronistic or imperialistic assumptions about what concerns are most important or relevant in women's lives.

Twenty-first-century rhetorics of gender—from the "Me Too" movement to ongoing debates over parental leave and work-life balance—also indicate the centrality of work to cultural understandings of gender. Whether in the home or the workplace, the gendered division of labor continues to be one of the primary modes through which the effects of gender are felt. Without discounting the significance of women's political and civic participation, this study suggests that women's economic status and day-to-day working conditions are equally fundamental to women's lived experience of gender. Indeed, women's economic and political lives are intertwined: economic status has direct consequences for women's political agency. As Karen Sacks argues, many societies base social adulthood in production, not voting rights (222). And Kessler-Harris concludes that, "given the paramount duty of the citizen to work, restrictions on women's opportunities in that sphere have assigned women to a secondary citizenship based on their roles as family members" (12). A full understanding of contemporary rhetorics of gender demands attention to the role of work in discourses of gender.

Finally, scholarship on rhetorics of gendered labor responds to calls for increasing intersectionality—what I am calling interactionality—in feminist rhetorics. As the archival analysis in the prior chapters demonstrates, the lens of gender discloses some truths while obscuring others.[3] And as David Gold cautions, when applying any heuristic, it is important not to "mistak[e] the map—and mapping—for the territory" (21). In particular, we must consider how other identities interact with and intervene in the gender relations we are mapping. By thus broadening our perspective, we undertake, in Biesecker's words, "to write the story not only of the difference between women's and men's subject (re)formation but, also, to write into that account the story of the differences between women as well" (351). For instance, it is nearly impossible to ignore class tensions among women when examining material and rhetorical structures of women's work. And yet, when historical archives represent women's experience largely through the words and perceptions of white, middle-class women, historiographers must read between the lines to grasp the significance of gendered labor for women across divergent subject positions. Indeed, writing class, race, ethnicity, religion, and education into the rhetorical history of gender requires a redeployment of feminist stances such as Jacqueline Jones Royster's "critical imagination," initially introduced as a "paradigm for the recovery and reenvisioning of experience" (*Traces* 83–84), and Susan Jarratt's classic defense of "the speculative leaps required to initiate feminist history" (391).

Beyond academia, interactional approaches not only foster disciplinary subtlety and rigor but also confront the rhetorical failures of white, middle-class Western feminism. Indeed, U.S. feminism has embraced as one of its central tenets the right of women to leave the home and go to work, ideally in their chosen profession. However, as bell hooks explains, such "right to work" rhetorics can alienate potential allies among women of color and working-class women (populations that crucially overlap). Not only is it true that "few black women have had a choice as to whether or not they will become workers" but also that "working for pay neither liberated them from sexist oppression nor allowed them to gain any measure of economic independence" (82, 144). For women who have historically been denied access to the privileged role of housewife, a fixation on middle-class white women's vocational and professional fulfillment can ring hollow. In this vein, *Utopian Genderscapes* illustrates not only the gendering of men's and women's work but also how changing labor practices—and well-intentioned attempts at labor or gender reform—often deepen and cement divides among women of different socioeconomic classes, races, ethnicities, religions, and educational backgrounds.

NOW: UTOPIAN RESPONSES TO GENDERED WORK

The three forms of women's work at the heart of this study—domestic, professional, and reproductive labor—endure as sites of struggle for gender equity in the present. Indeed, in some ways, public attitudes regarding problems and solutions in these arenas echo the logic of our nineteenth-century forebears. As I explore below, public accounts continue to turn to material solutions as a panacea for inequality, overlooking gendered rhetorics that inform how those innovations play out in the lives and experiences of gendered individuals. As these material solutions work to overcome problematic gender norms—often without seeking or requiring the direct participation of men—they reinforce divides among women based on class, race, citizenship, education, and sexuality. Perhaps less predictably, contemporary discussions also betray increasing interest in cultural solutions, grounded in an understanding of gender as a question of socialization. Unfortunately, this approach tends to blame women for their choices or their susceptibility to conventional gender norms, disregarding the ways that men's and women's behaviors and choices are not equally rewarded or disciplined.

Tidying Up

One recurring factor in the gendered division of labor from Brook Farm to the present is that women continue to do more housework than men. A recent report confirmed that, globally, women complete three times more "care work" than men (four to five hours a day) (Barker).[4] On the whole, men do more paid work than women, but when paid work and unpaid care work is combined, women work more hours than men on average. But the problem lies deeper than the question of men's involvement. For instance, some studies show that, in heterosexual households where the woman is the primary earner, the more money she earns, the less housework her partner will contribute (Burkeman). Moreover, housework is associated with women regardless of who does it. A 2016 study found that survey participants presented with fictional descriptions of gay and lesbian households reliably "assigned the stereotypically female tasks to the partner described as having the more stereotypically feminine interests, such as a fondness for shopping or romantic comedies" (Burkeman). The gendered status of housework functions independently of the bodies that complete this labor and is constructed in opposition to work outside the home.

One material solution to the problem of housework is to outsource this labor. In the United States, the number of in-home or domestic workers is growing (Sanchez).[5] But the fact that this work is compensated doesn't mean that it is afforded more social value. As Eileen Boris and Rachel Salazar Parreñas explain, "When intimacy becomes employment, it loses status as a labor of love and becomes regarded as unskilled work that anyone can perform because women have undertaken such activities without payment" (11). As at Brook Farm, compensating individuals for this labor doesn't change the idea—reality—that housework is women's work: between 93 and 95 percent of domestic workers are women (Sanchez; Enlow). Importantly, paid domestic labor is not characterized solely by gender. Around one-fourth of in-home workers live below the poverty line (Sanchez), and most of the two million domestic workers in the United States are African American or immigrant women (Bick). In addition, a disproportionate number are immigrants: unauthorized workers vulnerable to wage theft and other abuses facilitated by the threat of deportation (Holder). Finally, they lack basic workers' rights: domestic and eldercare workers are one of the only classes excluded from the 1935 National Labor Relations Act (Bick).[6] While some argue that middle-class women can't afford to concern themselves with the politics of hiring domestic workers—noting that "a man hiring a male cleaner would be seen as a simple act of employment" (Enlow)—others maintain that we can't ignore the history of this work. Pointing out that, historically, "if domestic work wasn't done by the woman of the house and her female kin . . . it was done by slaves or indentured servants, also for free," journalist Callie Enlow suggests that economically privileged women should be wary of adopting the logics that have devalued women's work for centuries.

Other solutions operate at the level of culture. For instance, authors like Stephen Marche (*The Unmade Bed*) and Tiffany Dufu (*Drop the Ball*) suggest that we address the problem by lowering our standards: "Housework is perhaps the only political problem in which doing less and not caring are the solution. . . . Leave the stairs untidy. Don't fix the garden gate. Fail to repaint the stained ceiling. Never make the bed" (Burkeman). Yet the suggestion that we "drop the ball" affects women differently than men. Men have not been raised to see the cleanliness and orderliness of their surroundings as a measure of self-worth: "A man who places a high priority on domestic cleanliness is just a clean man; a woman who doesn't is a bad woman" (Burkeman). The current preoccupation with the Netflix phenomenon *Tidying Up with Marie Kondo* underscores both the continuing association of housework with women and the desire to elevate this work to a lifestyle as a means to eschew its menial status (echoing Catharine Beecher, Martha Stewart, and other voices in generations prior). While Kondo's mission—"to spark joy in the world through tidying"—is in theory equally applicable to men and women, the families she coaches repeatedly turn to "mom" as the one who needs the intervention, whose work will be lessened, and whose emotional well-being is irretrievably bound up with the physical state of the home.

Brook Farm's lessons and warnings, it seems, are just as relevant today as they were in the 1840s. Compensating individuals for housework (and other devalued labor) does not raise the estimation of that work. And while the common practice of hiring other women to do this work—as with the middle-class members who aimed to "recruit" housekeepers to Brook Farm—are troubling, fixating on women's obligations to other women obscures men's role in the continued unequal distribution of household labor. Finally, the promise that housework will be less demeaning if only we can do this work *better*—whether through domestic management at Brook Farm or its contemporary joy-sparking equivalents—continues to disappoint. What we have learned since Brook Farm is that increasing women's paid work outside the home does not meaningfully alter women's responsibility for the work *of* the home. No wonder, then, if younger generations of women are finding a return to more conventional domestic roles attractive compared to the frenzied pursuit of "work-life balance" and "having it all."

Leaning In

The figure of the professional woman remains a contested site as well, with much attention to the gender wage gap and dearth of women in leadership positions. Proposed solutions in this arena also target material changes to women's work. For instance, one common approach is to grant more flexible work arrangements and longer parental leaves. In theory, such policies would allow women to better balance personal and professional roles, keeping them in the workforce and progressing through the ranks. However, research shows that women who use flexible policies are often penalized: while men who work flexibly are seen as likable and dedicated workers, "women are perceived as using flexible scheduling to accommodate family demands. Thus, even if women are using flexible schedules to be more productive, the impression of their peers might be the opposite" (Zarya). Other research supports these findings and suggests that "a great set of policies means little when employees think their careers will be derailed" (O'Connor and Cech). These differential outcomes also apply to parental leave: recent research shows that "some countries that offer more liberal parental leave policies have higher pay gaps among men and women ages 30 to 34," perhaps due to the fact that women are more likely than men to use this leave and that, despite assurances to the contrary, time out of the workforce is linked to lower wages (Livingston).

Another proposed panacea for women's professional advancement is to secure women in leadership positions in business and politics. Presumably, such women would be more likely to endorse and advance the careers of other women, thus promoting diversity from within. Indeed, research shows that women may estimate other women's abilities more highly and are "more likely than men to see structural barriers and uneven expectations holding women back" in professional contexts (Horowitz, Igielnik, and Parker). And yet women leaders may, in practice, suffer penalties for hiring or promoting other women and minorities in ways that white men do not. A study of 350 executives across 26 industries found that "white women and nonwhite executives" who promoted diversity "were rated as being less competent and having lower performance" in contrast to white male executives displaying the same behaviors (Lam, "Workplace-Diversity"). While the notion of women in leadership positions as the rising tide that floats all boats is attractive, evidence suggests that women leaders are forced to compromise between their own careers and their commitment to equality. Another unenviable alternative is to help other women by whistleblowing rather than working within the system.[7]

As with domestic self-help literature, cultural solutions to women's workplace dilemmas have also risen to the fore. Cultural commentators increasingly point to women's socialization and femininity as roadblocks to professional success. Popular texts such as *Lean In* and *The Confidence Code* promote the idea that women suffer from a "confidence gap" that prevents them from broadcasting their accomplishments and seeking rewards or promotions. Another version of this hypothesis suggests that women don't achieve as much as men do because they simply do not aspire to ambitious and competitive career paths. For instance, men in STEM tend to ascribe the dearth of women to women's lack of interest in these fields (Funk and Parker). To overcome their socialization, these texts suggest, women must engage in the workplace as men do. Unfortunately, women who employ so-called "masculine" strategies and attitudes aren't received in the same manner as men. While women are encouraged to display more confidence, research shows that, "unless women can temper their assertiveness with more stereotypically feminine traits like empathy and altruism, confidence will do little to advance their careers" (Thomson). In this light, a sensible fear of backlash is a more likely culprit for women's lack of self-promotion than their purported lack of confidence.

In light of the double bind facing women leaders in business and industry today, it is harder to fault Gertrude Rapp for failing to advocate for other women more than a century ago. Emphasizing her own gender in order to argue for the qualifications and aptitude of women entrepreneurs more broadly would have risked Rapp's already tenuous standing vis-à-vis the midcentury silk community. While Rapp chose to correspond with her associates in a distanced, gender-neutral, professional voice, today's professional women are encouraged to display their purportedly natural gifts for empathy and intuition on the job. Rapp's willingness to eschew expected gender norms may have something to do with the fact that, as a member of a celibate German community, she was already irredeemably outside the parameters of midcentury true womanhood.

Having It All

Finally, as at Oneida, contemporary workplace ideologies struggle to reconcile the identities of worker and mother. Many women experience straightforward discrimination along these lines, as in the case of Peggy Young, a UPS driver who was put on unpaid leave when she was unable to lift seventy pounds during pregnancy, as well as other routine egregious violations of the Pregnancy Discrimination Act (Zhou). But even when mothers do not suffer overt discrimination, marriage and motherhood affect women's careers in ways that do not correlate to men. As a 2016 *Atlantic* article reported, "Women who never married earn 94 percent of their male counterparts, while married women earn only 78 percent" (Lam, "How Do We Close"). The so-called "motherhood penalty" refers to these less visible, long-term effects of family responsibilities on women's professional lives. The issue is not just that women take time away from work for family but that they are penalized for doing so: a 2018 Pew survey showed that mothers are twice as likely as fathers to say that taking time off negatively impacted their job or career (Graf, Brown, and Patten). And the facts support these perceptions: when mothers cut back hours at work, their hourly wage (not just their take-home pay) suffers, and they are paid less than men for the hours they do work (C. Miller, "Gender Pay Gap").

One material solution to this problem invokes the logic of birth control in the Oneida Community: women should control and time their pregnancies so as not to interfere with their careers. How, exactly, women should do this is less clear, as "experts" debate the benefits and drawbacks of having children early to pursue professional goals versus delaying pregnancy until a level of professional standing has been achieved. Moreover, such rhetorics of control laud scientific agency by "medicalizing" pregnancy such that "scientific and medical expertise becomes valued over experiential knowledge" (Jensen 2). Applied to the workplace, such rhetorics blame women for failing to time their children to minimize the impact on their careers, justifying the professional penalties working mothers incur as the natural consequence of their "choices." In addition, the rhetoric and realities of choice via birth control differ by race and class. The history of birth control in the United States reveals a pattern where less reversible, riskier methods are promoted for women of color and working-class women. Thus, a focus on individual choice belies the reality that contraceptive technologies foster "stratified reproduction," where "members of some demographic groups are encouraged to reproduce and others are not" (Jensen 7).

Even as motherhood is opposed to cultural notions of professionalism, connotations of motherliness follow women to work. Women are tracked into low-pay nurturing and caring professions, such as healthcare and teaching, deepening the gender gap (K. Parker). Insisting again that women need to overcome their own gendered socialization, some advocates suggest that the solution is for women to pursue highly paid, conventionally masculine careers. Setting aside the frankly depressing fact that women's entry into a given field typically lowers its prestige and compensation, women who seek high-power positions find that making different choices doesn't resolve the issue.[8] For one thing, male-dominated fields are often hostile workplaces for women: a 2018 Pew survey found that 34 percent of women who work primarily with men say their gender has a negative impact on their working lives (K. Parker). And gendered expectations affect women's ability to perform in these positions: for instance, while male attorneys are expected to be aggressive and domineering, female attorneys are penalized for attempting to conform to these norms

(Wingfield). Finally, regardless of the profession, women are associated with emotional labor in the workplace. In academia, women's leadership is often misdefined as "service," and men spend, on average, 7.5 more hours per week on their own research (Detweiler et al. 453, 456). In other words, even when women move beyond fields with explicit ties to the labor of motherhood, they continue to suffer from expectations that they will perform "mothering work" on the job.

When it comes to reproduction and work, women are often encouraged to adopt the mindset of the Oneida Community, seeing motherhood and work as irreconcilable options to choose between. As with birth control at Oneida, the idea of controlling and timing children for career advancement pervades advice to professional women. Similarly, women are encouraged to manage and control their bodies during pregnancy so as to minimize effects on their work. And, as at Oneida, where biological motherhood was comparatively rare, the associations of women with motherly behavior contribute to the kinds of professions women are expected and able to pursue as well as to the division of labor within those professions.

As we tinker with the spaces and practices of work in our own lives and consider the larger spaces of work for gendered individuals across the nation and around the globe, we should be conscious of the operation of utopian and antiutopian rhetorics that can take the form of "magic bullet" material solutions or promote inertia through slippery slope appeals playing to our fear of change. And yet an awareness of the problematic accompaniments to some utopian appeals should not blind us to the necessity of the utopian impulse as a primary means through which alternatives are imagined and materialized.

THEN: REMEMBERING UTOPIA

As this chapter suggests, utopia isn't just the site for the three primary cases of this study; it is also an integral part of rhetorics of gendered labor in the past and present. But what of utopia itself? Is there a place for the dream called utopia in contemporary society? All too often, utopian dreaming is relegated ceaselessly to the past in narratives that position utopias as the inevitable failures of hapless dreamers or extremist ideologues. If we want to revive utopia, we will need to work past the antirhetorical and antiecological mindset that haunts discussions of utopian projects and possibilities, past and present.

Certainly, there is some public interest in remembering the communities of this study, as well as other nineteenth-century intentional communities. Six acres of the Harmonist site in Ambridge, Pennsylvania, were purchased by the state in 1916, and "Old Economy Village" became a State Historic Site in 1919. The Brook Farm site was recognized as a Boston Landmark (the city's highest recognition for historic sites) in 1977 and purchased by the State of Massachusetts in 1988. In 1987, the Oneida Community Mansion House was chartered by the New York State Education Department as a 501c3 nonprofit historic house and museum. All three of the communities in this study are now National Historic Landmarks, a distinction enjoyed by just 3 percent of the over ninety thousand places listed on the country's National Register of Historic Places. As such, Oneida, Brook Farm, and Old Economy Village—as well as sites of other communities such as Hancock Shaker Village, Canterbury Shaker Village, the Amana Colonies, and Zoar Village—are recognized as "icons of ideals that shaped the nation" and "places characterizing a way of life" ("National"). Contemporary interest in historical utopian communities is also demonstrated by Eric Reese's 2016 *Utopia Drive*, a travelogue through the historical narratives and contemporary landscapes of nineteenth-century communities, and *Nice Try! Utopian*, a 2019 podcast series exploring utopian projects ranging from Oneida to Chandigarh, India.

Yet in spite of this public interest, the dominant theme in popular discussions of utopia is failure. After introducing the wide variety of communities discussed in the first season of *Nice Try*, host Avery Trufelman intones, "Their motivations vary, but these projects share one thing in common: in one way or another, they all fail" ("Introducing"). Similarly, a 2016 *New Yorker* retrospective on historical intentional communities concludes that "the biggest problem—at least, in any attempt to harness these nineteenth-century projects to twenty-first-century reforms—is one less of evil than of ineffectuality. A spectre hangs over these places—the spectre of failure" (Kapur). These "failure stories" typically categorize utopian communities as impractical dreamers or predatory cults. Thus, Trufelman's podcast juxtaposes Charlotte Perkins Gilman's pacifist all-female *Herland* (the inspiration for Wonder Woman's Amazonian origin story) with the Third Reich's architectural plans for a "Berlin for a New Order." In this light, given the association of twentieth-century utopian movements with genocide and mass terror, their purportedly inevitable failure might be met with relief rather than regret. Even when we sympathize with the ends of a community, we express concern over the means—and the Promethean temperament of those who would strive for perfection.[9] After the heyday of nineteenth-century utopian experimentation, the undeniable trend in the twentieth century is toward dystopia—in common parlance the terms are nearly interchangeable.

The practical effect of this "spectre of failure" is to discourage utopian dreaming and experimentation. If we ascribe to Nathan Stormer's view of public memory as a "conduit of contestation," failure stories of nineteenth-century communities function "as a way of orienting struggle around new ways of living" (4). Indeed, public accounts often position contemporary efforts as latter-day equivalents of historical communities. For instance, an account of Factor e Farm—a sustainable living experience based in open-source design led by Marcin Jakubowski—compares the community to Brook Farm, aligning the *ethos* of these very different communities. "In one video, Jakubowski appears onscreen in rubber boots, grinning broadly and munching a radish. ('Happy, hapless, *sansculottes*,' Emerson called the Brook Farmers)" (Eakin). Noting that "the historical record is not auspicious in this regard," the article backhandedly concludes that Jakubowski's resolve and dedication seem "simultaneously heroic and insane." The consensus take that "failure is baked into the very idea of utopia" puts any group who might attempt to carve out a different kind of life on the defensive (Kapur). In the terms of Stacy Sheriff's heuristic grammar of rhetorical failure, the perceived inevitable failure of utopian projects has evolved from a "failure of situation," where communities ahead of their time are too radical to succeed, to a "failure of genre," where their very association with "utopia" brands them as failures (193–94).

Teleological accounts of utopia as inevitable failures also depict the current socioeconomic system as inevitable and natural. As Akash Kapur suggests, "The example of America's nineteenth-century intentional communities suggests that there is something elemental in what John Maynard Keynes, writing during the Great Depression, called 'the resilience of capitalism.'" Such accounts indicate that capitalism is better suited to human nature than any other model: "Egoism, acquisitiveness, competitiveness, and all the other ills of human flesh bob repeatedly to the surface, like a cork that will not be submerged." In this framing, our problems are rooted in human nature, not socioeconomic structures. Such "nothing new under the sun" rhetorics—like dismissive references to "hippie communes" of the 1960s and 1970s—function to squelch and discredit contemporary cohousing communities and other alternative living arrangements. By insistently positioning utopianism as a phase in America's past—whether in the mid-nineteenth or mid-twentieth century—public memories of utopia forestall opportunities for utopian imagination and experimentation in the present and future.

To reconsider utopia, we will need to reconsider its rhetorical shadow: failure. Revisiting the failure of intentional communities from a rhetorical and ecological standpoint might help us preserve rather than foreclose utopian projects. I want to suggest that failure is, in large part, a question of scope. A broader scale—a widened scope of space and time—can help us rewrite narratives of failure. There are spatial dynamics at work in public views of intentional communities: their separation from the larger society promotes their perception as discrete ventures that will either succeed or fail. Similarly, my temporal reconsideration of failure is indebted to Lindal Buchanan's enunciation of "the power and importance of articulating alternatives to the status quo. Even when such arguments are vilified or rejected, so long as they continue to circulate within the rhetorical ecology, they have the potential to effect change over the long term" ("Few Good" 47). Buchanan notes that rhetorics that fail in their initial moment are often successfully recirculated in the future. Ironically, with intentional communities, the opposite may hold true: members' testimonies suggest that these communities were successful at their initiation, yet their lack of continuance is interpreted as failure. When it comes to failure (of rhetoric or utopia), we must ask: Failure for whom, or for what? Failure when, or where? By framing the existence of a community as rhetorical—and as having rhetorical effects across time and space—I engage Royster and Kirsch's "strategic contemplation," which "becomes especially useful . . . when the ecologies of person, time, and space stretch beyond anointed assumptions about the ways and means of rhetorical performance" (21). At the close of this project, I take a longer and wider view, resisting the idea of intentional communities as bounded units and cultivating an attunement to their participation in broader networks and ecologies.

For one thing, this broader view resituates the purpose of an intentional community. If rhetorical success or failure lies in confronting a particular exigence, then we should rethink utopian communities. As I suggested in my introduction, midcentury intentional communities formed in response to a complex socioeconomic situation that, for some, demanded a response. The same might be said of the flourishing of intentional communities in the decades after World War II. In this view, intentional communities form in waves as problems arise that people feel moved to address *in community*: some of these innovations stick, some are abandoned, and life goes on.[10] As the exigencies that prompted a particular community (or wave of communities) shift, those communities evolve, dissolve, or otherwise change in response. For instance, the Huntington Open Women's Land (HOWL), a lesbian utopian community in Vermont, formed in the 1980s to offer an escape from patriarchal oppression: "Women came seeking a new life after leaving behind first marriages, families and neighborhoods where living openly was unsafe" (Raphael). The community is currently struggling to recruit members in part because that exigence has changed. As one leader remarked, "Honestly, in Burlington, the patriarchy has a lower volume" (qtd. in Raphael). Interpreting this situation as HOWL's failure seems like a missed opportunity to observe something more profound. The notion that the only possible goal of an intentional community is to *continue living in the same location in the same manner* is a narrow perspective: ecologically speaking, stasis is not success.

We can also reconsider the temporal dynamics of intentional communities. The notion that a community "begins" when it sets up a communal living arrangement and "fails" when that arrangement ends beleaguers utopian projects. At Oneida, we might reconsider the community's evolution into a unique business endeavor. The Oneida Community's incorporation may have marked *an* end, but it didn't dissolve the community of individuals associated with the project. Most Oneida members continued to work for the corporation, producing the flatware that comprised half of the silverware in use in the United States as recently as the 1980s. Even today, many members' descendants live and work in the immediate area, keeping the legacy of the community alive and active in the present. The Harmony Society also lived on as a business venture after its communal phase: many members lived in Economy for the rest of their lives, while others, having been helped through their initial years in the United States as German immigrants, moved elsewhere and pursued other projects in their new land. The current site serves as an educational and communal center for Ambridge, Pennsylvania, helping to articulate the broader contributions of German immigrants in Pennsylvania in the past and present. Finally, though Brook Farm has not been materially preserved to the same extent as the other communities of this study, the future uses of the farmers' land—as a Union training camp during the Civil War and an orphanage from 1872 to 1943—were in line with the community's values. In this way, Brook Farm's lasting influence might be understood in terms of Jensen's notion of "percolation," where "old ideas and arguments do not disappear when their chronological time . . . has passed but, instead, percolate at subsequent, often seemingly disconnected moments to combine and contend with newer arguments, appeals, and narratives" (5). The heritage of Brook Farm seems to inform future uses of its space.

If we move away from the terministic screens of success and failure, we will be better equipped to perceive alternative ways of living in our midst. Jakubowski has received a good deal of media attention through his TED Talks and charismatic public presentations, but those qualities haven't served as well in the day-to-day matters of leading and sustaining Factor e Farm. If we want to find utopia, we may need to listen better. Less flamboyant communities—often purposefully off the grid—may better indicate the promise and possibilities of intentional communities today. Like Brook Farm, these communities embrace the philosophy that "a steady endeavor to embody these ideas more and more perfectly in life, would give the best answers, both to the hopes of the friendly and the cavils of the skeptical, and furnish in its results the surest grounds for any larger efforts" ("Signs"). The community of Twin Oaks, Virginia, was founded in 1967 and has continued its communal lifestyle since, sparking several other communities either inspirationally or practically, as members split off to start their own groups, such as the East Wind Community in the Ozarks of southern Missouri. Indeed, the number of intentional communities listed in the Foundation for Intentional Community's directory nearly doubled between 2010 and 2016, and the foundation's executive director attributes this growth to interest from millennials, who "get this intentional community thing more than people in the past" (Mariani). Rather than focusing on leaders' visions, we might inquire into members' experiences. A 2017 study from the Norwegian Institute of Public Health found that North Americans living in intentional communities ranked on par with the highest previously published scores on the Satisfaction with Life Scale (a globally recognized measurement) (Grinde et al.). Tellingly, the most important predictors for the reported happiness of individuals in communities were "meaning in life" and "social support." Despite a surge in public interest in happiness in recent decades, intentional communities continue to be undervalued as a source of inspiration or model for our individual or collective lives. The failure is ours: we overlook these alternative ways of living to our detriment.

Our blind spot when it comes to perceiving and acknowledging alternative lifestyles also obscures the historical contributions of utopian communities. Though the examples are too many to enumerate here, some of the existential effects of these communities particularly germane to this study include: Brook Farm's role in sparking the communal housekeeping[11] movement of the late nineteenth and early twentieth centuries; the Harmony Society's validation of U.S. manufacturing and the inclusion of women in manufacturing (regarding which Frederick Rapp testified to Congress); and the Oneida Community's effect on feminism and the birth control movement.[12] Other traces of these communities are distributed throughout our mundane, everyday spaces and practices. Have you lived in a home with an Amana fridge or Oneida stove? Has the international obsession with enduring and adaptive Shaker-style cabinetry struck you? Did you send your children to kindergarten? Do you or have you engaged in family planning with some form of birth control? Do you take note of Oneida silverware when dining out? Have you wondered at the waste of individual dishwashers and washing machines in every house on your street? Do you pride yourself on buying American rather than from factories abroad? Are you a woman who wears pants or cuts your hair short?

In the end, the collective effects of intentional communities may be more crucial than the individual impact of any one community. As one observer noted in an 1844 edition of the *New York Herald*, "Though of little influence individually, . . . the impulses which they communicated to the popular mind, and the variety of elements they combine and exercise, make them powerful" ("Wonderful Progress of the New Philosophy"). Indeed, even if intentional communities primarily serve to spark the "utopian impulse" that too often lies dormant in each of us, this is no small feat (Jameson 51). As humans, we may never achieve perfection, but we cannot thrive without our drive toward the good, toward the *better.*

NOTES

WORKS CITED

INDEX

NOTES

1. Ecologies of Women's Work

1. Sanborn is likely most directly responding to Parson's *The Family* (1906), which advocated for trial marriages, divorce, and contraception, and Gilman's *The Home, Its Work and Influence* (1903) and *Human Work* (1904), nonfiction works that critiqued domesticity and argued for women's economic independence well before Gilman's better-known feminist utopia, *Herland* (1915).

2. I use the terms "utopian" and "intentional" community more or less interchangeably throughout this project as a means of acknowledging both the participation of these projects in a larger utopian tradition and the preference of some modern-day communitarians for the latter term.

> The term intentional community dates to the late 1940s, when the Inter-Community Exchange—an organization formed in Yellow Springs, Ohio, in the wake of World War II to help promote peaceful, cooperative living arrangements (in the hope of eradicating war altogether)—changed its name to the Fellowship of Intentional Communities; the founders felt the new title better conveyed the deliberateness with which these groups were assembling. (Mariani)

3. See M. Smith, "Containment Rhetoric," for a fuller discussion of antiutopian rhetoric in public accounts of the Amana Community, a German pietist community in Iowa. While the "free love" Oneida Community was accused of "living in a state of vile concubinage" ("Perfectionism and Polygamy"), the celibate, pietistic Harmony Society also raised concerns about "what remodeling of the family constitution was found necessary . . . to carry out practically the celibate law" (Nevin). Secular communities such as Hopedale and Brook Farm were similarly described as damaging "the distinctions of marriage" and threatening "the family tie" (Hinds, "Hopedale").

4. This aspect of utopian communities is beginning to receive scholarly attention. See, among others, Foster's two monographs considering gender

roles across several nineteenth-century communities (*Religion and Sexuality*; *Women, Family, and Utopia*). Chmielewski, Kern, and Klee-Hartzell's edited collection also offers a glimpse of women's experiences in communities spanning the nineteenth century to the present.

5. This approach is indebted to material rhetoricians such as Carole Blair, who maintains that a scholarly focus on rhetoric's symbolicity impedes our understanding of its consequentiality and partisanship (19–20).

6. I join other feminist rhetoricians in demonstrating the interconnection of reproductive and professional gendered rhetorics. See, for instance, Jessica Enoch's analysis of how the ideograph of <home> was used first to support and then to undermine working mothers ("There's No Place"). Similarly, Robin Jensen's analysis of infertility articulates the intersections of women's reproductive and professional roles: "Long before the twentieth century, women's lack of success in bearing children was attributed to immorality, sexual perversion, strenuous intellectual work, and so-called masculine professional aspirations" (6).

7. Despite recent discussions about naming, I retain the term "feminist rhetorics" to describe my area of study. For an elaboration of these discussions, see M. Smith, "Feminist."

8. Indeed, several material feminists are concerned that the discursive turn has gone too far, eschewing the body (Hekman 86). For instance, Susan Hekman argues that feminist theorists must reclaim ontology to grapple with women's embodied experiences and assert truth claims about women's status (90, 107).

9. Scholars such as Cheryl Glenn, Shirley Wilson Logan, Jacqueline Jones Royster, Karlyn Kohrs Campbell, and others have worked to recover the women who have, indeed, always been practicing rhetoric. And, as Lindal Buchanan and Kathleen J. Ryan explain, "Once its prototypical elite male speaker was replaced by a woman, the discipline required deep revision in order to accommodate the constraints and particular strategies of a new constituency" (xvi).

10. Similarly, Sarah Hallenbeck calls for feminist rhetorical historiography to shift its gaze "from women-as-rhetors towards a broader, more descriptive project that interrogates *all* the ways that rhetoric alternately supports, complicates, and subverts dominant understandings of gender" ("Toward" 13). For an introduction to rhetorics of gendering, see M. Smith, "Indoor Duties." For more exemplars of the transition from women's rhetorics to rhetorics of gendering, see Mattingly on the gendering of women's bodies and dress on the platform and Lindal Buchanan's exploration of the gendering of bodies through public speaking (*Regendering*).

11. My use of intra-action borrows from material feminist Karen Barad, who proposes intra-activity as an alternative to mediation as a way of understanding the iterative agency of material and discursive practices (140–41).

12. Historian Bruce Laurie emphasizes the uneven transition to an industrial economy: "While the factory was the most visible manifestation of industrialism, it was a relatively small part of the industrial scene before the Civil War. As late as 1860, more wage earners worked in farmhouses and small workshops than in factories, and most used hand tools, not power-driven equipment" (16). He continues, noting that, "into the 1840s, nimble hands in Northern and Southern homes yielded more yarn and cloth than textile factories" (17).

13. In 1846–47, "the number of immigrants rose from 82,000 to over 142,000 and climbed steadily thereafter, reaching the antebellum high of 267,000 in 1851" (Laurie 26).

14. As historian Edith Abbott notes, the 1850 national census was the first to be "in the least complete" when it came to women's work (79).

15. Despite newly available manufactured goods, contemporary documents show that nineteenth-century housewives were exhausted and overworked. Ruth Schwartz Cowan attributes this to several factors: men working outside the home contributed less to household chores; labor-saving devices raised domestic standards; and technological innovations eliminated or eased stereotypically masculine occupations but not those gendered feminine (45–65).

16. Outworkers earned an estimated $0.75–1.50/week, which barely amounted to a subsistence wage for a young woman and put single mothers in an impossible financial situation (Stansell 111). The system's profitability and popularity are undeniable: by 1860, Brooks Brothers had seventy workers inside and two to three thousand outside (109).

17. This language crucially operated at the intersection of midcentury ideas of gender and slavery, suggesting that, "unlike the bondsman, the hireling could count himself free because the sale of his labor ensured his property in his domestic dependents" (Stanley 90).

18. Eliza Leslie's 1841 domestic advice text, *The House Book*, observed that "complaints are incessantly heard of the deterioration of servants," and Frances Trollope's 1832 *Domestic Manners of the Americans* blamed the inadequacy of "help" on a want of refinement in the new nation (qtd. in Dudden 4). Immigration and class divides among women surfaced in the rhetoric of the "servant problem," which implied that "one could not really *be* a lady if one did not have a problem with servants" (Stansell 161).

19. Religious differences supported ethnic prejudice against recent Irish immigrants. One "Wanted" ad seeking a "GIRL, to take care of children and do plain sewing" stipulated: "None but Protestants need apply" (Dudden 70).

20. Another prototype of the working-class woman, the "factory girl," became an object of social concern in the 1830s and was differentiated both from the "spotless" Lowell girls and the "victimized" sewing woman (Stansell 125).

This factory girl embodied "a more disturbing kind of female independence," specifically a form of insubordination that undermined both class and gender distinctions—factory girls were reportedly dismissive and disrespectful toward their husbands (125).

21. As Dudden explains:

> Supervising domestics could also be interpreted as a form of benevolence, since it was the occasion of considerable contact between women across class lines, and it helped to effect the transition into leisure and consumption since the same domestics who secured a woman some ease also demanded of her a work role similar to that of entrepreneurial men. (7)

The "ideology of domesticity thus provided the initial impetus for what would become a class intervention, the movement of reformers into the working-class neighborhoods and the households of the poor between 1830 and 1860" (Stansell 65).

22. One exception is Lindal Buchanan's *Regendering Delivery*, whose profound observations about the careers of women speakers might just as readily apply to other professions.

23. The idea that feminist rhetorics should take as its subject the lived experience of gender is one I have discussed elsewhere in greater detail (see "Indoor Duties"). Ideally, methodologies of lived experience would serve the goal of moving past binary gender frames toward "broader, more expansive definitions of gender that more closely mirror the complexities of lived gender" (Rawson 42). In a materialist vein, this approach speaks to the "*mutuality* of material practice, embodied experience, and discursive representation" (Edbauer 21, emphasis in original). This project thus joins feminist and material rhetoricians in exploring rhetoric as a constitutive part of "lives as they are actually lived," which are often "at odds with abstract normative theories or official ideologies" (Coole and Frost 27).

24. Recent theory in and beyond rhetoric has encouraged the discipline to eschew traditional models of rhetorical situation and intention. For instance, material rhetoricians have complicated sender-receiver models and exploded conventional rhetorical triangles (or quartets), questioning "whether notions of rhetorical situation adequately account for the 'constitutive circulation' of rhetoric in the social field" (Edbauer 7). As Carole Blair warned twenty years ago, we must avoid limiting the efficacy of rhetoric to the intentions of a rhetor: "We must ask not just what a text means but, more specifically, what it does; and we must not understand what it does as adhering strictly to what it was supposed to do" (23). Systemic power relations—such as gender, race, class, and so on—outstrip the apprehension and will of individual actors even as

those actors re/produce those structures. "There are events. I never *act*; I am always slightly surprised what I do. That which acts through me is also surprised by what I do, by the chance to mutate, to change, and to bifurcate" (Latour, *Pandora's Hope* 281).

25. Rhetoricians and feminists alike have been skeptical of Latour's assertion that tracing networks itself reveals power dynamics insofar as "the more associations a node has, the greater power it has in the network" (Walsh et al. 406).

26. Latour's methodology of *translation* or *delegation* explores the transformation of a major effort into a minor one by shifting roles between humans and nonhumans: "Every time you want to know what a nonhuman does, simply imagine what other humans or other nonhumans would have to do were this character not present" ("Mixing" 299).

2. Domestic Rhetorics

1. As Amy Dru Stanley explains, gender roles were undermined by wage labor because the conversion of labor to a commodity demasculinized men, according to the Enlightenment tradition that persons who labored for others were dependents (84–85). Historically, wage labor was associated with the household and legally categorized (along with marriage and slavery) as a domestic relation (85).

2. Brook Farm's protofeminist reputation increased after the shift to Fourierism in 1844, which made women's rights an explicit goal. An 1856 article on "Social Communities" in the *United States Magazine* described Brook Farm as one of many communities "which have sprung up . . . to establish better relations between man and man, and more harmonious relations between the sexes" (445). Such accounts positioned Brook Farm as part of a groundswell of women's rights activism, a reputation that might have taken the community's founders by surprise.

3. That women workers in the Lowell mills were paying close attention to Brook Farm is perhaps due to the efforts of John Allen and John Orvis, who "spoke to a large and deeply interested audience" in Lowell in 1846 ("Brook Farm Lecturers" 175).

4. Canadian political philosopher C. B. Macpherson coined the term "market society," which he defines as follows: "Where labour has become a market commodity, market relations so shape and permeate all social relations that it may properly be called a market society, not merely a market economy" (qtd. in Stanley 75).

5. Wage cuts in the 1830s sparked labor protests across the nation, including strikes at the Lowell mills in 1834 and 1846. These strikes "fit a national pattern,

in which the language of republicanism and the spirit of the Revolution were invoked to mobilize workers against what was seen as an emerging tyranny of economic power" (Freeman 66–67). In the 1840s, labor protests united under the banner of "radicalism" fought for bread-and-butter causes such as shorter hours, higher wages, and better working conditions rather than systemic overhaul (Margo 30–31).

6. Transcendentalist reformers such as Ripley and Brownson differed markedly from the strand of transcendentalism embodied by Emerson, which highlighted introspection, self-reliance, and self-culture. Gura describes this friction as the identifying marker of transcendentalism as a movement (xiv).

7. This innovation was seen as remarkable, even humorous, to neighbors and onlookers. As Emerson later recounted, the community's rural neighbors "naturally were surprised to observe that one man ploughed all day and one looked out of the window all day, and perhaps drew his picture, and both received at night the same wages" (qtd. in Sams 224).

8. The language of drones refers to male worker bees. In the nineteenth century, the term became associated with individuals who lived off others without contributing active labor, especially members of the "leisure classes."

9. Underlying the rhetoric of drudges and drones, the view of physical labor as degrading and demeaning continued. Hawthorne's famous declarations that "a man's soul may be buried and perish under a dungheap or in a furrow of the field, just as well as under a pile of money" and that "labor is the curse of this world, and nobody can meddle with it, without becoming proportionately brutified" are only the boldest statements of a common attitude (qtd. in Sams 21, 30). Even Elizabeth Peabody's idealistic description of the community articulated this sense that "as the labor becomes merely bodily, it is a greater sacrifice to the individual laborer" and that "intellectual labor involves in itself higher pleasures, and is more its own reward, than bodily labor" ("Plan").

10. In 1855, 224 of 400 single workingwomen in Christine Stansell's study of women in New York City were living independently of uncles, aunts, grandparents, and parents (84).

11. Marianne Dwight came to Brook Farm an unmarried woman, but her letters from her time in the community were published under her married name, Orvis. I refer to her as Dwight—her name when these letters were written.

12. Hawthorne left the community on October 17, 1842.

13. The ten women listed with their own profession comprise three students, four teachers, and three seamstresses (Rose 234–38).

14. Fuller never did join the community, though she seems to have enjoyed her visit, remarking, "I have found myself here in the amusing position of a conservative" (qtd. in Sams 218).

15. Brook Farm had comparatively generous working conditions for physical laborers. Members were expected to work six ten-hour days during spring and summer and six eight-hour days in the fall and winter (Delano, *Brook Farm* 67). It is possible, of course, that these expectations applied more to men's outdoor agricultural work than women's domestic work, which would not vary seasonally to the same extent.

16. The fancy group, originated by Dwight and other women, is one of many aspects of Brook Farm taken up somewhat sardonically in Hawthorne's *The Blithedale Romance.* In the novel, a young recruit named Priscilla sews small purses described as useless, an echo of her general ineptitude at housework. In contrast, the actual fancy group at Brook Farm successfully sold their goods at market, and this work was viewed as an escape from, not a component of, the women's housework.

17. This focus on profit is further expressed by Dwight in a letter to her brother: "Mrs. Ripley took in four fans last week, sold two for $1.50 cts each, 1 for $1.00 and 1 for $1.25. Was it not grand? Now Amelia and I feel encouraged" (Brook Farm Association, *Records*, Correspondence, May 18, 1845).

18. Faye Dudden describes the diary of Phebe Eastman, a New York farm-woman in the 1820s: "Cooking for large numbers of hired men and caring for the children who arrived at regular intervals did not seem like accomplishments to her; carding, warping, dyeing, and weaving did. She always noted in her diary how many yards she wove" (15). Such accounts confirm that selling one's work or products on the market may have given American women a greater sense of accomplishment and self-worth than their housework.

19. Women's occupations were included from the Seventh Census in 1850 onward. Yet gendered discrepancies in census-taking methods meant that the "occupations tables" are less complete for women, as one official noted regarding the 1870 census:

> It is taken for granted that every man has an occupation, and the examination of tens of thousands of pages of schedules returned in the present census has satisfied the superintendent that only in rare cases, too inconsiderable to be taken into account in such a discussion, have assistant marshals failed to ask and obtain the occupation of men, or boys old enough to work with effect. It is precisely the other way with women and young children. The assumption is, as the fact generally is, that they are not engaged in remunerative employments. Those who are so engaged constitute the exception, and it follows from a plain principle of human nature, that assistant marshals will not infrequently forget or neglect to ask the question. (Abbott 353–54)

20. The racial dynamics of service are further illustrated by the fact that free blacks in service were routinely denied the title of help and white domestics commonly objected to working alongside blacks (Dudden 33, 223).

21. In the midcentury United States, paid housework transitioned from flexible forms of "help" to the more rigid structure of "domestics." In Dudden's account, "helping" was less an occupation than an activity—and helpers were likely to deny the name of "servant." Domestics had longer hours and more work discipline; native-born women who were happy to help did not want to be domestics and withdrew to other forms of work (7–8). The transition from help to domestics coincided with the midcentury influx of immigrant, especially Irish, women (60). Employers expressed nostalgia for the time of "help" and expressed their ethnic and economic superiority through the rhetoric of the "servant problem"—difficulties finding and keeping good servants.

22. In this vein, one might ask whether Marianne Dwight's account illustrates the frustrations of a woman who is actually overworked or of one experiencing a conflict between the community's expectations and her own entitlement: "We need more leisure, or rather, we should like it. There are so many, and so few women to do the work, that we have to be nearly all the time about it" (8).

23. Indeed, such archival silences and absences are one reason why feminist rhetorical historiography has invested in methodologies such as Jacqueline Jones Royster's "critical imagination" (83) and Susan Jarratt's defense of "the speculative leaps required to initiate feminist history" (391).

24. Similarly, while the women's accounts do not describe particular machines or inventions that aided in their housework, outside accounts associated Brook Farm with "progress" in this regard as well. Without providing details, articles make reference to Brook Farm women benefiting from "the present state of science" and "the devices of our mechanical age" (Lane 352; Brownson 493).

25. Another former member remembered Ripley's laundry acumen a bit differently: "The elegant Mrs. Ripley is said to have worked ten hours in the day in the laundry at times; but what I would imply is that a skilled laundress might have done the same work in six hours, perhaps better" (Salisbury).

3. Professional Rhetorics

1. As Donald Durnbaugh points out, there's something of a paradox in the fact that the most successful utopian communities—largely German pietist communities like the Harmonists—have received less public and scholarly attention than the infamous failures of the transcendentalists, Owenites, and Fourierists (72). This paradox is likely attributable to the ideological resonances between the latter experiments and contemporary political and social norms,

but I also explore the popular preoccupation with utopia and failure in my final chapter.

2. A terminological clarification: while the community's name is the Harmony Society, their settlement in Pennsylvania was called Economy. As a result, I refer to both the "Harmonists" or the "Harmony Society" and to life "in Economy" throughout this chapter as I consider women's work in this community.

3. As I discuss below, the Harmonists' policy on celibacy was an on-again, off-again affair.

4. For example, Deborah Cannarella emphasizes that Gertrude Rapp continued in her grandfather's tradition as a leader in business rather than religion (40). Emily Lapisardi's more recent article focuses on how Gertrude Rapp managed to be accepted as a cultured lady by the worldly model and still a much-respected member of the Harmony Society (32).

5. My use of "anagrammatical" derives from Christina Sharpe's *In the Wake* and is discussed in greater detail in the conclusion to this chapter.

6. Pennsylvania as a whole experienced rapid industrialization in the nineteenth century, with workers in agriculture dropping from 68 percent of the workforce in 1820 to just 17 percent in 1900 (Greenwald 3).

7. One exception is a covenant adopted on February 15, 1805, which included a commitment to extend "to the widows and orphans of any member, the same rights and maintenance . . . as long as they shall live or remain members of the community" (Williams 50). Still, this provision refers to a special class of women, not to female members as a whole.

8. The revised 1827 constitution includes a preface explaining that the community's principles, "being faithfully derived from the sacred Scriptures, include the Government of the Patriarchal Age, united to the Community of Property" (qtd. in Arndt, *George Rapp's Harmony Society* 355). Of course, "patriarchal" here referred more to Rapp's unquestioned authority over *all* members than to women's position vis-à-vis men's.

9. At the same time, familial and paternalistic structures continued to operate in the community: for instance, when signing the community's articles, men's signatures were witnessed by Rapp and two elders, while women's signatures were witnessed by a father, older brother, or husband (A. Ott 26).

10. Visitors compared Harmonist workers with the degraded and downtrodden status of impoverished workers in the United States and Europe. As James Buckingham, a visitor and member of the British Parliament, wrote:

> The great charm about these labours of the Rappists, is, that no one appears to be over-worked, or under-fed; none are without abundance of clean and comfortable apparel; there are in their factories no children,

> whose strength is taxed beyond its power to bear: there is no anxiety on the mind of a single being, as to a stoppage of the works, a loss of employment, a reduction of wages, or any of those vicissitudes, which place before many an English operative the choice between a prison, a poor-house, or emigration. (qtd. in Arndt, *George Rapp's Years of Glory* 477)

11. The *Silk Letter Book* contains outgoing correspondence from 1842 to 1847. Of the approximately seventy-five letters in the book, around a third are signed "Gertrude Rapp," another third are unsigned, and a handful of the remaining third are written on Gertrude's behalf by other Harmonists involved in the silk business. Other than Gertrude, Harmony trustee Romelius (R. L.) Baker is the most frequent letter writer, with occasional letters from George Rapp or Jacob Henrici, another trustee. Many of the unsigned letters respond to letters addressed to Gertrude Rapp, but the identity of the respondents is impossible to determine. As the letters in the *Silk Letter Book* are copies and were most likely not transcribed by the original authors, a handwriting analysis would be inconclusive. In addition, because Rapp's English was superior to several of the male leaders', George Rapp's in particular, several scholars have noted that her role in his correspondence is difficult to determine (Lapisardi 29). Here, I have focused my analysis on letters signed "Gertrude Rapp."

12. Material feminist Susan Hekman deploys Andrew Pickering's term "mangle" as a noun or verb to describe combinations of material and social agencies (94).

13. See M. Smith, "In Rosie's Shadow," for an examination of patriotism as a method of expanding notions of women's work during World War II.

14. As Anne Witz explains, professionalism is boundary work that distinguishes between professions and practitioners. Witz identifies two primary tactics used to create or enforce professional boundaries: legalistic tactics, which enlist the state, and credentialist tactics, "which describe the use of educational certificates and accreditation to monitor and restrict access to occupational positions" (676).

15. In the end, the tariff sought by Rapp and other advocates of the silk cause was unsuccessful. It applied only to finished goods, making it easy to procure unfinished silk from abroad, and this legislative failure, along with the technological improvements that made it possible for large mills to produce silk cloth from unfinished silk, undermined hand-raising, -reeling, and -weaving ventures like the Harmonists' (Field et al. xxii).

16. Louise Weil, a German visitor from the Württemberg region, described her treatment in America as follows: "People who are cultured and educated are treated brutally . . . not much better than slaves. . . . everywhere in America

the spirit and the heart are ignored while money is everything. One hears: 'She is worth $10,000' or 'She is worth nothing'" (19). Assumed to be uneducated and gullible, German emigrants were subject to a host of schemes and manipulations, starting from their voyage overseas. Agents offered free passage to America only to entrap the travelers once they had arrived: those "who didn't have the funds or money found they had to stay on the ship until they were sold. . . . The chosen one is bound in writing on paper for five or ten years; they can't read English" (Boke 51). For the most unfortunate, passage to America bore the high cost of entering oneself or one's children into indentured servitude.

17. James Daybell and Andrew Gordon's recent collection on women's epistolary agency usefully expands our understanding of the gendered functions of this historical genre.

18. Briefly, the process of silk raising is as follows: the silk eggs are stored in a cool place until they are warm and prepared to hatch; the caterpillar, or silkworm, emerges from the egg and feeds on mulberry leaves (this stage lasts about thirty days); the silkworm expels a sticky liquid and spins a cocoon from roughly half a mile of liquid silk; the creature left inside the cocoon, the chrysalis, is killed with steam, boiling water, or frost; and, finally, the silky threads of the cocoon are unwound, washed, and twisted into silk thread. Among the other intricacies of this process, Harmonist women were responsible for dyeing the silk: instructions in the Old Economy Village Archives record methods such as creating blue silk using "a mixture of cyanide potassium and sulphuric acid" ("Instructions").

19. This passage most likely refers to the practice of placing silkworm eggs in a tin box enclosed in a wood one and lowered into a hole in an ice house (Field et al. 47).

20. Wells notes that, though it is hard for us "to imagine the contingency and openness of nineteenth-century medicine," at the time it was easier to become a doctor than a minister (7).

21. Schetterly was not alone in pondering textile manufacture as an employment for women and children: Frederick Rapp was subpoenaed by a U.S. House of Representatives committee to report on the Harmonists' woolen manufactory, including, among other things, the sex and age of the workers (Arndt, *George Rapp's Harmony Society* 386).

22. In 1845, just 7 percent of the Lowell workforce was Irish—by the early 1850s, half the textile workers in Lowell and other mill towns were Irish (Freeman 74).

23. As William Passavant explained, the central street was occupied by "the most influential members, and those who originally invested the largest capital," while those "whose interest was little or nothing, inhabit the squares most distant from the center" (qtd. in Arndt, *George Rapp's Years of Glory* 485).

24. In 1829, the community received a letter from a "Count Leon" claiming to be a European aristocrat desirous of joining the community. Upon his arrival, the community learned that Count Leon was really Bernhard Müller, a professional explorer who staunchly opposed celibacy. Eventually George Rapp bribed him to leave, but the damage had been done: Müller took with him a sizable group of Harmonists, an event that became known as the Secession of 1832.

25. This framing underscores the argument that women's work is less threatening when presented as the result of happenstance or serendipity rather than ambition, intention, or curiosity (see Hallenbeck, "Inventing," and Greer).

26. Women who worked in mills seem to have developed a taste for a different kind of life: mill girls tended to marry later than women who stayed at home, were far less likely to marry a farmer, and were more likely to live in a city (Freeman 63). As Joshua Freeman explains, "the mill experience accelerated the transition out of a world of semi-subsistence agriculture into an emerging commercial society" (63).

27. Weil notes that the Economy hotel is run by "four ladies in ages from 50–70," including Melina Wagner, an immigrant who moved her entire family to Economy, "where she happily is working as a servant in the hotel" (16). In addition, Jacob Silvan of the Zoar community in Ohio corresponded with Baker about both communities' need for maids, noting that "when German immigrants passed Zoar on their way West via the Ohio Canal, it was easier to find German maids than now when the train passes through Cleveland" (qtd. in Arndt, *George Rapp's Harmony Society* 565).

28. See, for example, Arndt, *George Rapp's Harmony Society* (651, 838).

29. The community's celibacy brought them "a world-wide, unenviable notoriety," including a satirical memorialization in Lord Byron's "Don Juan": "When Rapp the Harmonist embargo'd marriage/ In his harmonious settlement,/ Why called he 'Harmony' a state sans wedlock?/ Now here I've got the preacher at a dead-lock" (Nevin). New England clergy intensely opposed lay vows of celibacy. Celibacy was seen as a threat to political and social order and a disavowal of manifest destiny's exhortation to be fruitful and multiply. The fear and distrust of individuals outside family structures is exemplified by the weekly twenty-shilling tax on "lone-men" in Hartford, Connecticut, for the "selfish luxury of living alone" (Seeman 405).

30. On the one hand, middle-class women were meant to be passionless and pure; the cult of true womanhood held that the ideal woman was essentially asexual. On the other hand, attitudes toward celibate women focused less on their sexuality than on their childlessness and lack of maternal qualities. One ex-Shaker, for example, noted that celibacy made women unwomanly: they had unusually harsh voices and "belched" their words (qtd. in Chmielewski et al.

140). At its most extreme, the public consensus on celibate women viewed them as monstrous beings. Such attitudes manifest in occurrences like the physical attack on Mother Ann Lee, founder of the Shakers, to determine whether a leader who advocated celibacy could actually be a biological woman.

31. For instance, Applegarth shows how female anthropologists at times portrayed an unrealistically welcoming view of the field as a "not-yet-realized vision" of the profession they hoped to build and a means of recruiting other women ("Field Guides" 203).

32. As Enoch explains regarding the relationship between domestic scientists and feminism,

> Domestic scientists may not have been feminists, but they were active rhetorical agents who creatively engineered spaces to invent a new ethos for themselves and claim new educational as well as professional opportunities. I suspect that as feminist scholars continue to explore rhetorical questions concerning women and work, they may find even more evidence of tense relationships with feminism. For many working women, to associate with feminist causes might have come at too high a cost—financially, professionally, educationally, ideologically, or personally. (*Domestic Occupations* 116)

4. Reproductive Rhetorics

1. This area was a rich hub of revivalist activity. Besides Oneida, the region housed three Owenite communities, seven Fouriest phalanxes, and the Millerites (later the Seventh Day Adventists). Joseph Smith received his revelations regarding the Mormon faith ninety miles west of Oneida, in Palmyra, New York.

2. In Putney, charges of adultery followed on the heels of Noyes's decree that he and his community would begin practicing complex marriage in 1847. After his indictment, Noyes fled Putney and eventually settled in Oneida, New York, in early 1848.

3. See Mattingly for a detailed account of the relationship between nineteenth-century women's rights rhetorics and changes in women's dress. Among others, Mattingly details the innovative dress of Frances Wright, an early female rhetorician whose "Turkish trousers" were inspired by women's dress in Robert Owen's New Harmony community. Wright went on to found her own intentional community, Nashoba, an infamous and short-lived interracial venture in Tennessee.

4. This passage from Noyes's autobiographer Robert Allerton Parker is representative in its approach to Oneida and other midcentury intentional communities:

> No theory of social organization seemed so fantastic that it could not attract a little band of fanatical adherents. The very expanse of the North American continent, across which, even at the middle of the nineteenth century, the white race had as yet but faintly penciled in a vague outline of its civilization, invited social experimentation. . . . To the dissatisfied, the gullible, the maladjusted and the adventurous, excursion rates to Utopia were offered by reformers, fanatics, or mere madmen gifted with the power of persuasion. (145)

Such accounts are equally ungenerous to the leaders and followers of these movements.

5. While the physical processes of reproduction are hardly universal, as the increasing medicalization of conception, pregnancy, and childbirth have demonstrated, the cultural associations of motherhood—with their attending notions of good and bad, fit and unfit mothers—also differ dramatically with context and circumstance. For instance, the contemporary construct of intensive mothering—based in the assumptions that women are not complete without children, that women make the best primary caretakers, and that motherhood requires extreme devotion and self-sacrifice—arose as recently as the 1980s (see O'Reilly and Douglas and Michaels). Yet some resist this dominant construct, as in African American communities where "othermothering" or "community mothering," informal or formal arrangements where individuals care for a child that is not their own, are common (see James).

6. As feminist rhetoricians have shown, nineteenth-century women rhetors often deployed reproductive rhetorics that articulated motherhood as a motive and qualification for their activism and engagement beyond the home (see Harris; Tonn; and Buchanan, *Rhetorics*). Such women used "maternalism," a rhetorical strategy that "accepted, even idealized, women's traditional role as wife and mother but at the same time insisted that women had a duty to extend their female skills and concerns beyond their own homes" (Clapp 3). At the same time, such rhetorics were circumscribed by the nineteenth-century code of motherhood, which opposed maternity to public and civic roles, including work outside the home.

7. Here, I join other feminist rhetoricians who have demonstrated the interconnection of reproductive and professional rhetorics. See, for instance, Jessica Enoch's analysis of how the ideograph of <home> was used first to support and then undermine working mothers ("There's No Place"). Similarly, Robin Jensen's analysis of infertility articulates the intersections of women's reproductive and professional roles: "Long before the twentieth century, women's lack of success in bearing children was attributed to immorality, sexual

perversion, strenuous intellectual work, and so-called masculine professional aspirations" (6).

8. Noyes's *Slavery and Marriage* satirized the similarities between "the arguments southerners used to justify slavery and northerners used to defend indissoluble marriage" (Passet 66). Among the more trenchant aspects of this comparison is Noyes's counterargument to the notion that married women seem happier, superficially, than unmarried women and old maids: "These outsiders, my friend, are the '*free negroes*' of the marriage system—that is, their position and degradation result from the existence of Marriage, just as the degradation of the free blacks results from the existence of Slavery" (*Third Annual Report* 32).

9. The practice of mutual criticism is usually attributed to the Oneida Community, but Noyes claims he learned the practice from a "select society" of missionaries for the Congregational Church that he met during his time at the Theological Seminary at Andover, Massachusetts (J. Noyes 5).

10. For one thing, the practice of ascending and descending fellowship meant that young women who spurned older lovers were seen as less sincere in their faith. Furthermore, unwillingness to participate might be interpreted as evidence of harboring "special love": one account reported that some women would entertain multiple partners "without complaint simply to gain the confidence of those in charge of such things so that she would be allowed to associate with some one she loved" (Van de Warker 789–90). Due to these and other pressures, the female refusal rate at Oneida was "probably low," and never "a problem" (Dalsimer 115). Grimace.

11. This number was calculated as follows: roughly 100 women of child-bearing age in Oneida bore 36 children—5 planned and 31 accidental—over 21 years (1848–69) (Carden 51). This figure (children born annually to each woman—.0171) was multiplied by 1,000 to correspond with the practice used in calculating the national fertility rate.

12. Noyes was not the only leader who realized that unregulated reproduction would compound the challenges of communal life. Of the five hundred utopian communities in nineteenth-century America, most—including the celibate Harmony Society—practiced some form of population control (Cirillo 261).

13. As George Bernard Shaw explained, many "members of the community" had "succeeded so well in capitalistic commerce and in conventional society that they desire nothing but the completest possible oblivion for their extremely unconventional origin" ("To Hope Emily Allen," 19 Nov. 1924).

14. Among the gendered conventions exposed and challenged, the change to women's hair and dress was perhaps the most discussed in the community's publications. As one article in the *Circular* explains, the women's defense of the costume was directly linked to women's work:

> The short dress worn in our Communities. . . . is already adopted, quite extensively we should judge, as a form of *convenience.* It is the kitchen costume in many of the farm-houses and rural villages around here. . . . Many a kitchen door discovers a woman in pantalettes. She is a little shy, possibly, and steps one side if too strictly observed. . . . But her apology is the work she is about at the sink or wash-tub, which is lightened one-half by her riddance from the trammels of long petticoats. ("About Dress," emphasis in original)

The discussion of dress at Oneida echoed the larger dress reform movement in its connection to women's rights. As one writer proclaimed, "Woman cannot be free or great, with limbs swathed in long skirts, the vital organs compressed to half their natural size, and bound in stays" ("Bloomer Dress in Winter"). Urging other women on, they insisted that if women were not "brave enough to resist the despotism of the avaricious and silly of their own sex, they can never hope to become great states-women or to throw off the yoke of that tyrant man. . . . Short dresses are absolutely essential to women's rights" ("Dress Question").

15. The community's greatest early challenge was determining how to support itself. Fortunately, Noyes was effective at recruiting members with capital: by 1857, members had invested $108,000, $40,000 of which was drained before the community started to turn a profit (Carden 39).

16. Oneida would eventually make and sell six sizes of traps to buyers in the United States, Canada, South America, Russia, and Australia (Myers 193).

17. Such separations were not unique: other offenses such as "special love"—engaging in a monogamous relationship—were addressed through criticism, or, if that proved ineffectual, by sending one of the parties to the community at Wallingford ("Special Love"). Noyes was also known to restrict sexual privileges, though this punishment was more often applied to men (Vickers 15).

18. Criticisms of women often focused on their failure to submit to male authority or comply with gender roles. For instance, Harriet Matthews "received a sincere criticism . . . in regard to my relations to my brothers" and found herself "criticised for lack of meekness & respect, for assuming superiority & making them feel small" (19).

19. Predictably, some women protested the conflict between the community's idealistic attack on traditional gender roles and practical reliance on the idea of women as inherent nurturers. As the prominent leader Harriet Worden intoned in a sardonic letter to Noyes:

> If it were right to envy, I should envy the men. They are so wise and strong; and so confident, withal, in their wisdom & strength. They form such great plans, and are able to talk about them in such a large,

> disinterested way . . . that their opinions *pass for what they are worth*, every time. But woman, *per contra*, is such a creature of feeling she can scarcely give her views entirely free from personalities, and hence her judgment is received doubtfully. . . . She may feel as deeply, know as intelligently, & understand as thoroughly the premises in a certain case as her 'lord & master' man! But being a woman is evidence against her—she meekly bows to fate, and retires from the field of argument to attend babies and make pancakes. (Klaw n135, emphasis in original)

As this passage illustrates, though the realities of life at Oneida did not always live up to its ideals, those ideals inspired some women to critique sexism and misogynism in the community.

20. Lindal Buchanan ("Few Good") and Sarah Moseley explore this dynamic with relation to women in the navy and women firefighters, respectively.

21. Jordynn Jack's analysis of female factory workers and scientists in World War II suggests that these rhetorical strategies of difference extended across blue- and white-collar jobs: "Like their industrial worker counterparts, women scientists found themselves mostly channeled into appropriately 'feminine' areas of science or subordinate positions on wartime projects" (*Science* 2). Kristy Maddux describes similar patterns in the late nineteenth century regarding male-dominated fields such as finance (117).

22. Bronzing is a printing method where wet ink is dusted with bronzed powder to create an iridescent, metallic effect.

23. Similar arguments designated clerical work as "women's work" in the late nineteenth and early twentieth centuries (see England and Boyer).

24. As Jessica Enoch explains, ideographs like <home>—or, in this case, <family>—are flexible designators whose deployment has direct consequences for the nature and valuing of women's work ("There's No Place" 429).

25. Motherly behavior can also serve as a rhetorical strategy to negotiate gender in the workplace, as Enoch describes: "In the lab, [Ellen] Richards defused the perceived strangeness of the gendered situation by taking on traditional domestic duties, from mending her male classmates' clothes to sweeping the laboratory floor" (*Domestic Occupation* 87).

26. Midcentury domestic literature emphasized this role. For instance, Catharine Sedgwick's 1837 *Live and Let Live; Or, Domestic Service Illustrated* framed supervision of servants as benevolence "to the domestic and through her to all the poor" (Dudden 166).

27. The interanimation of Oneida's social and labor systems meant that women faced a potentially hostile work environment and were subject to implicit or explicit quid pro quo intimidation. The narrative of birth control at Oneida

thus supports the contentions of feminist scholars who caution that "'control' in sexual and reproductive matters too often supports a view of 'sex without consequences' that in fact alienates women from their bodies and, rather than freeing them to explore their sexuality, actually subjects them to male sexual dominance" (Ruhl 643).

28. Daniel Smith's research demonstrates that the presumed inverse relation of work and motherhood does not hold true in the nineteenth century. Ninety percent of nineteenth-century American women married, and 95 percent of those women did not work outside the home, "yet women progressively bore fewer and fewer children" (122). Between 1800 and 1900 the total U.S. fertility rate decreased by half, with at least half to three-quarters of the decline attributable to the reduction of fertility in marriage (122).

29. Nineteenth-century eugenics debates are examined in *Evolutionary Rhetoric*. As Wendy Hayden contends, those earlier eugenics arguments, unlike those of the twentieth century, were focused less on class and race issues directly than on women's health, productivity, and notions of ideal motherhood resulting in exceptional children (212–13).

30. Similarly, Enoch's *Domestic Occupations* shows how nondeliberate spatial rhetorics "enabled the respectable white middle-class woman to move from one iteration of domestic space to another. Because the school was now a home, the woman could now become a teacher" (57).

5. Arguments on the Landscape

1. Similar arguments about women's work countering an exaggerated focus on civic rhetorics and suffrage are articulated by Hallenbeck and Smith, as well as Maddux.

2. Drafted by Elizabeth Cady Stanton and presented at the Seneca Falls Convention of 1848, the Declaration includes the following in its list of grievances men have inflicted on women: "He has taken from her all right in property, even to the wages she earns," and "he has monopolized nearly all the profitable employments, and from those she is permitted to follow, she receives but a scanty remuneration" (qtd. in Kraditor 185). At the last session, Lucretia Mott added the following, which was unanimously adopted: "Resolved, That the speedy success of our cause depends upon the zealous and untiring efforts of both men and women, for the overthrow of the monopoly of the pulpit, and for the securing to woman an equal participation with men in the various trades, professions, and commerce" (qtd. in Kraditor 188). Importantly, the Declaration includes both the right to work and the vote *within its understanding of citizenship*.

3. My use of "disclosure" is inspired by Hekman's definition of the term, which she adapts from philosopher of science Joseph Rouse (95, 111).

4. While men's weekly hours of housework (four) has doubled from that same measure in 1965, that number has remained fairly constant since 1995 (Bianchi et al.). And these patterns are continuing into the next generation: a 2018 *New York Times* article reported that girls spend more time on household chores than boys do, are paid less for doing chores, and receive smaller allowances (C. Miller, "Generationally Perpetuated").

5. Domestic workers staff the homes not only of the wealthy but also of middle-class professionals and people of modest means: a recent survey of New Yorkers found that one-fifth of those surveyed employed domestic workers, and most employers had household incomes of $99,999 or less (Enlow).

6. This exclusion is due in large part to racism: southern congressional representatives refused to support the labor law provisions of the New Deal if they included farm and domestic workers, two populations composed largely of African Americans (Feliciano and Segal). To this day, these groups are excluded from the National Labor Relations Act and the Fair Labor Standards Act.

7. For instance, Ellen Pao's prominent but unsuccessful lawsuit against her former employer Kleiner Perkins likely inspired other women to speak out against their own professional discrimination—a phenomenon dubbed "the Pao effect" (Zhou).

8. The *Atlantic* reports that, "as women take over male-dominated fields, pay drops by double-digit percentage points" (Lam, "Socialization").

9. A recent account of a modern-day utopian settlement describes its leader as "indifferent" to a lack of food and "obsessive" in focus, similar to *Star Trek*'s Spock in his "deliberate diction" and "unwavering high-mindedness" (Eakin).

10. Public memories of utopia, it seems, also move in waves: Oneida and Brook Farm were designated as National Historic Landmarks in 1965, the same year that Old Economy was added to the National Register of Historic Places.

11. As the nineteenth century progressed, other communal housekeeping experiments followed in the footsteps of Brook Farm. Among the more radical of these efforts was Melusina Fay Peirce's series of proposals in the *Atlantic Monthly* in 1868. Peirce later claimed, with some justice, that the acclaimed utopian novels of Edward Bellamy (*Looking Backward*, 1888) and Charlotte Perkins Gilman (*Herland*, 1915) stole her ideas. Gilman's lesser known *What Diantha Did* (1912) also imagined housework as an industry. Dolores Hayden's *Grand Domestic Revolution* traces the history of cooperative housekeeping, locating the first demand for pay for housework in 1868 and the end of the movement with the Hoover Report on Home Building and Home Ownership in 1931, which advocated single-family home ownership (8).

12. In the short term, Oneida's use of birth control alongside complex marriage was so reviled that the community was a direct target of the 1873

Comstock Laws, federal obscenity laws that "classified all information concerning contraception as lewd, lascivious and obscene, and forbade the dissemination by the United States mails of all literature on the subject" (R. Parker 267). But there is also a significant positive link between Oneida and the early birth control movement. Historian Linda Gordon describes the Oneidans as part of a small group of radicals whose "influence was greater than their size," especially when it came to women's and reproductive rights (72). She maintains that "the specific ideology that stimulated feminism was the exploration of sex radicalism by American perfectionists" (89).

WORKS CITED

Abbott, Edith. *Women in Industry*. Arno, 1969.

"About Dress." *Circular*, 18 July 1864, Box 17, Oneida Community Collection, Special Collections Research Center, Syracuse University Libraries.

Adams, Heather. "Goodbye, 'Post-pill Paradise:' Texturing Feminist Public Memories of Women's Reproductive and Rhetorical Agency." *Quarterly Journal of Speech*, vol. 105, no. 4, 2019, pp. 390–417.

Apple, Rima D. "Constructing Mothers: Scientific Motherhood in the Nineteenth and Twentieth Centuries." *The Society for the Social History of Medicine*, vol. 8, no. 2, 1995, 161–78.

Applegarth, Risa. "Field Guides: Women Writing Anthropology." *Women and Rhetoric Between the Wars*, edited by Ann George, M. Elizabeth Weiser, and Janet Zepernick, Southern Illinois UP, 2013, pp. 193–208.

———. *Rhetoric in American Anthropology: Gender, Genre, and Science*. U of Pittsburgh P, 2014.

Aristotle. *Physics*. Translated by R. P. Hardie and R. K. Gaye, 350 B.C.E. *The Internet Classics Archive*, classics.mit.edu/Aristotle/physics.html. Accessed 15 Mar. 2020.

Arndt, Karl J. R. *George Rapp's Harmony Society 1785–1847*. U of Pennsylvania, 1965.

———. *George Rapp's Years of Glory: Economy on the Ohio, 1834–1847*. Peter Lang, 1987.

Baker, R. L. Letter to Jacob Henrici and Jonathan Lenz. 26 Jan. 1861. Translated by Hilda Kring, Site History Files, Women's History Project. Old Economy Village Archives, Pennsylvania Historical and Museum Commission, Ambridge, PA.

Ballif, Michelle. "Victor J. Vitanza." *Twentieth-Century Rhetorics and Rhetoricians: Critical Studies and Sources*. Greenwood, 2000, pp. 336–42.

Barad, Karen. "Posthumanist Performativity: Toward an Understanding of How Matter Comes to Matter." *Signs*, vol. 28, no. 3, 2003, pp. 801–31.

Barker, Gary. "Why Men's Aversion to Housework Is Stalling Women's Careers." *World Economic Forum*, 7 Mar. 2018, www.weforum.org/agenda/2018/03/mens-aversion-to-housework-stalling-womens-careers. Accessed 16 Mar. 2019.

Baron, Ava, ed. *Work Engendered: Toward a New History of American Labor.* Cornell UP, 1991.

Bazerman, Charles. "Letters and the Social Grounding of Differentiated Genres." *Letter Writing as a Social Practice*, edited by D. Barton and N. Hall, John Benjamins, 2000, pp. 15–30.

Bazerman, Charles, and James G. Paradis, editors. *Textual Dynamics of the Professions: Historical and Contemporary Studies of Writing in Professional Communities.* U of Wisconsin P, 1991.

Beecher, Catharine E. *Domestic Receipt Book.* Harper and Brothers, 1850.

———. *Treatise on Domestic Economy.* Harper and Brothers, 1848.

Beecher, Catharine E., and Harriet Beecher Stowe. *The American Woman's Home.* J. B. Ford, 1869.

Bennett, Jane. *Vibrant Matter: A Political Ecology of Things.* Duke UP, 2009.

Bianchi, Suzanne M., Liana C. Sayer, Melissa A. Milkie, and John P. Robinson. "Housework: Who Did, Does or Will Do It, and How Much Does It Matter?" *Social Forces*, vol. 91, no. 1, 2012, pp. 55–63.

Bick, Carolyn. "Invisible Women: Domestic Workers Underpaid and Abused." *Aljazeera*, 21 Oct. 2017, www.aljazeera.com/news/2017/10/invisible-women-domestic-workers-underpaid-abused-171019104144316.html. Accessed 16 Mar. 2019.

Biesecker, Barbara. "Coming to Terms with Recent Attempts to Write Women into the History of Rhetoric." *Walking and Talking Feminist Rhetorics: Landmark Essays and Controversies*, edited by Lindal Buchanan and Kathleen J. Ryan, Parlor, 2010, pp. 337–51.

Blackwell, Marilyn S. "The Republication Vision of Mary Palmer Tyler." *Mothers and Motherhood: Readings in American History*, edited by Rima D. Apple and Janet Golden, Ohio State UP, 1997, pp. 31–51.

Blair, Carole. "Contemporary US Memorial Sites as Exemplars of Rhetoric's Materiality." *Rhetorical Bodies*, edited by Jack Selzer and Sharon Crowley, U of Wisconsin P, 1999, pp. 16–57.

"The Bloomer Dress in Winter." *Circular*, 8 Feb. 1852, Box 17, Oneida Community Collection, Special Collections Research Center, Syracuse University Libraries.

Boke, Liwwat. *Liwwat Boke 1807–1882 Pioneer.* Minster Historical Society, 1987.

Bordelon, Suzanne. "'Private Letters' for Public Audiences: The Complexities of Ethos in Louise Clappe's The Shirley Letters from the California Mines, 1851–52." *Rhetoric Review*, vol. 37, no. 8, 2017, pp. 1–13.

Boris, Eileen, and Rachel Salazar Parreñas, editors. *Intimate Labors: Care, Sex, and Domestic Work.* Stanford UP, 2010.

Bourdieu, Pierre. *Outline of a Theory of Practice.* Cambridge UP, 1977.

Boydston, Jeanne. *Home and Work: Housework, Wages, and the Ideology of Labor in the Early Republic.* Oxford UP, 1990.

———. "To Earn Her Daily Bread: Housework and Antebellum Working-Class Subsistence." *Radical History Review*, vol. 35, 1986, pp. 7–25.

———. "The Woman Who Wasn't There: Women's Market Labor and the Transition to Capitalism in the United States." *Journal of the Early Republic*, vol. 16, no. 2, 1996, pp. 183–206.

"Brook Farm." *Voice of Industry*, 18 Oct. 1847.

"Brook Farm: A Social Enterprise." *Frank Leslie's Illustrated Newspaper*, 25 Apr. 1874, p. 102.

"Brook Farm: Seven Golden Years of an Experiment." *American Socialist*, 12 June 1879.

"Brook Farm Association." *Boston Cultivator*, 20 July 1844.

Brook Farm Association. *Brook Farm Records.* Microfilm edition, 1 reel, Boston, Massachusetts Historical Society.

———. *Constitution of the Brook Farm Association, for Industry and Education, West Roxbury, Mass. With an Introductory Statement.* I. R. Butts, 1844.

"Brook Farm Did 'Pay.'" *New Haven Register*, 15 Apr. 1895.

"Brook Farm Lecturers." *Harbinger*, 21 Feb. 1846.

Brownson, O. A. "Brook Farm." *United States Magazine and Democratic Review*, Nov. 1842, pp. 481–95.

Buchanan, Lindal. "A Few Good (Wo)Men: Integrating the US Submarine Force." *Rhetoric Review*, vol. 35, no. 1, 2016, pp. 35–48.

———. *Regendering Delivery: The Fifth Canon and Antebellum Women Rhetors.* Southern Illinois UP, 2005.

———. *Rhetorics of Motherhood.* Southern Illinois UP, 2013.

Buchanan, Lindal, and Kathleen J. Ryan, editors. *Walking and Talking Feminist Rhetorics: Landmark Essays and Controversies.* Parlor, 2010.

Burkeman, Oliver. "Dirty Secret: Why Is There Still a Housework Gender Gap?" *Guardian*, 17 Feb. 2018.

Butler, Judith. "Performative Acts and Gender Constitution: An Essay in Phenomenology and Feminist Theory." *Theatre Journal*, vol. 40, no. 4, 1988, pp. 519–31.

Campbell, Karlyn Kohrs. *Man Cannot Speak for Her: A Critical Study of Early Feminist Rhetoric.* Praeger, 1989.

Cannarella, Deborah. "The Story of Gertrude Rapp: Piety, Prosperity, and Lovely Silk Ribbons." *Piecework*, 1994, pp. 43–49.

Carden, Maren. *Oneida: Utopian Community to Modern Corporation.* Syracuse UP, 1998.

"Certificate of Indenture for Hannah, a Woman of Color." 20 Oct. 1817, Manuscript Group 437: Karl Arndt Collection of Harmony Society Materials, Legal File. Old Economy Village Archives, Pennsylvania Historical and Museum Commission, Ambridge, PA.

Chmielewski, Wendy E., Louis J. Kern, and Marlyn Klee-Hartzell, editors. *Women in Spiritual and Communitarian Societies.* Syracuse UP, 1992.

Christoph, Julie Nelson. "Reconceiving Ethos in Relation to the Personal: Strategies of Placement in Pioneer Women's Writing." *College English*, vol. 64, no. 6, 2002, pp. 660–79.

Cirillo, Vincent. "Birth Control in Nineteenth-Century America: A View from Three Contemporaries." *Yale Journal of Biology and Medicine*, vol. 27, 1974, pp. 260–67.

Clapp, Elizabeth. *Mothers of All Children: Women Reformers and the Rise of Juvenile Courts in Progressive Era America.* Penn State UP, 1998.

Coole, Diana, and Samantha Frost, editors. *New Materialisms: Ontology, Agency, and Politics.* Duke UP, 2010.

Coolidge, Mary Roberts. *Why Women Are So.* Henry Holt, 1912.

Cooper, Marilyn M. "Rhetorical Agency as Emergent and Enacted." *College Composition and Communication*, vol. 62, no. 3, 2011, pp. 420–49.

Cowan, Ruth Schwartz. *More Work for Mother: The Ironies of Household Technology from the Open Hearth to the Microwave.* Basic Books, 1985.

"Criticism of ML Prindle." 1871, Box 16, Oneida Community Collection, Special Collections Research Center, Syracuse University Libraries.

Curtis, Edith Roelker. *A Season in Utopia: The Story of Brook Farm.* Thomas Nelson and Sons, 1961.

Dalsimer, Marlyn Hartzell. "Women and Family in the Oneida Community, 1837–1881." Diss., New York University, 1975.

Davis, Rebecca Harding. "The Harmonists." *Atlantic Monthly*, vol. 17, 1866, pp. 529–38.

Daybell, James, and Andrew Gordon, editors. *Women and Epistolary Agency in Early Modern Culture, 1450–1690.* Routledge, 2016.

Delano, Sterling F. *Brook Farm: The Dark Side of Utopia.* Harvard UP, 2004.

———. "'We Have Abolished Domestic Servitude': Women and Work at Brook

Farm." *Toward a Female Genealogy of Transcendentalism*, edited by Jana L. Argersinger and Phyllis Cole, U of Georgia, 2014, pp. 179–206.

Detweiler, Jane, Margaret LaWare, and Patti Wojahn. "Academic Leadership and Advocacy: On Not Leaning In." *College English*, vol. 79, no. 5, 2017, pp. 451–65.

Dingo, Rebecca. Foreword. *Transnational Feminist Rhetorics and Gendered Leadership in Global Politics*, by Rebecca S. Richards, Lexington, 2014, pp. ix-xii.

———. *Networking Arguments: Rhetoric, Transnational Feminism, and Public Policy Writing*. Pittsburgh UP, 2012.

Domosh, Mona, and Joni Seager. *Putting Women in Place: Feminist Geographers Make Sense of the World*. Guilford, 2001.

Douglas, Susan J., and Meredith Michaels. *The Mommy Myth: The Idealization of Motherhood and How It Has Undermined Women*. Free Press, 2004.

Dow, Bonnie J. "Historical Narratives, Rhetorical Narratives, and Woman Suffrage Scholarship." *Rhetoric and Public Affairs*, vol. 2, 1999, pp. 321–40.

"The Dress Question." *Circular*, 8 May 1870, Box 17, Oneida Community Collection, Special Collections Research Center, Syracuse University Libraries.

Dudden, Faye E. *Serving Women: Household Service in Nineteenth-Century America*. Wesleyan, 1985.

Durnbaugh, Donald F. "Work and Hope: The Spirituality of the Radical Pietist Communitarians." *Church History*, vol. 39, no. 1, 1970, pp. 72–90.

Durrwachter, Elisabeth, and Magdalena Weidenbach. Letter "To the Small Community." Undated. Translated by Hilda Kring, Site History Files, Women's History Project. Old Economy Village Archives, Pennsylvania Historical and Museum Commission, Ambridge, PA.

Eakin, Emily. "The Civilization Kit." *New Yorker*, 16 Dec. 2013.

Edbauer, Jenny. "Unframing Models of Public Distribution: From Rhetorical Situation to Rhetorical Ecologies." *Rhetoric Society Quarterly*, vol. 35, no. 4, 2005, pp. 5–24.

England, Kim, and Kate Boyer. "Women's Work: The Feminization and Shifting Meanings of Clerical Work." *Journal of Social History*, vol. 43, no. 2, 2009, pp. 307–40.

Enlow, Callie. "We Need to Talk About the Domestic Workers Making Our Lives Possible." *Make Change*, 25 June 2017, www.makechange.aspiration.com/articles/2017/6/25/we-need-to-talk-about-the-domestic-workers-making-our-lives-possible. Accessed 16 Mar. 2019.

Enoch, Jessica. *Domestic Occupations: Spatial Rhetorics and Women's Work*. Southern Illinois UP, 2019.

———. "Releasing Hold: Feminist Historiography without the Tradition." *Theorizing Histories of Rhetoric*, edited by Michelle Ballif, Southern Illinois UP, 2013, pp. 58–73.

———. "There's No Place Like the Childcare Center: A Feminist Analysis of <Home> in the World War II Era." *Rhetoric Review*, vol. 31, no. 4, 2012, pp. 422–42.

"Family Register." 1 Jan. 1849, Box 7, Oneida Community Collection, Special Collections Research Center, Syracuse University Libraries.

Featherstonhaugh, George, W. *A Canoe Voyage up the Minnay Sotor.* Vol. 1, Minnesota Historical Society, 1970.

Feliciano, Ivette and Corinne Segal. "'You're Mostly Isolated and Alone': Why Some Domestic Workers are Vulnerable to Exploitation." *PBS News Hour*, 12 Aug. 2018, www.pbs.org/newshour/nation/ai-jen-poo-domestic-workers-exploitation. Accessed 16 Mar. 2019.

Felton, R. Todd. *A Journey into the Transcendentalists' New England.* Roaring Forties, 2006.

Field, Jacqueline, Marjorie Senechal, and Madelyn Shaw. *American Silk, 1830–1930: Entrepreneurs and Artifacts.* Texas Tech UP, 2007.

First Annual Report of the Oneida Association: Exhibiting Its History, Principles, and Transactions to Jan. 1, 1849. Digital ed., Department of Special Collections, Syracuse University Library, 2000, pp. 1–66, library.syr.edu/digital/collections/f/FirstAnnualReportOfTheOneidaAssociation. Accessed 19 Mar. 2019.

Fleming, David. "The Space of Argumentation: Urban Design, Civic Discourse, and the Dream of the Good City." *Argumentation*, vol. 12, 1998, pp. 147–66.

Fogarty, Robert S. *Dictionary of American Communal and Utopian History.* Greenwood, 1980.

———. "Oneida: A Utopian Search for Religious Security." *Labor History*, vol. 14, 1973, pp. 202–27.

Foster, Lawrence. "Free Love and Feminism: John Humphrey Noyes and the Oneida Community." *Journal of the Early Republic*, vol. 1, no. 2, 1981, pp. 165–83.

———. *Religion and Sexuality: The Shakers, the Mormons, and the Oneida Community.* Oxford UP, 1981.

———. "The Rise and Fall of Utopia: The Oneida Community Crises of 1852 and 1879." *Communal Societies*, vol. 8, 1988, pp. 1–17.

———. "Sex and Conflict in New Religious Movements: A Comparison of the Oneida Community under John Humphrey Noyes and the Early Mormons under Joseph Smith and His Would-Be Successors." *Nova Religio: The Journal of Alternative and Emergent Religions*, vol. 13, no. 3, 2010, pp. 34–58.

———. *Women, Family, and Utopia: Communal Experiments of the Shakers, the Oneida Community, and the Mormons.* Syracuse UP, 1991.

The Fourth Exhibition of the Massachusetts Charitable Mechanic Association, at Quincy Hall, in the City of Boston, September 16, 1844. Crocker and Brewster, 1844.

Freeman, Joshua B. *Behemoth: A History of the Factory and the Making of the Modern World.* Norton, 2018.

Freibert, Lucy. "Creative Women of Brook Farm." *Women in Spiritual and Communitarian Societies in the United States*, edited by Wendy E. Chmielewski, Louis J. Kern, and Marlyn Klee-Hartzell, Syracuse UP, 1993, pp. 75–88.

Funk, Cary, and Kim Parker. "Women and Men in STEM Often at Odds over Workplace Equity." *Pew Research Center*, 9 Jan. 2018, www.pewsocialtrends.org/2018/01/09/women-and-men-in-stem-often-at-odds-over-workplace-equity. Accessed 16 Mar. 2019.

Gaard, Greta. "Reproductive Technology, or Reproductive Justice? An Ecofeminist, Environmental Justice Perspective on the Rhetoric of Choice." *Ethics and the Environment*, vol. 15, no. 2, 2010, pp. 103–29.

Gamber, Wendy. *The Female Economy: The Millinery and Dressmaking Trades, 1860–1930.* U of Illinois P, 1997.

Garrison, Stephen, and Joel Myerson. "Elizabeth Curson's Letters from Brook Farm." *Resources for American Literary Study*, vol. 12, 1982, pp. 1–28.

"George Ripley and the Brook Farm Association." *Littell's Living Age*, 1 Dec. 1860, pp. 571–73.

Gere, Anne Ruggles. *Intimate Practices: Literacy and Cultural Work in U.S. Women's Clubs, 1880–1920.* U of Illinois P, 1997.

Gilman, Charlotte Perkins. *Women and Economics.* Small, Maynard, and Co., 1898.

"A Girl's Recollections of Brook Farm School." *Overland Monthly and Out West Magazine*, Sept. 1918, p. 233.

Glenn, Cheryl. *Rhetoric Retold: Regendering the Tradition from Antiquity through the Renaissance.* Southern Illinois UP, 1997.

Gold, David. "Remapping Revisionist Historiography." *College Composition and Communication*, vol. 64, no. 1, 2012, pp. 15–34.

Golden, Janet. "The New Motherhood and the New View of Wet Nurses, 1780–1865." *Mothers and Motherhood: Readings in American History*, edited by Rima D. Apple and Janet Golden, Ohio State UP, 1997, pp. 72–89.

Gordon, Linda. *Woman's Body, Woman's Right: Birth Control in America.* Penguin, 1990.

Graf, Nikki, Anna Brown, and Eileen Patten. "The Narrowing, but Persistent, Gender Gap in Pay." *Pew Research Center*, 9 Apr. 2018, www.pewresearch.org/fact-tank/2018/04/09/gender-pay-gap-facts. Accessed 16 Mar. 2019.

Greenwald, Maurine. "Women and Pennsylvania Working-Class History." Pennsylvania Historical and Museum Commission Staff Seminar, January 1993, Site History Files, Women's History Project. Old Economy Village Archives, Pennsylvania Historical and Museum Commission, Ambridge, PA.

Greer, Jane. "Profiting from Rhetorical Domesticity: Fashion Magnate Nell Donnelly Reed's Discursive Seams, 1916–1956." *Women and Work: Rhetorics of Gender and Labor*, edited by David Gold and Jessica Enoch, U of Pittsburgh, 2019, pp. 158–71.

Grinde, Bjorn, Ragnhild Bang Nes, Ian F. MacDonald, and David Sloan Wilson. "Quality of Life in Intentional Communities." *Social Indicators Research*, vol. 137, 2018, pp. 625–40.

Grosz, Elizabeth. *Volatile Bodies.* Indiana UP, 1994.

Gura, Philip F. *American Transcendentalism: A History.* Hill and Wang, 2007.

Haines, Michael. "Fertility and Mortality in the United States." *EH.Net Encyclopedia*, edited by Robert Whaples, 19 Mar. 2008, eh.net/encyclopedia/fertility-and-mortality-in-the-united-states/. Accessed 15 Mar. 2020.

Hallenbeck, Sarah. "Inventing Feminine Ingenuity: The Gendered Tropes of Space, Motive, Training, and Scope." *Rhetoric Review*, vol. 37, no. 3, 2018, pp. 259–72.

———. "Resituating Rhetorical Failure: The Case of Nineteenth-Century Metallurgist Carrie Everson." *Women and Work: Rhetorics of Gender and Labor*, edited by David Gold and Jessica Enoch, U of Pittsburgh, 2019, pp. 69–83.

———. "Toward a Posthuman Perspective: Feminist Rhetorical Methodologies and Everyday Practices." *Advances in the History of Rhetoric*, vol. 15, 2012, pp. 9–27.

Hallenbeck, Sarah, and Michelle Smith. "Mapping *Topoi* in the Rhetorical Gendering of Work." *Peitho*, vol. 17, no. 2, 2015, pp. 200–25.

Halloran, S. Michael. "From Rhetoric to Composition: The Teaching of Writing in America to 1900." *A Short History of Writing Instruction*, edited by James J. Murphy, Hermagoras, 1990, pp. 151–82.

Haraszti, Zoltan. *The Idyll of Brook Farm: As Revealed by Unpublished Letters in the Boston Public Library.* Trustees of the Public Library, 1937.

Hardy, Robert. "'Housekeeping Hereafter': The Preservation of Domesticity in a Technological Utopia." *Utopian Studies*, vol. 13, no. 2, 2002, pp. 53–66.

Harris, Leslie. "Motherhood, Race, and Gender: The Rhetoric of Women's Antislavery Activism in the *Liberty Bell* Giftbooks." *Women's Studies in Communication*, vol. 32, no. 3, 2009, pp. 293–319.

Hawthorne, Nathaniel. *The Blithedale Romance.* Ticknor and Fields, 1852.

Hayden, Dolores. *The Grand Domestic Revolution: A History of Feminist Designs for American Homes, Neighborhoods, and Cities.* MIT, 1981.

———. *Seven American Utopias: Architecture of Communitarian Socialism, 1790–1975.* MIT, 1976.

Hayden, Wendy. *Evolutionary Rhetoric: Sex, Science, and Free Love in Nineteenth-Century Feminism.* Southern Illinois UP, 2013.

Hekman, Susan. "Constructing the Ballast: An Ontology for Feminism." *New Materialisms: Ontology, Agency, and Politics*, edited by Diana Coole and Samantha Frost, Duke UP, 2010, pp. 85–119.

Hinds, William Alfred. *American Communities and Cooperative Colonies.* Porcupine, 1975.

———. "The Hopedale and Brook-Farm Communities." *American Socialist*, 22 June 1876.

"History of the Printing Business of the O.C." 1872, Box 67, Oneida Community Collection, Special Collections Research Center, Syracuse University Libraries.

History of Wages in the United States from Colonial Times to 1928. 1st ed., United States Bureau of Labor Statistics, 1934.

Holder, Sarah. "The Price of Domestic Workers' Invisible Labor in U.S. Border Towns." *Citylab*, 25 June 2018, www.citylab.com/equity/2018/06/the-price-of-domestic-workers-invisible-labor-in-us-border-towns/563087. Accessed 16 Mar. 2019.

hooks, bell. *Ain't I a Woman: Black Women and Feminism.* South End, 1981.

Horowitz, Juliana Menasce, Ruth Igielnik, and Kim Parker. "Women and Leadership 2018." *Pew Research Center*, 20 Sept. 2018, www.pewsocialtrends.org/2018/09/20/women-and-leadership-2018. Accessed 16 Mar. 2019.

"Instructions for Dyeing Silk." Translated by Hilda Kring. Old Economy Village Research Files, Pennsylvania Historical and Museum Commission, Ambridge, PA.

"Introducing: Utopian." *Nice Try!* Curbed, 3 May 2019, www.curbed.com/2019/5/7/18514684/nice-try-podcast-utopian-avery-trufelman.

Jack, Jordynn. "Acts of Institution: Embodying Feminist Rhetorical Methodologies in Space and Time." *Rhetoric Review*, vol. 28, no. 3, 2009, pp. 285–303.

———. *Science on the Homefront: American Women Scientists in World War II.* U of Illinois P, 2009.

James, Stanlie. "Mothering: A Possible Black Feminist Link to Social Transformation?" *Theorizing Black Feminisms: The Visionary Pragmatism of Black Women*, edited by Stanlie M. James and Abena P. A. Busia, Routledge, 1993, pp. 44–54.

Jameson, Fredric. "The Politics of Utopia." *New Left Review*, vol. 25, 2004, pp. 35–54.

Jarratt, Susan. "Rhetoric and Feminism: Together Again." *College English*, vol. 62, no. 3, 2000, pp. 390–93.

Jeacle, Ingrid, and Tom Brown. "The Construction of the Credible: Epistolary Transformations and the Origins of the Business Letter." *Accounting, Business, and Financial History*, vol. 16, no. 1, 2006, pp. 27–43.

Jensen, Robin E. *Infertility: Tracing the History of a Transformative Term.* Penn State UP, 2016.

Johnson, Nan. *Gender and Rhetorical Space in American Life, 1866–1910.* Southern Illinois UP, 2002.

Kanter, Rosabeth Moss. *Commitment and Community: Communes and Utopias in Sociological Perspective.* Harvard UP, 1972.

Kapur, Akash. "The Return of the Utopians." *New Yorker*, 3 Oct. 2016.

Kelley, Mary. *Learning to Stand and Speak: Women, Education, and Public Life in America's Republic.* U of North Carolina P, 2008.

Kern, Louis J. *An Ordered Love: Sex Roles and Sexuality in Victorian Utopias—The Shakers, the Mormons, and the Oneida Community.* U of North Carolina P, 1981.

Kessler-Harris, Alice. *In Pursuit of Equity: Women, Men, and the Quest for Economic Citizenship in Twentieth-Century America.* Oxford UP, 2003.

Kinsley, Jessie. "Community Work." 1933, Box 63, Oneida Community Collection, Special Collections Research Center, Syracuse University Libraries.

Kirby, Georgiana Bruce. *Years of Experience: An Autobiographical Narrative.* Putnam, 1887.

Klaw, Spencer. *Without Sin: The Life and Death of the Oneida Community.* Penguin, 1994.

Klee-Hartzell, Marlyn. "Family Love, True Womanliness, Motherhood, and the Socialization of Girls in the Oneida Community, 1848–1880." *Women in Spiritual and Communitarian Societies in the United States*, edited by Wendy E. Chmielewski, Louis J. Kern, and Marlyn Klee-Hartzell, Syracuse UP, 1993, pp. 182–200.

Knoedler, Christiana. *The Harmony Society.* Vantage Press, 1954.

Kolmerten, Carol A. *Women in Utopia: The Ideology of Gender in the American Owenite Communities.* Indiana UP, 1990.

Kraditor, Aileen S., editor. *Up from the Pedestal: Selected Writings in the History of American Feminism.* Quandrangle, 1968.

Kring, Hilda. "Getting to Know Harmonist Women." Unpublished manuscript, 1994. Old Economy Village Research Files, Pennsylvania Historical and Museum Commission, Ambridge, PA.

———. *The Harmonists: A Folk-Cultural Approach.* Scarecrow, 1973.

Kunkel, Benjamin. *Utopia or Bust: A Guide to the Present Crisis.* Verso, 2014.

La Moy, William T., and Geo. Edward Cragin. "Two Documents Detailing the Oneida Community's Practice of Complex Marriage." *New England Quarterly*, vol. 85, no. 1, 2012, pp. 119–37.

Lam, Bourree. "How Do We Close the Wage Gap in the U.S.?" *Atlantic*, 8 Mar. 2016, www.theatlantic.com/business/archive/2016/03/equal-pay/472407. Accessed 16 Mar. 2019.

———. "The Socialization of Women and the Gender Pay Gap." *Atlantic*, 10 Aug. 2016, www.theatlantic.com/notes/2016/08/the-socialization-of-women/495200. Accessed 16 Mar. 2019.

———. "A Workplace-Diversity Dilemma." *Atlantic*, 7 Apr. 2016, www.theatlantic.com/business/archive/2016/04/status-diversity/477228. Accessed 16 Mar. 2019.

Lane, Charles. "Brook Farm." *Dial*, Jan. 1844, pp. 351–57.

Lapisardi, Emily. "Harmony Society Silk: A Celebration of Aesthetics, Craftsmanship, and Ideology." *Communal Studies*, vol. 26, no. 1, 2006, pp. 27–44.

"The Last of a 'Community.'" *Daily National Intelligencer*, 26 Mar. 1855.

Latour, Bruno. "Mixing Humans and Nonhumans Together: The Sociology of a Door-Closer." *Social Problems*, vol. 35, no. 3, 1988, pp. 298–310.

———. "On Actor-Network Theory: A Few Clarifications." *Soziale Welt*, vol. 47, no. 4, 1996, pp. 369–81.

———. *Pandora's Hope: Essays on the Reality of Science Studies.* Harvard UP, 1999.

———. *The Pasteurization of France.* Translated by Alan Sheridan and John Law, Harvard UP, 2004.

Laurie, Bruce. *Artisans into Workers: Labor in Nineteenth-Century America.* Hill and Wang, 1989.

Leavitt, Sarah H. *From Catharine Beecher to Martha Stewart: A Cultural History of Domestic Advice.* U of North Carolina P, 2002.

Leonard, Charlotte M. *Journals of Charlotte M. Leonard.* Box 63, pp. 1–54, Oneida Community Collection, Special Collections Research Center, Syracuse University Libraries.

Lewis, Jan. "Mother's Love: The Construction of an Emotion in Nineteenth-Century America." *Mothers and Motherhood: Readings in American History*, edited by Rima D. Apple and Janet Golden, Ohio State UP, 1997, pp. 52–71.

Livingston, Gretchen. "The Link between Parental Leave and the Gender Pay Gap." *Pew Research Center*, 20 Dec. 2013, www.pewresearch.org/fact-tank/2013/12/20/the-link-between-parental-leave-and-the-gender-pay-gap. Accessed 16 Mar. 2019.

Logan, Shirley Wilson. *We Are Coming: The Persuasive Discourse of Nineteenth-Century Black Women.* Southern Illinois UP, 1999.

Maddux, Kristy. "Without Touching Upon Suffrage: Gender and Economic Citizenship at the World's Columbian Exposition." *Rhetoric Society Quarterly*, vol. 47, no. 2, 2017, pp. 105–30.

"Maids of All Work." *Godey's Lady's Book*, vol. 54, Mar. 1857, p. 286.

Male Continence. Digital ed., Department of Special Collections, Syracuse University Library, 2000, pp. 1–20, library.syr.edu/digital/collections/m/MaleContinence-51k. Accessed 19 Mar. 2019.

Margo, Robert A. United States, National Bureau of Economic Research. *The Labor Force in the Nineteenth Century.* Historical paper no. 40, 1992.

Mariani, Mike. "The New Generation of Self-Created Utopias." *New York Times*, 22 Jan. 2020.

Matthews, Harriet. *Journal.* Box 64, pp. 1–38, Oneida Community Collection, Special Collections Research Center, Syracuse University Libraries.

Mattingly, Carol. *Appropriate[ing] Dress: Women's Rhetorical Style in Nineteenth-Century America.* Southern Illinois UP, 2002.

May, Ernestine Ott. "Harmony Society: History and Information Gathered by Ernestine Ott May." Unpublished manuscript, 1966. Old Economy Village Research Files, Pennsylvania Historical and Museum Commission, Ambridge, PA.

McClymond, Michael J. "John Humphrey Noyes, the Oneida Community, and Male Continence." *Religions of the United States in Practice*, edited by Colleen McDannell, vol. 1, Princeton UP, 2001, pp. 218–33.

Miller, Claire Cain. "The Gender Pay Gap Is Largely Because of Motherhood." *New York Times*, 13 May 2017, www.nytimes.com/2017/05/13/upshot/the-gender-pay-gap-is-largely-because-of-motherhood.html?module=inline. Accessed 16 Mar. 2019.

———. "A 'Generationally Perpetuated' Pattern: Daughters Do More Chores." *New York Times*, 8 Aug. 2018, www.nytimes.com/2018/08/08/upshot/chores-girls-research-social-science.html. Accessed 16 Mar. 2019.

Miller, Tirzah C. "Parentage at Oneida." 25 Dec. 1877, Box 66, Oneida Community Collection, Special Collections Research Center, Syracuse University Libraries.

———. "To Mary." 23 Feb. 1871, Box 66, Oneida Community Collection, Special Collections Research Center, Syracuse University Libraries.

Moseley, Sarah. "'A Strong Leadership That Does Not Show': Ladies Auxiliaries as Women's First Entrance Points into the Fire Department." *Rhetoric Review*, vol. 36, no. 4, 2017, pp. 348–62.

Mountford, Roxanne. *The Gendered Pulpit: Preaching in American Protestant Spaces.* Southern Illinois UP, 2005.

Myers, Eleanor. "Oneida Community." *National Genealogical Quarterly*, vol. 54, 1966, pp. 193–210.

"National Historic Landmark." *Wikipedia.* Wikipedia.org, 11 Dec. 2019, en.wikipedia.org/wiki/National_Historic_Landmark. Accessed 18 Mar. 2020.

Nevin, D. E. "The Late George Rapp and the Harmonists." *Scribner's Monthly, An Illustrated Magazine for the People*, vol. XVII, 1878–79, pp. 703–12.

Norton, Mary Beth. *Founding Mothers and Fathers: Gendered Power and the Forming of American Society*. Vintage, 1997.

Noyes, George Wallingford, and Lawrence Foster. *Free Love in Utopia: John Humphrey Noyes and the Origin of the Oneida Community*. U of Illinois P, 2001.

Noyes, Harriet. *History of M.A.H.* Box 67, Oneida Community Collection, Special Collections Research Center, Syracuse University Libraries.

Noyes, John Humphrey. *Mutual Criticism*. Office of the American Socialist, 1876.

O'Brien Hallstein, D. Lynn. "Introduction to Mothering Rhetorics." *Women's Studies in Communication*, vol. 40, no. 1, 2017, pp. 1–10.

Ockershausen, Jane. "Harmony in the Wilderness: A Walk through Old Economy Village." *Pennsylvania Heritage*, vol. 21, no. 1, 1995, pp. 20–27.

O'Connor, Lindsey Trimble, and Erin Cech. "Your Flex Work Culture Doesn't Help Employees if It Hurts Their Careers." *Harvard Business Review*, 12 June 2018, hbr.org/2018/06/your-flex-work-culture-doesnt-help-employees-if-it-hurts-their-careers. Accessed 16 Mar. 2019.

O'Reilly, Andrea. *Mother Outlaws: Theories and Practices of Empowered Mothering*. Women's Press, 2004.

Orvis, Marianne (Dwight). *Letters from Brook Farm, 1844–1847*. Edited by Amy L. Reed, Porcupine, 1972.

Ott, Alice T. "Community in 'Companies': The Conventicles of George Rapp's Harmony Society Compared to Those in Wurttemberg Pietism and the Bruderunitat." Unpublished manuscript. Old Economy Village Research Files, Pennsylvania Historical and Museum Commission, Ambridge, PA.

Ott, Nannette Ritter. Letter to Gertrude Rapp. 10 Aug. 1849. Translated by Hilda Kring, Site History Files, Women's History Project. Old Economy Village Archives, Pennsylvania Historical and Museum Commission, Ambridge, PA.

Ott, Sarah. Letter to Rebecca Feucht. 11 Sept. 1866. Translated by Hilda Kring, Site History Files, Women's History Project. Old Economy Village Archives, Pennsylvania Historical and Museum Commission, Ambridge, PA.

Packer, Barbara L. *The Transcendentalists*. U of Georgia, 2007.

Palmer, Phyllis. *Domesticity and Dirt: Housewives and Domestic Servants in the United States, 1920–1945*. Temple UP, 1991.

Parker, Kim. "Women in Majority-Male Workplaces Report Higher Rates of Gender Discrimination." *Pew Research Center*, 7 Mar. 2018, www.pewresearch

.org/fact-tank/2018/03/07/women-in-majority-male-workplaces-report-higher-rates-of-gender-discrimination. Accessed 16 Mar. 2019.

Parker, Robert Allerton. *A Yankee Saint: John Humphrey Noyes and the Oneida Community.* Archon, 1973.

Passet, Joanne E. *Sex Radicals and the Quest for Women's Equality.* U of Illinois P, 2003.

Peabody, Elizabeth P. "The Community at West Roxbury, Mass." *Gannett's Monthly Miscellany*, Aug. 1841.

———. "Plan of the West Roxbury Community." *Dial*, Jan. 1842.

Pear, Robert. "Average Size of Household in U.S. Declines to Lowest Ever Recorded." *New York Times*, 15 Apr. 1987.

"Perfectionism and Polygamy." *New York Observer and Chronicle*, 22 Jan. 1852.

Pfeffer, Friedrich. Letter to George Rapp. 20 May 1828. Translated by Hilda Kring, Site History Files, Women's History Project. Old Economy Village Archives, Pennsylvania Historical and Museum Commission, Ambridge, PA.

Pitzer, Donald E., editor. *America's Communal Utopias.* U of North Carolina P, 1997.

Raphael, Rina. "Why Doesn't Anyone Want to Live in This Perfect Place?" *New York Times*, 24 Aug. 2019.

Rapp, Gertrude. Letter to Christopher Muller. 5 June 1832. Translated by Hilda Kring, Site History Files, Women's History Project. Old Economy Village Archives, Pennsylvania Historical and Museum Commission, Ambridge, PA.

———. Letter to Rosina Rapp. 13 Aug. 1824. Translated by Hilda Kring, Site History Files, Women's History Project. Old Economy Village Archives, Pennsylvania Historical and Museum Commission, Ambridge, PA.

Rapp, Rosina. Letter to Gertrude Rapp. 12 Sept. 1824. Translated by Hilda Kring, Site History Files, Women's History Project. Old Economy Village Archives, Pennsylvania Historical and Museum Commission, Ambridge, PA.

Rawson, K. J. "Queering Feminist Rhetorical Canonization." *Rhetorica in Motion: Feminist Rhetorical Methods and Methodologies*, edited by Eileen E. Schell and K. J. Rawson, U of Pittsburgh P, 2010, pp. 39–52.

Reibel, Daniel B, editor. *Readings Concerning the Harmony Society in Pennsylvania Drawn from the Accounts of Travelers and Articles in the* Harmonie Herald *for Use as a Research Tool by Guides, Docents and Volunteers at Old Economy Village.* Unpublished manuscript, 1978. Old Economy Village Library, Pennsylvania Historical and Museum Commission, Ambridge, PA.

Rich, Adrienne. *Of Woman Born: Motherhood as Experience & Institution.* 2nd ed., Norton, 1986.

Richards, Rebecca S. *Transnational Feminist Rhetorics and Gendered Leadership in Global Politics.* Lexington, 2014.

Rickert, Thomas. *Ambient Rhetorics: The Attunements of Rhetorical Being.* U of Pittsburgh P, 2013.

Ripley, Sophia. "Woman." *Dial*, Jan. 1841.

Rose, Anne C. *Transcendentalism as a Social Movement, 1830–1850.* Yale UP, 1981.

"Roster." Box 58, Oneida Community Collection, Special Collections Research Center, Syracuse University Libraries.

Royster, Jaqueline Jones. *Traces of a Stream: Literacy and Social Change among African American Women.* U of Pittsburgh P, 2000.

Royster, Jacqueline Jones, and Gesa E. Kirsch. *Feminist Rhetorical Practices: New Horizons for Rhetoric, Composition, and Literacy Studies.* Southern Illinois UP, 2012.

Ruhl, Leslie. "Dilemmas of the Will: Uncertainty, Reproduction, and the Rhetoric of Control." *Signs*, vol. 27, no. 3, 2002, pp. 641–63.

Russell, Amelia Eloise. *Home Life of the Brook Farm Association.* Little, Brown, and Co., 1900.

Sacks, Karen. "Engels Revisited: Women, the Organization of Production, and Private Property." *Woman, Culture, and Society*, edited by Michelle Zimbalist Rosaldo and Louise Lamphere, Stanford, 1974, pp. 207–22.

Salisbury, Annie M. "The Real Brook Farm II." *Boston Evening Transcript*, 3 Nov. 1894.

Sams, Henry W. *Autobiography of Brook Farm.* Prentice Hall, 1958.

Sanborn, Alvan F. "The Revolt from Family Ties." *Good Housekeeping*, Aug. 1907, pp. 167–70.

Sanchez, Rebecca Lee. "America's Domestic Workers, Mostly Female Immigrants, 'Undervalued and Underpaid.'" *Public Radio International*, 9 Dec. 2013, www.pri.org/stories/2013-12-09/americas-domestic-workers-mostly-female-immigrants-undervalued-and-underpaid. Accessed 16 Mar. 2019.

Sargent, Lyman Tower. "The Social and Political Ideas of the American Communitarians: A Comparison of Religious and Secular Communes Founded Before 1850." *Utopian Studies*, vol. 3, 1991, pp. 37–58.

———. "The Three Faces of Utopianism Revisited." *Utopian Studies*, vol. 5, no. 1, 1994, pp. 1–37.

Scott, Joan W. "Deconstructing Equality-versus-Difference: Or, the Uses of Poststructuralist Theory for Feminism." *Feminist Studies*, vol. 12, no. 1, 1988, pp. 32–50.

Second Annual Report of the Oneida Association: Exhibiting its Progress to February 20, 1850. Digital ed., Department of Special Collections, Syracuse

University Library, 2000, pp. 1–31, library.syr.edu/digital/collections/s/SecondAnnualReportOfTheOneidaAssociation. Accessed 19 Mar. 2019.

Sedgwick, Catharine Maria. *Live and Let Live; Or, Domestic Service Illustrated.* Harper and Brothers, 1837.

———. "A Plea for Children." *Ladies Magazine*, vol. 8, 1835, pp. 93–97.

Seeman, Erik R. "'It Is Better to Marry than to Burn': Anglo-American Attitudes toward Celibacy, 1600–1800." *Journal of Family History*, vol. 24, 1999, pp. 397–419.

Shapiro, Laura. *Perfection Salad: Women and Cooking at the Turn of the Century.* Farrar, Straus, and Giroux, 1986.

Sharpe, Christina. *In the Wake: On Blackness and Being.* Duke UP, 2016.

Shaw, George Bernard. "To Hope Emily Allen." 19 Nov. 1924, Box 77, Oneida Community Collection, Special Collections Research Center, Syracuse University Libraries.

Sheriff, Stacy. "Rhetoric and Revision: Women's Arguments for Social Justice in the Progressive Era." Diss., Pennsylvania State University, 2009.

Siebers, Tobin. "Disability Experience on Trial." *Material Feminisms*, edited by Stacy Alaimo and Susan Hekman, Indiana UP, 2008, pp. 291–307.

"Signs of the Times: Brook Farm Association." *Present*, 1 Mar. 1844.

Sigourney, Lydia H. *Letters to Mothers.* Hudson and Skinner, 1838.

Silk Letter Book. Manuscript Group 185: Harmony Society Papers, Business File. Old Economy Village Archives, Pennsylvania Historical and Museum Commission, Ambridge, PA.

Skinner, Carolyn. "'The Purity of Truth': Nineteenth-Century American Women Physicians Write about Delicate Topics." *Rhetoric Review*, vol. 26, no. 2, 2007, pp. 103–19.

———. *Women Physicians and Professional Ethos in Nineteenth-Century America.* Southern Illinois UP, 2014.

Smart, Carol. "Disruptive Bodies and Unruly Sex: The Regulation of Reproduction and Sexuality in the Nineteenth Century." *Regulating Womanhood: Historical Essays on Marriage, Motherhood, and Sexuality*, edited by Carol Smart, Routledge, 1992 pp. 7–32.

Smith, Daniel Scott. "Family Limitation, Sexual Control, and Domestic Feminism in Victorian America." *Clio's Consciousness Raised: New Perspectives on the History of Women*, edited by Mary S. Hartman and Lois Banner, Harper & Row, 1974, pp. 119–36.

Smith, Michelle. "Containment Rhetoric and the Public Sphere: Imagining Amana, Inscribing America." *Rhetoric Society Quarterly*, vol. 40, no. 2, 2010, pp. 128–45.

———. "'Indoor Duties' in Utopia: Archival Recalcitrance and Methodologies of Lived Experience." *College English*, vol. 80, no. 6, 2018, pp. 517–38.

———. "In Rosie's Shadow: WWII Recruitment Rhetoric and Women's Work in Public Memory." *Women and Work: Rhetorics of Gender and Labor*, edited by David Gold and Jessica Enoch, U of Pittsburgh, 2019, pp. 186–208.

———. "Review: Feminist Rhetorical Questions and the Broadening Imperative." *College English*, vol. 82, no. 3, 2020, pp. 326–41.

"Social Communities." *United States Magazine*, Nov. 1856.

"Special Love." Box 14, Oneida Community Collection, Special Collections Research Center, Syracuse University Libraries.

Stage, Sarah, and Virginia Vincenti, editors. *Rethinking Home Economics: Women and the History of the Profession*. Cornell UP, 1997.

Stanley, Amy Dru. "Home Life and the Morality of the Market." *The Market Revolution in America*, edited by Melvyn Stokes and Stephen Conway, Virginia UP, 1996, pp. 74–96.

Stansell, Christine. *City of Women: Sex and Class in New York, 1789–1860*. Illinois UP, 1987.

Stokes, Melvyn. "Introduction." *The Market Revolution in America*, edited by Melvyn Stokes and Stephen Conway, Virginia UP, 1996, pp. 1–20.

Stormer, Nathan. *Sign of Pathology: U.S. Medical Rhetoric on Abortion, 1800s–1960s*. Penn State UP, 2015.

Strasser, Susan. *Never Done: A History of American Housework*. Holt, 2000.

Third Annual Report of the Oneida Association: Exhibiting Its Progress to February 20, 1851. Digital ed., Department of Special Collections, Syracuse University Library, 2000, pp. 1–32, library.syr.edu/digital/collections/t/ThirdAnnualReportOfTheOneidaAssociation. Accessed 19 Mar. 2019.

Thomson, Stephanie. "A Lack of Confidence Isn't What's Holding Back Working Women." *Atlantic*, 20 Sept. 2018, www.theatlantic.com/family/archive/2018/09/women-workplace-confidence-gap/570772. Accessed 16 Mar. 2019.

Tonn, Mari Boor. "Militant Motherhood: Labor's Mary Harris 'Mother' Jones." *Quarterly Journal of Speech*, vol. 82, no. 1, 1996, pp. 1–21.

Van de Warker, Ely. "A Gynecological Study of the Oneida Community." *American Journal of Obstetrics and Diseases of Women and Children*, vol. 27, no. 8, 1884, pp. 785–810.

Vickers, Jason. "'That Deep Kind of Discipline of Spirit': Freedom, Power, Family, Marriage, and Sexuality in the Story of John Humphrey Noyes and the Oneida Community." *American Nineteenth Century History*, vol. 14, no. 1, 2013, pp. 1–26.

Vitanza, Victor. "Taking A-Count of a (Future-Anterior) History of Rhetoric as 'Libidinalized Marxism' (A PM Pastiche)." *Writing Histories of Rhetoric*, edited by Victor J. Vitanza, Southern Illinois UP, 1994, pp. 180–216.

Walsh, Lynda, Nathaniel A. Rivers, Jenny Rice, Laurie E. Gries, Jennifer L. Bay, Thomas Rickert, and Carolyn R. Miller. "Forum: Bruno Latour on Rhetoric." *Rhetoric Society Quarterly*, vol. 47, no. 5, 2017, pp. 403–62.

Wan, Amy. "Republicanism, Religiosity, and the Rhetoric of Women's Labor Reform in Lowell, Massachusetts, 1830–1850." *Women and Work: Rhetorics of Gender and Labor*, edited by David Gold and Jessica Enoch, U of Pittsburgh, 2019, pp. 17–30.

Warner, Michael. *The Letters of the Republic*. Harvard UP, 1990.

Wayland-Smith, Ellen. "The Status and Self-Perception of Women in the Oneida Community." *Communal Societies*, vol. 8, 1988, pp. 18–53.

Wayland-Smith, Francis. "What Held the OC Together." Box 76, pp. 1–11, Oneida Community Collection, Special Collections Research Center, Syracuse University Libraries.

Wayne, Tiffany K. *Woman Thinking: Feminism and Transcendentalism in Nineteenth-Century America*. Lexington, 2005.

"Wedding Journal of Amanda Adams 1837." *Harmonie Herald*, 1978, p. 2.

Weil, Louise. *From the Swabian Manse to America: Travel Views by Louise Weil*. Stuttgart, 1860. Translated by Hilda Kring. Old Economy Village Research Files, Pennsylvania Historical and Museum Commission, Ambridge, PA.

Wells, Susan. *Out of the Dead House: Nineteenth-Century Women Physicians and the Writing of Medicine*. U of Wisconsin P, 2001.

Whidden, Graham. "A Brook Farm Survivor." *Outlook*, 9 Apr. 1904.

Williams, Aaron. *The Harmony Society*. W. S. Haven, 1866.

Wingfield, Adia Harvey. "How 'Service With a Smile' Takes a Toll on Women." *Atlantic*, 26 Jan. 2016, www.theatlantic.com/business/archive/2016/01/gender-emotional-labor/427083. Accessed 16 Mar. 2019.

Witz, Anne. "Patriarchy and Professions: The Gendered Politics of Occupational Closure." *Sociology*, vol. 24, no. 4, 1990, pp. 675–90.

"Wonderful Progress of the New Philosophy—Fourierism in the Ascendant—A Great Political and Social Revolution at Hand." *New York Herald*, 8 Jan. 1844.

Worden, Harriet M. *Old Mansion House Memories: By One Brought Up in It*. 1950.

Worden, Susan. "1851–1868 File of letters to Marcus L. Worden." Box 77, Oneida Community Collection, Special Collections Research Center, Syracuse University Libraries.

Zarya, Valentina. "Working Flexible Hours Can Hurt Your Career—But Only if You're a Woman." *Fortune*, 21 Feb. 2017, fortune.com/2017/02/21/flexible-schedule-women-career. Accessed 16 Mar. 2019.

Zhou, Li. "Year in Review: The Biggest Stories about Gender Inequality at Work." *Atlantic*, 31 Dec. 2015, www.theatlantic.com/business/archive/2015/12/gender-equality-workplace-2015/422328. Accessed 16 Mar. 2019.

INDEX

Italicized page numbers indicate figures

MICHELLE C. SMITH is an assistant professor of English at Clemson University. Her teaching and research interests include feminist rhetorics, rhetorical theory, and historiography. Her writing has appeared in *College English*, *Rhetoric Society Quarterly*, and *Peitho*, as well as in other journals and edited collections.